THE GUIDE TO
ELECTRIC
HYBRID & FUEL-EFFICIENT CARS

CIVIC CENTER

Project Manager: Agnès Saint-Laurent
Copy Editor: Robert Ronald
Proofreader: Elizabeth Lewis
Translators: Matthew Brown, Duggan Richard Cayer
Art Direction & Design: François Daxhelet
Graphics Designers: Chantal Landry, Johanne Lemay
Photo Retouching: Johanne Lemay
Coordinator: Julien Rodrigue

EXCLUSIVE DISTRIBUTOR:

For Canada and the United States:
Simon & Schuster Canada
166 King Street East, Suite 300
Toronto, ON M5A 1J3
phone: (647) 427-8882
          1-800-387-0446
Fax: (647) 430-9446
simonandschuster.ca

Bibliothèque et Archives nationales du Québec and Library
and Archives Canada cataloguing in publication

Breton, Daniel, 1962-

    Breton, Daniel, 1962-

    [Auto électrique, hybride et écoénergétique. English]

    The guide to electric, hybrid & fuel-efficient cars :
85 vehicles reviewed, plus everything you need to know
about going electric

    Translation of : Guide de l'auto électrique, hybride et
écoénergétique.
    Includes bibliographical references.

    ISBN 978-1-9880024-4-6

    1. Electric automobiles. 2. Hybrid electric cars.
I. Duval, Jacques, 1934- . II. Juteau, Sylvain.
III. Langlois, Pierre, 1951- . IV. Title. V. Title : Guide de l'auto
électrique, hybride et écoénergétique. English. VI. Guide to
electric, hybrid and fuel-efficient cars.

TL220.B7313 2016   629.22'93   C2016-940843-4

06-16

© 2016, Juniper Publishing,
division of the Sogides Group Inc.,
a subsidiary of Québecor Média Inc.
(Montréal, Québec)

Printed in Canada
All rights reserved

Legal deposit: 2016
National Library of Québec
National Library of Canada

ISBN 978-1-988002-44-6

Conseil des Arts   Canada Council
du Canada   for the Arts

We gratefully acknowledge the support of the Canada
Council for the Arts for its publishing program.

We acknowledge the financial support of the
Government of Canada through the Canada Book Fund
for our publishing activities.

DANIEL BRETON - JACQUES DUVAL

THE GUIDE TO
ELECTRIC
HYBRID & FUEL-EFFICIENT CARS

85 vehicles reviewed, plus everything you need
to know about going electric

With the collaboration of Sylvain Juteau and Pierre Langlois

JUNIPER
PUBLISHING
A Quebecor Media Corporation

TABLE OF CONTENTS

USER MANUAL

ELEC	**HYBR**	**HYB**	**ECO**	**H**
100% Electric	Plug-in hybrid (PHEV) or an electric car with a range extender	Hybrid	Energy-Efficient	Hydrogen

①

PRICE: $39,200
FUEL CONSUMPTION: 6.7 L/100 km (35 mpg)
ELECTRIC RANGE: 50 km (31 mi)
CHARGE TIME: 120 V: 8 h; 240 V: 2.2 h
② GREENHOUSE EMISSIONS: 98.7 g/km (158 g/mi)
③ GHG EMISSIONS RATING: 10/10
④ CALIFORNIA SMOG RATING: n/a

① LEAF RATING
A score (from 1 to 10 leaves) given to a vehicle, 10 being the highest. We compare vehicles from the same category: electric, plug-in hybrid, hybrid or energy-efficient. A traditional vehicle can therefore receive a higher score than a hybrid. That doesn't make it a "greener" vehicle than the hybrid, but only more so than others in its category.

② GHG (GREENHOUSE GAS)
Grams of CO_2 emitted per kilometer driven. GHG emissions contribute to global warming.

③ GHG EMISSIONS RATING
The ratings are from 1 to 10, 10 being the highest. The higher the rating, the lower the GMG emissions.

④ CALIFORNIA SMOG RATING
Score based on polluting emissions that contribute to air pollution and create environmental problems (smog) and health problems (lung disease, cancer).

ZEV: Zero-Emission Vehicle (the cleanest): 10/10
PZEV: Partial Zero-Emission Vehicle: 9/10
SULEV II: Super-Ultra-Low-Emission Vehicle: 8/10
ULEV 70-50: Ultra-Low-Emission Vehicle: 7/10
ULEV II: Ultra-Low-Emission Vehicle: 6/10
LEV II: Low-Emission Vehicle: 5/10
LEV II option I: Low-Emission Vehicle: 4/10
SULEV II/Light Truck: 2/10
ULEV and LEV II/Light Truck: 1/10

MY RACE FOR
THE ENVIRONMENT

JACQUES DUVAL

Many people would probably assume that I'm the last person who should take on the task of writing about an area in which I was something of a destructive force for a good chunk of my life. For those who don't know, I spent 20-odd years driving race cars all over North America and Europe and singing the praises of high-performance automobiles on television and the radio, in newspapers and magazines, and above all in a book that just celebrated its 50th anniversary: *Le Guide de l'auto* [English: *The Car Guide*]. I started up this yearly publication and ran it for some 40 years, focusing mainly on sports cars—extravagant, gas-guzzling sports cars. My work on *Le Guide de l'auto* continued until a point came when I realized that in pursuing my own enjoyment, I was helping to put that of future generations at great risk.

I had planned to retire after publishing the 50th edition of the car guide, but here I am back at it at the age of 81. Holiday travels and idle pleasures will have to wait. Instead, I want to devote my energy and expertise to a cause that is very close to my heart—the electric car—in order to shine a spotlight on information that might be unclear with respect to this technology of the present and future. Calling it a "cause" might lead to confusion here. I am not implying that a battle has to be won to pave the way for this important conversion in technology; on the contrary, I am quite certain that the shift is inevitable.

Calming fears

I won't deny that a certain amount of anxiety comes with such a radical change. The aim of our group—me, Daniel, Pierre, Jean-François and last but not least Sylvain, the most fervent proponent of the electric vehicle—is to lift the veil on questions surrounding the subject, regarding both the nature of cutting-edge solutions that have emerged and the different vehicles that are currently on the market. Because available electric cars are still fairly few in number, we decided to address all vehicles that can be "plugged in"; in other words, rechargeable vehicles. And for those who are still hesitating to take the plunge, we have also selected some gas-powered cars that at least have the advantage of using gas sparingly.

We also asked three women, who are specially keen on electric cars, to share with us their family experience of a green automobile. They helped us to clarify and counter many myths and prejudices.

Whole chapters will address any worries you may have, and you will find helpful articles on the energy performance of vehicles that have been exactingly tested.

With that in mind, cast your fears aside and get ready to drive electric and save.

I LOVE CARS, BUT I'D PREFER A VIABLE PLANET

DANIEL BRETON

I love cars

I grew up in a world, in a family, where cars played a central role in our lives. Plus, my uncle Chuck, cousins Kirk and Denis, and myself have all worked in the automobile industry (in Canada and the U.S.). We've been talking cars our whole lives.

There were oil refineries just a couple of blocks from where I grew up. As long as I can remember, I witnessed spills, fires and even a fatal tanker explosion about a football field away from my childhood home.

These events caused a total shift in how I approached transportation and cars some 20 years ago. From what I could see and what I learned, I had come to believe that, as a species, we couldn't successfully continue:

- burning more oil
- emitting more greenhouse gases
- polluting more
- becoming increasingly dependent on oil companies
- spending larger sums of money abroad and diving deeper into deficit
- suffering more environmental disasters, spills, fires and explosions
- waging oil wars

Environmental activist

So I began studying the matter in depth with engineers, scientists, ecologists, economists and researchers. I went back to school to expand on what I already knew. I became an environmental activist.

And I purchased a little 2001 Honda Insight that I still have to this day, 15 years later.

Twelve years ago, I started writing articles on hybrid and fuel-efficient vehicles, the environment and alternate modes of transportation. Other car columnists thought I was a real nut job.

Later, I took over as Québec's Environment Minister, the first elected official in Canada to be charged with writing and implementing a transportation electrification strategy.

So I come from a milieu that's highly conscious of the environmental challenges we face and our dependence on oil and cars.

When oil prices fall, a majority of people worry less about how much they're spending on gas, but an increasing number of people want to change their habits.

Useful guide

So after fielding questions from all kinds of people on what they can do to reduce their energy consumption and impact on the environment, it felt like the perfect time to write *The Guide to Electric Cars and Fuel-Efficient Vehicles*.

This book is meant for the majority of the population that wants a solution to decrease their reliance on oil, pollutants and greenhouse gases. They've asked about carpooling, ridesharing and driving more efficient or zero-emissions vehicles.

The guide was designed for people who want feasible and concrete solutions to their day-to-day transit needs.

It was written for those who take an interest in energy issues, electric vehicle (EV) battery life cycles, the hydrogen vs. electric debate, and the future of transportation.

Lastly, it also targets skeptics and/or people who want to convince them.

All that in one guide.

We hope you like it.

For a viable planet

As you read earlier, I love cars—but I'd prefer a viable planet. That's why my partner and I drive electric cars when we can't take public transit or our bicycles.

When we went to the COP 21 in Paris, we saw how committed the countries of the world were to an agreement on reducing global warming emissions for the future of our planet.

We invite you to sign your own agreement with yourself to do the same.

Happy reading!

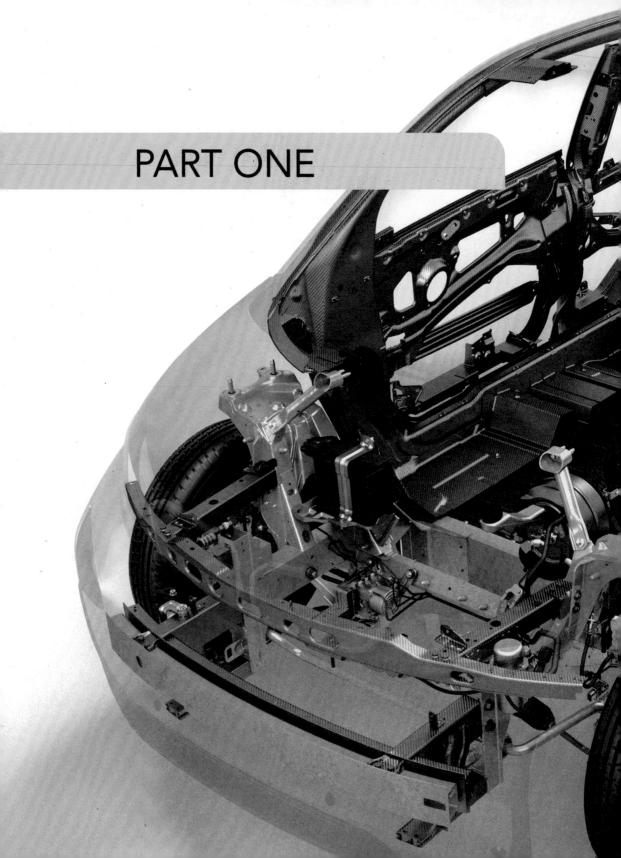

PART ONE

MYTHS
AND REALITIES

La Jamais Contente

BACK TO SQUARE ONE: ELECTRIC TRANSPORT IN 2016

DANIEL RUFIANGE

It looks like we're the lucky witnesses of a major and historic shift in motorized transport. We're seeing the gradual, and sometimes massive, arrival of vehicles propelled by something other than the combustion engine. This time around, the vehicles are here for good.

At the beginning of the last century, the gasoline engine faced its first serious competition and one of its main competitors was the electric motor. Let's take a look at the latter's initial foray into private and public transport.

Private transit

You'd have to go back to the first half of the 1800s to see the first electric vehicles (EVs), which basically came in the form of a carriage powered by a one-charge battery system. Next, the rechargeable battery was invented and perfected in the second half of the same century, leading to a whole slew of electric transport companies being founded.

The Columbia Automobile Company of Hartford, Connecticut, is an interesting case study. While most auto manufacturers were producing gas-powered vehicles one by one at the end of the 19th century, this Connecticut company was building hundreds of units of its

Electric Coach every year, and the car was able to travel faster than 50 km/h (31 mph), thanks to its two-horsepower engine. The willingness and know-how were all there.

In 1899, *La Jamais Contente* (English: The Never Satisfied) was the first road vehicle to drive faster than 100 km/h (62 mph). The manufacturer behind the new land speed record was France's *Compagnie internationale des transports automobiles électriques*.

The first hybrid car would soon follow—a little someone by the name of Ferdinand Porsche was behind the endeavor.

In the United States, the Woods Motor Vehicle Company of Chicago would put out an electric vehicle in 1911. It was too pricey, too slow and too expensive to maintain—all that to say it did not last long.

The most famous EV-producing outfit would have to be the Anderson Electric Car Company (called the Detroit Electric Car Company from 1920 onward). They used to manufacture the Detroit Electric—some

13,000 of them to be exact—from 1907 to 1939. At the dawn of the 20th century, the Anderson plant produced between 1,000 and 2,000 cars every year. During World War I and amid inflated gas prices, Detroit Electric sales soared to new heights.

But wait

EV technology was on borrowed time. The price tag, weight and lackluster range of electric cars were major handicaps. As the combustion engine got better, the end of electric cars grew nigher. Canada saw its first provincial highway department in Quebec in 1914. Come 1916, the federal government of the U.S. legislated its first major funding campaign for highways in the country. North Americans took to the roads in droves shortly thereafter, discovering the pleasures of traveling long distances by car. Contemporary EVs were not up to the task. Also, environmental concerns were not exactly foremost on people's minds at the beginning of the 20th century.

The Detroit Electric

The tram nicknamed "Rocket"

Public transit

The city of Montréal's public transit system is an excellent case study of how electric power similarly blew up and fizzled out.

Montréal streetcars first took to the rails in 1892. The Montréal City Passenger Railway Co.'s *The Rocket*, which was able to move at a neckbreaking speed of 13 km/h (8 mph), traveled up and down Sainte-Catherine Street. The advent of *The Rocket* signaled the end of horse-drawn trams and two years later, the horses were sent back to their stables.

With electric streetcars in service, the company was able to grow and extend its network, and became a driver for economic development in the city. The population embraced the new technology, which fed their thirst for modernism.

In just a few years, the network grew from 50 to 358 kilometers (222 miles). The number of annual passengers multiplied by 15, reaching 107 million in 1910.

These were the golden years of the city's electric tram system.

Electric buses

What became the Montréal Tramways Company acquired seven trolleybuses in 1937. Ontario tested out trolleybuses in Windsor (1922) and Toronto (1926), but Montréal was the first Canadian city to put them into service. The network grew mainly in the northern parts of the city. The company would purchase another 105 vehicles between 1947 and 1952.

Still, just like streetcars, trolleybuses were doomed to extinction as well.

Starting in 1951, tramway lines started disappearing to make way for bus routes. On August 30, 1959, the last tramway serving the last electric line (Tram 3057, Papineau-

Bélanger) was put to rest in its municipal garage. The city marked the end of an era with a giant parade. Come June 18, 1966, just before the Montréal subway system opened to the public, the very last trolleybus was retired from service. At the time, 103 of the 105 vehicles ordered between 1947 and 1952 were still in service. One hundred were sold to Mexico City.

Our modern reaction to the premature decline of electric-powered public transit is one of sadness and surprise. In the beginning of the 1950s, car culture started to dominate. No matter how you try to spin it, this movement has negatively affected public transit as a whole. People wanted their own car and the freedom that came with it. The public transit system was up to the challenge and needed to stay competitive. Gas-powered buses allowed transport farther and farther from the city center, to places that electric transit just couldn't reach. The subway, of course, was the exception.

The same challenges are relevant today.

The future

These days, we're back at square one. Electric cars are widely available and better than ever. Nonetheless, consumer enthusiasm is bridled by questions of cash and range. Fortunately, these obstacles are being surmounted and won't be relevant within a few years, or even a few months.

North American public transit authorities are using more and more hybrid buses, plug-in hybrids and electric vehicles on their routes. That being said, some of these companies are also moving toward natural gas to power their extensive fleets.

So what's the difference a hundred years later? Today, there's a new willingness and motivation behind the change.

Humanity had a choice at the beginning of the last century. That's not the case now—our future depends on electric power.

100-percent-electric bus

FIRST SPIN: APPREHENSION

JACQUES DUVAL

A bit like a novice pilot flying solo for the first time, when one gets behind the wheel of a Tesla Model S on a long trip alone, it can be very stressful. Failures, however, are bound to be far less catastrophic on the road than in the air.

When I went to the big electric car rally at Summerside in Prince Edward Island, I had the trusted backing of Sylvain Juteau (Québec's EV hot shot). I took him for a spin in my recently acquired Tesla Model S.

With Juteau by my side, I had nothing to worry about. The guy knows everything about everything, including how to drive an electric vehicle with about 430 kilometers (270 miles) of range over long distances. We covered some 2,300 kilometers (1,500 miles) without "running out of juice." The experience led me to what I call my first long-range solo mission a few weeks later.

430 kilometers (270 miles) of range

I was expected to make an appearance at an Ottawa-area high school to give a talk on electric cars. The night before I left, I was careful to recharge the batteries to the max, which would normally allow me to drive about 430 kilometers (270 miles). Remember: You're not supposed to fully recharge a Tesla on a regular basis to avoid damaging the 7,500 batteries that are built into the floor of the car, which lower its center of gravity. You may do a full recharge occasionally, though.

My GPS told me that I had 223 kilometers (140 miles) to drive from my home in Saint-Bruno to my final destination in Ontario. It didn't take the closure of the Champlain Bridge into account—I had to take the Mercier Bridge instead, adding 18 kilometers (11 miles) to my trip. With 430 kilometers (270 miles) of range and only a 240-kilometer (150-mile) drive ahead of me, I had all the wiggle room I needed, even though I needed to turn on the heat (it was -8°C/18°F outside) and there was some faster highway driving ahead. The ride there went smoothly and I arrived at my destination around noon, having left my home at 9:15 a.m. that morning.

Wise calculations

Upon arrival, I was directed to a 40-amp charging station at the school. Since my charge was at 140 kilometers (87 miles), the five hours I spent at the youth book fair would give me the opportunity to bank an extra 200 kilometers (125 miles) to get back to Saint-Bruno. The charging station, however, wasn't as generous as I thought and when I unplugged the vehicle I was left with enough electricity to drive 310 kilometers (190 miles) in total. A 241-kilometer (150-mile) drive with a 310-kilometer (190-mile) charge seemed to be cutting it close with an ambient temperature of -14°C (7°F). That's why the right foot of yours truly needed to tread lightly and I might have been in for a chilly behind. All this meant that I needed to stay on the right trajectory, too. Any

error in my itinerary would be problematic. Everything went well for the first 90 minutes, but when the range meter started displaying double digits, I decided to turn off the heat. It's a well-known fact that electric cars, which include plug-in hybrids, lose about 20 percent of range in cold weather. If I wanted to get home, I'd have to deal with the cold to avoid getting stuck roadside, out of juice.

Small scare

A feeling of mild panic started setting in when the range meter read 50 kilometers (30 miles). I pulled over to the side of the road to check the PlugShare site on the vehicle's 17-inch screen. It didn't matter, though, because recharging stations were not as common as they are today. There were hundreds at the time, but they were far away from my current location. I got back on the road and, after having gotten my bearings, I breathed a sigh of relief. The 37 kilometers (23 miles) left on my range meter would be enough to get me home to a nice bottle of red wine and my Tesla Model S to a warm garage for a recharge. When I parked, I read 29 kilometers (18 miles) on the dashboard and saw pretty much every warning light go off.

Moral of the story

Driving an EV requires prior planning, which involves locating public charging stations along the way. If you want to get the most out of your electric car, you need to plan ahead—before you hit the road. It's a new approach to travel.

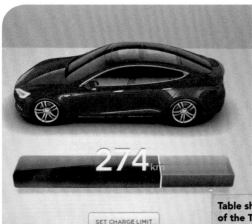

Table showing the range of the Tesla Model S

SET CHARGE LIMIT

274 km

THE ABCs
OF HYBRID, PLUG-IN AND ELECTRIC CARS

DANIEL BRETON

Hybrid cars

The first hybrid car was unveiled at the 1900 Salon de Paris by Viennese Jacob Lohner, who had called on a young engineer by the name of Ferdinand Porsche to perfect the vehicle. It was the first car to combine an internal combustion engine to two in-wheel motors.

Afterward, the hybrid engine pretty much fell into obscurity for decades. Worldwide crises, in tandem with automobile-related atmospheric pollution and the 1973 Oil Crisis, created the perfect storm for the hybrid engine. It was given a new life and perfected by Andrew Alfonso Frank (1971) and Victor Wouk (1974), the latter actually developing a regenerative braking system.

The hybrid engine really took off in 1997 when Toyota rolled out its first generation of

Priuses. Since then, millions of hybrid cars have been sold worldwide. Despite the misgivings and disparaging remarks of onlookers and "specialists," hybrids would only increase in number over the following years.

Hybrid engines are characterized by the combination of an internal combustion engine and an electric motor. The battery is charged by the combustion engine and braking, which makes revving up a hybrid vehicle less energy intensive. It's a sort of "electric turbo" that allows the vehicle to perform like a car with a bigger engine, but with better fuel economy, and greenhouse gas emissions closer to those from a smaller engine. The electric motor comes online when the combustion engine becomes less efficient, such as during acceleration, at low speeds or when stopping.

Three kinds of hybrid architecture exist:

Series hybrid. While the electric motor moves the vehicle forward, the combustion engine powers a generator that charges the battery. The combustion engine isn't connected to the wheels, so it operates at peak efficiency. That's how the Chevrolet Volt works most of the time.

Parallel hybrid. The engines are connected by the transmission. The combustion and electric motors are connected to the same shaft. The Honda Insight is an example of a parallel hybrid car.

Power-split hybrid. The combustion and electric motors come together in a more elaborate manner, allowing the engines to rotate at different speeds. The Toyota Prius is a perfect example of a power-split hybrid that can work in 100-percent electric mode, 100-percent gas mode and sometimes both.

Hybrid engines and highway driving

Keep the following in mind when driving a hybrid engine on a highway:

- When a hybrid car is not in motion, the engines are also at rest.
- During a slow start, it's most often the electric motor that propels the car forward (until it hits 30 km/h or 50 mph).
- During a quick start, the engines work together for more vigorous acceleration.
- At higher speeds, the combustion engine kicks in and progressively takes over for the electric motor.
- When you slow down, whether you're going downhill or braking, the engine/generator converts some of the kinetic energy into electricity that recharges the battery. This means you get enhanced engine braking, which makes the mechanical brakes' job easier.

Plug-in hybrids

Plug-in hybrid car motors are much like the motors on board regular hybrids. What's the difference, then? Basically, you can plug these cars into an external power source to recharge them. You can recharge a plug-in hybrid car using the power grid (at home, for example) or various public charging stations at work, in public parking lots, on the street, at service stations and so on.

You can also produce electricity with the hybrid's small gas engine when the battery is running low. You can power on your car with this little engine at full blast while the battery recharges and then turn it off when you want to lower your emissions.

The father of plug-in hybrid cars is considered to be Andrew Alfonso Frank, professor emeritus at UC Davis (in California).

Pierre Couture's in-wheel motor

One of the first plug-in hybrid vehicles was designed by Pierre Couture's team at Hydro-Québec in 1994...using a Chrysler Intrepid. The car's gas engine was replaced by four in-wheel motors that were dreamed up at the Institut de recherche en électricité du Québec (IREQ). In lab and road testing, wheel engine performance trounced the classic engine both in terms of energy efficiency and power.

The electric system was designed to work in tandem with a gas-powered generator to provide the energy required to charge the battery, which in turn reduced the car's fuel consumption by nearly 80 percent. The car could be recharged by plugging it in. Couture believed that such an electric vehicle could be plugged in only once a day.

In 1995, the project was dropped. Twenty years later, it's still controversial.

The Chevrolet Volt: The first best-selling plug-in hybrid

In dealerships since 2010, this plug-in hybrid car (Chevrolet insists on calling the Volt an "extended-range electric car") is a feat of technological prowess that hasn't really been rivaled in recent decades—except by the Toyota Prius, of course.

The Volt is especially reliable and it's tailored to the needs of the average driver who wants an electric car that they won't have to worry about over long distances. Most Volt drivers see their gas consumption drop by 60 to 90 percent. It's so remarkable that loyal Toyota Prius fans have started paying attention to the Chevrolet Volt. Incredible!

There's no doubt in my mind that the technology used for this car will have a brilliant career. I project that it will even be part of the primary solutions for the future of private, carbon-friendly transport.

You'll also find other, more traditional plug-in hybrids on the market. There's the Toyota Prius Plug-in, the Ford Fusion Energi, the Porsche Cayenne S E-Hybrid and others.

Electric cars

Electric cars are powered by one or more electric motors that derive their energy from an electric battery or fuel cell. An electric battery gets its energy from an external power source (home-charging station, level 2 or 3 public-charging station). Depending on the model, an electric battery can also recharge and act like a generator when you decelerate or go downhill.

In 2016, electric cars boast ranges between 100 and 500 kilometers (62 to 310 miles) and their recharge time is directly proportional to the size of the battery and the onboard charger.

The two current best-sellers are:

• **The Nissan Leaf.** This affordable electric car has a range of up to 250 kilometers (155 miles) with the 30 kWh version (average range of 200 kilometers or 124 miles). It's been in dealerships since 2010.

• **The Tesla Model S.** This vehicle is a 100-percent electric luxury car that, is revolutionizing the high-end market. High-performance, quiet as a mouse and safe as can be, it outclasses the German and Japanese competition. It's been so successful that several auto manufacturers have recently announced the launch of their own luxury EVs. You gotta give it to Tesla—this little outfit from Silicon Valley has really shaken up the world of cars.

The near future

Other market-shaking EVs (like the Chevrolet Bolt EV and Tesla Model 3) are not far off on the horizon. The coming years promise to be nothing short of captivating when it comes to electric cars.

We'll soon be the judges...

Tesla Model 3

The ABCs of hybrid, plug-in and electric cars

Bixi bike-sharing system

DO YOU REALLY NEED A CAR?

DANIEL BRETON

The question is pertinent. When thinking about your future mode of transportation, it's certainly a question that you should ask yourself.

This guide to electric cars is not designed solely to help you transition from your current vehicle to a cleaner one. It's *also* here to open up a discussion on how you get from point A to point B and how that impacts the world around you.

The less frequently you travel solo by car, the less you'll pollute via exhaust, greenhouse gases, energy consumption and contributing to extra traffic.

Must you own your own vehicle?

Manufacturing a car requires a considerable amount of raw materials, energy and water. That's why it's important to ask yourself the following: Do I need to own a car? Should I really own my own car or could I carpool, use ride shares, take public transit or even taxis for my daily transportation needs?

You *must* ask yourself this question.

City dwellers

If you live in or around a city, it's almost a certainty that these kinds of transportation services are available to you. They're probably also very efficient and thus viable alternatives to owning your own vehicle to get around for your day-to-day activities. Did you know that 90 percent of North American motorists travel fewer than 60 kilometers (40 miles) a day? That includes travel for work and family.

All you city dwellers are no doubt aware of just how inconvenient it can be to have your own car in town with parking, theft, tickets, snow removal, traffic, increasing insurance premiums—and the list goes on. When it comes down to it, keeping a car in the city can quickly become a headache.

Long-distance travel

If you really need a car to go longer distances, you can always use the services of a car rental company. More and more North American companies are offering hybrid, plug-in hybrid and 100-percent electric rental cars. Some of them even specialize in electric rentals, which means they offer better service and know-how than your everyday rental company.

Country dwellers

If you live in the suburbs or a rural area, transportation (carpooling, car shares, public transit, active commuting and so on) is less of an option than elsewhere—if it's even an option at all.

After a stint downtown in the busy metropolis of Montréal, I now live in the country, and I see how necessary it is for many people to own their own vehicle, especially in rural areas. No matter what your transportation needs are, however, know that owning a personal vehicle (electric or not) has a real impact on the environment. And your footprint only gets bigger when you drive solo.

Montréal subway ("the Metro")

Chevrolet Spark EV plugged in at a charging station on the street

ELECTRIC CARS: MYTHS AND PREJUDICES

DANIEL BRETON, ÈVE-MARY THAÏ THI LAC, JENNIFER ST-YVES-LAMBERT AND ELVIRE TOFFA JUTEAU

I've been writing about hybrid and electric cars for some time now, and I've come to realize that there are many of myths and prejudices on the subject. If it was 15 years ago, I would understand the widespread ignorance about these vehicles, but with the things I hear and read today, I'm astonished at the lack of knowledge that still exists. That's why we have invited three people who own electric cars to report on their experience, to help demystify the subject and clear up some of the misinformation that's out there.

Myth 1: Cost a lot more

While some electric cars are quite expensive, other models are very affordable ($20,000 [CAD]/$15,000 [USD] or less): for example, the Smart Fortwo Electric Drive (ED) and the Mitsubishi i-MiEV. You can certainly find electric cars that are a lot pricier—just as some gas-powered cars are more expensive. But the price of electric cars is gradually dropping, while that of gas-powered cars is rising. In five years, their prices should be more or less on par.

Former Canadian MP Ève-Mary Thaï Thi Lac describes her experience:

"The maintenance and repair costs for my last gas-powered car were mind-boggling. In 2014, the total came to more that $2,000 (CAD)/$1,500 (USD). Then there's the average fuel efficiency of 11 L/100 km (21 mpg). It was time for me to find a new vehicle. I knew I wanted a convertible, absolutely. But in 2014, there was only one fully electric convertible: the Smart Fortwo ED Convertible. As it happened, my lifestyle at the time was well-suited to this two-seater model.

At the dealer, our representative was extremely professional. After taking the car for a test drive, I was convinced. I wanted it! *But,* signing the contract means negotiating with the director of financial services. That's where things got a little rocky. The rep wanted to sell me a prepaid service plan that included oil changes—for an electric car! So, potential buyers, beware.

While my gas-powered car cost me $450 (CAD)/$337 (USD) a month on average (gas, maintenance and insurance, since my car was paid for), my payments are about $325 (CAD)/$243 (USD) per month (monthly installments, electricity, annual inspection and insurance included). With the money I'm saving, I take a trip south every year!

So, for anyone who claims they can't afford an electric car, I would tell them that for me the savings have been incredible."

Myth 2: Batteries for electric cars or hybrids last only two to three years

Totally false. Batteries in hybrid and electric vehicles are made to last just as long as the cars themselves, if not longer. These batteries are also usually guaranteed for a minimum of eight years and 160,000 kilometers (100,000 miles). Ask a taxi driver who uses a Prius and you'll see. And the battery for my own car, a Honda Insight, is still working well—after more than 15 years.

Toyota Prius

Ford Focus EV

Myth 3: Only for summers, only for cities

Electric cars start much more easily in winter than gas-powered cars, since an electric motor has far fewer moving parts than a gas engine, and contains no oil to turn to the consistency of molasses. That means there's less friction and less energy loss. Let's hear from Jennifer St-Yves-Lambert, who lives in the country and drives frequently in the winter:

"You often hear that electric vehicles are only useful in the city. Not true! I've always lived in the country, and during winter storms, the roads are frequently covered in snow when I leave for work in the morning. That's one reason why I bought an SUV in 2010. I thought I was protected from mudslides and from losing control on slippery roads. But in fact, the weight of the battery makes my electric Ford Focus very heavy, which gives the tires excellent traction. During snowstorms, this car is just as effective as any light truck!

Also, if electric vehicles were only made for the city, I'd be in trouble, since I drive 90 kilometers (56 miles) to work every day. Obviously, when the range drops in cold weather, it's essential one's employer offers charging. But all in all, I would never go back. For me, gas-powered vehicles, SUVs or otherwise, are a thing of the past."

Myth 4: Can't go more than 100 kilometers (62 miles) without being plugged in

While some electric cars still have a range of less than 100 kilometers, such vehicles are becoming fewer and fewer. A growing number of electric cars can drive 150, 200 or even 300 kilometers (93, 124 or 186 miles) in poor conditions. Batteries are advancing rapidly and are increasingly effective and affordable.

Myth 5: More pollution

Except for in a few U.S. states, where more than 70 percent of electricity production still comes from coal-fired plants, an electric car pollutes less than a gas-powered car. And the place where electric cars have the lowest pollution is Québec. Since the electricity produced there is 99 percent renewable, it's a win-win. But even in states like California, it's definitely a net gain. For the few states that still overuse coal for fuel, the hybrid is the best solution at hand (see the section that deals specifically with that subject).

Myth 6: Poor performance

Tesla punctured this myth with the Tesla Model S P90D, a car whose performance and acceleration surpasses the most exotic sports cars you can find anywhere on Earth for under $500,000 (CAD)/$375,000 (USD)—and the Tesla is a lot more affordable.

Myth 7: Not designed for families

To respond to that claim, let's listen to the experiences of Elvire Toffa Juteau, businesswoman and mother of three:

"I've been driving electric in a Chevrolet Volt for four years now. I work about five minutes from home and I go to business meetings now and then throughout the city. However, I can't even remember the last time I went to refuel. Oh, wait! The last time was last year. The car gave me a message asking me to put in a little bit of fuel. It's been so long that I've actually become intolerant of that unpleasant gas smell.

On the family side, I have three kids: Danyc, eight years old, David, five, and Marlène, two and a half. The Volt has enough space for us. Marlène's car seat fits comfortably in the back, and David sits beside her, so they can laugh and play and bug each other. The eldest sits up from with me, where he can be my copilot. The four-seat car is spacious and comfortable enough for my three kids and me.

I also often use the trunk to transport the things I need for my business, like boxes full of hair for my beauty salon, fabric supplies for the clothing I make, and so on. Basically, my electric car is ideal for my job as a mother and entrepreneur."

Coal-fired power plant

ELON MUSK: A REVOLUTIONARY SPIRIT

DANIEL RUFIANGE

At the beginning of the 20th century, the world saw numerous attempts at electric-powered transportation. Despite some promising initiatives, the historical context wasn't fertile soil for its development. Talented, ingenious and well-intentioned people were not able to make the electric car catch on. Humanity was on a different path.

Now, some 100 years later, conditions are different. The electric car is present in our everyday lives. Just as before, talented, ingenious and well-intentioned people are working on making the electric car a success.

Now, the stars have aligned to ensure its future in the long term.

This time around, the world is ready.

One of the founding fathers of the electric revolution that we're living today is Elon Musk. Never heard of him? You may have heard of the company he founded. Musk is the man behind Tesla Motors, a group that's pushing the envelope in the car industry and forcing the competition to move over.

Here is his story.

Business-minded visionary

Tesla was founded in 2003. At the time, Elon Musk was 32 years old. He had big dreams for his new company, perhaps ones that seemed too ambitious for an automobile industry outsider. If you took even a quick look at his journey, however, you'd understand how this man is a visionary.

Musk hails from South Africa, from Pretoria in the Transvaal to be exact. He developed a head for business quite early on—at the tender age of 10, he got his hands on his first PC, a Commodore VIC-20. He learned how to program on his own and two years later, he developed the code for a video game called Blastar. He sold the rights to a specialty magazine for about $500.

Off to Canada, and then the United States

In 1989, the ultra-talented young man arrived in Canada, obtained citizenship (his mother is from Regina, Saskatchewan) and enrolled at Queen's University in Kingston, Ontario. In 1992, Elon headed off to Pennsylvania where, at age 24, he earned a bachelor's degree in physics from the University of Pennsylvania's College of Arts and Sciences as well as a bachelor's in economics from the Wharton School of the University of Pennsylvania.

Life then took him to California, where he began a PhD in applied physics at Stanford. After just two days, he dropped his doctoral studies to go into the Internet business, which was barely off the ground at the time.

Made a fortune

In 1995, Elon and his brother Kimbal started a company called Zip2, where he developed software that provided content for websites. His two biggest clients were the *New York Times* and the *Chicago Tribune*. Four years later, Zip2 was sold to Compaq for no fewer than 307 million dollars.

Tesla Roadster

Elon Musk: a revolutionary spirit

That same year, Elon Musk cofounded X.com, an online payment solutions company. A subsidiary company acquired by X.com one year later would go on to become PayPal, a global juggernaut. In 2002, eBay would purchase the former for 1.5 billion dollars in stock. Before the sale, Musk owned an 11-percent stake in PayPal.

Several other players would cash in their fat checks and retire. Not Elon. In 2002, he founded SpaceX, an endeavor focused on space exploration and related technology. The goal: building commercial spacecraft. Some might not have taken the idea seriously in the beginning, but everyone soon discovered just how very real SpaceX's mission was. In 2008, NASA signed a contract with SpaceX to deliver supplies to the International Space Station. Their first mission was accomplished in 2012.

Tesla confounds convention

In 2003, Elon Musk founded Tesla Motors with four other partners. Five years later, he became CEO and product architect. Tesla has given him the most influence yet by far and it's the company that, up until today, touches the most people. Tesla owners are growing in number and Tesla is planning on selling new models soon. This year, they'll debut Model X and the order book is already quite full.

Tesla Motors products are so popular that other manufacturers such as Porsche have announced plans to sell 100-percent electric vehicles to compete with cars like the now famous Model S.

Tesla confounds conventions and the way it does business is changing transportation in a real way. The company's founder doesn't plan on stopping either. He's begin working on other projects, namely Hyperloop and Powerwall. The former is a kind of high-speed tube-based travel. The latter, a home battery that feeds on wind and solar energy. Everything is powered by lithium batteries. And Musk isn't even 45!

Musk, Edison and Tesla

Elon Musk should be viewed as a great visionary. He's often introduced as a businessman, an inventor and an entrepreneur. The decisions he makes have a direct influence on our collective history. We'll of course need to wait decades or even centuries to know exactly what his impact has been, but one thing is certain—his name will be remembered, just like his idol Thomas Edison.

Contrary to what you might think, Nikola Tesla is not Elon Musk's hero, even if the company does carry his name. It's true that Tesla cars have an electric motor that uses alternating currents and that technology comes from Nikola Tesla's 1882 invention. Musk's admiration for Edison, however, comes from how his inventions went from the drawing board to reality, a bit like Musk's own progress.

Funnily enough, Nikola Tesla often worked with Thomas Edison. It's often said that some of Edison's inventions should be partly attributed to Tesla. In any case, both were great creative minds that advanced the human race as a whole. And now, Elon Musk, in his turn, is getting his name into the history books as well.

Elon Musk at the unveiling of the SpaceX Dragon V2 spacecraft

Elon Musk at the Paris Climate Conference

Sommet des élus locaux pour le climat
Paris - Vendredi 4 décembre 2015

Elon Musk: a revolutionary spirit

WEATHERING WINTER WITH AN ELECTRIC CAR: A HOW-TO GUIDE

DANIEL BRETON

The author of this text, yours truly, lives in a part of North America where the cold weather can be particularly, well, *cold*. And winter 2014 to 2015 proved to be especially harsh here, with temperatures sometimes dipping below -30°C and plummeting to -50°C

(-22°F and -58°F) with the windchill factor! So it's a good thing that electric vehicle (EV) batteries aren't affected by windchill. My wife and I both drive plug-ins: a 2012 Chevrolet Volt and a 2014 Smart Fortwo Electric Drive. And just like the thousands of other drivers who have made the switch to electric, we've proved that it's entirely possible to get around in an electric car...even in the dead of winter!

Of course, driving an EV in chilly weather does require making a few slight adjustments, and of course, it has its pros and cons.

IMPORTANT: Whether you drive a fuel-powered, diesel or electric car, fuel economy invariably decreases with the mercury! Fuel consumption can increase by up to 50 percent, which is similar to the 50-percent increase in energy consumption of an electric vehicle during colder weather. It's also important to note that when temperatures go from +30 to -30°C (+86 to -22°F), air density increases by 25 percent. This means your car needs more energy to "slice" through air, rendering any movement more difficult than usual.

Let's start with the cons:

· **An electric car's operating range drops by 50 percent in extremely cold weather (between -20 and -40°C or -4 and -40°F)**. If you drive distances of up to 150 kilometers (93 miles) with your electric car in summer, be prepared for that number to drop to 75 kilometers (47 miles) in winter, especially if you turn on your heater. In milder weather, say between -5 and -10°C (23 and 14°F), your EV's range will decrease by 20 to 30 percent.

To maintain your car's range and protect your battery, it's recommended that you charge it as often as possible during the winter months. And if you can, store your vehicle in a heated garage to boost your vehicle's range.

· **In order to preserve as much range as possible, dress more warmly than you would when driving a vehicle with an internal combustion engine.** Most plug-in hybrid and electric vehicles come equipped with heated seats, and some even come with a heated steering wheel. These elements are designed to limit the need for your heater, which tends to burn through battery power. So to save on heating, dress warmly!

And there you have it: the inconveniences of driving an electric car in winter.

Weathering winter with an electric car: a how-to guide

And now for the pros:

· **An electric car will always start,** because the motor is always free of any liquid. So say goodbye to jumper cables for good!

· **You can heat your car ahead of time... without polluting.** Contrary to the remote starters on fuel-powered and diesel cars, which tend to encourage idling and pollute the air, warming up your EV is 100-percent environmentally friendly. It's great for keeping the inside of your car warm when traveling short distances. Plus, when you warm up your car while it's charging, you don't drain its battery, which in turn prolongs range. Once on the road, your heating system just has to maintain the desired temperature, which takes a lot of stress off the battery.

Another hands-down advantage: Warming up your car will defrost your windshield, side and rear windows, so you don't have to spend time scraping the ice yourself!

· **The battery in an electric car is usually located beneath the floor, lowering the car's center of gravity and making it more than capable of handling in snowy weather.** The bottom of an EV is usually flat, allowing it to glide across the snow, thus lowering the odds of you getting stuck in it.

· **A cold climate has a positive effect on EV battery life.** Although EV battery range drops in colder weather, its lifespan does not. That being said, it's important to avoid letting your battery freeze, so remember to always plug in your car during cold spells.

· Just as with any internal combustion vehicle, **it's strongly recommended that you not accelerate too quickly after starting your electric car.** This will allow all the car's parts (wheels, suspension, etc.) to warm up. Plus, if only for security reasons, it's best to drive below the speed limit, seeing as your car's tires have considerably less grip in extremely cold weather.

So there you have it: a short guide to driving an electric car in winter. For further information and to learn more about your model, make sure you read your vehicle's handbook.

AddÉnergie's Circuit Électrique charging stations: level 2 (left) and level 3 (right)

CHILD'S PLAY: CHARGING YOUR ELECTRIC CAR

SYLVAIN JUTEAU

Over the years, people who are interested in buying an electric vehicle, but are worried about charging, have been asking me some questions:

- Is it complicated to charge an electric car? Is it expensive?
- Will I need to change my main power supply at home?
- Will I be able to convince my employer to install charging stations at my workplace?
- How do I locate public charging stations?
- Are there enough of them, and can they be found everywhere?
- I live in a condo. Will the owners' association allow me to install a charging station?
- I live in an apartment and I park on the street. How do I charge each night?

You have to sympathize with these people: it's human nature to fear the new and unknown. Moreover, the entire industry directly or indirectly connected with fossil-fuel-based mobility (oil companies, car manufacturers, etc.) puts no small effort into maintaining fear and misconceptions about electric cars. Our goal here is to answer your questions. But we'll start by defining the different types of charging stations available in North America.

Types of charging stations:

Level 1: Portable 120-volt charger issued with the vehicle

This is the basic charger, since it works on 120-volt electric outlets, which are found everywhere. Normally, buildings have at least one 120-volt outlet available outside. This will probably be a backup solution in many cases, since it can take several days to charge some electric vehicles, like the Tesla or the Chevrolet Bolt, particularly if it's very cold out (almost all the 120-volt charger's energy will be used to keep the electric car at an optimal temperature). Also, the charger that normally comes with the vehicle is fragile and isn't designed to be used on a daily basis. And in harsh northern climates it is that much less effective outside.

Level 2: 240-volt charging stations

The 240-volt station is the key to enjoying the experience of electric driving and making it superior to driving with a conventional gas-powered car. The best place to install it is wherever you park your electric vehicle at night. The next best option is at one's workplace, which is where most of us spend a lot of our time. The vast majority of cars are parked 22 hours out of 24. If you're able to plug in your electric car during that time, it will always be fully charged when you want to take it out.

A 240-volt charging station must be installed by a certified electrician. However, it's much less complicated than you might think. It's very similar to installing an electrical outlet for a dryer or stove—a pretty common job for electricians. This charging station will charge

your vehicle in just a few hours. Stations of this kind have been installed all over the road network, particularly in places where people spend a lot of time. You'll see them at restaurants, at rest stops and at tourist attractions such as museums. You can charge your car while you go about your business in these places. Some networks may be free, while others will require you to pay in order to charge your car.

Level 3: 400-volt fast-charging stations

Fast charging is obviously the ultimate method: You can fully charge your vehicle in only a few minutes! These extraordinarily powerful chargers are almost always public. You'll mainly see them along major highways. The networks are being developed, and new fast-charging stations are appearing regularly. These stations allow drivers to go longer distances. But note that the fast-charging port, which allows you to use these stations, is not available on all electric cars. Be sure to ask your dealer whether your new car is equipped with this kind of port. With stations becoming more numerous, making use of them is very practical. In the U.S. there are three standard kinds of plug's for fast charging: the CCS Combo, the CHAdeMO and the Supercharger, for Teslas.

Charge networks

There are a number of charging networks along North American roads. Remember that each has different conditions of use, but they're all very simple to use. When you have to pay for the charge, you can operate the station with a

Tesla's Supercharger charge ports

prepaid card that you can buy on the network's website using an application on your smartphone, with a credit card or even with cash.

Main networks in North America include Electric Circuit, VERnetwork (Québec), Sun Country Highway, Tesla's Supercharger, ChargePoint and the Blink Network. Each one has its own website.

Frequently asked questions

Q: Is it complicated to charge my electric car? How do I find public charging stations?
A: Remember that it really isn't complicated to charge your car anywhere and at any time. Apps and websites list all the charging stations on North American roads. The PlugShare free app is definitely the most popular, since it's designed to be a map that uses a color code to precisely indicate each station. When you click on the symbol of a station, a complete description tells you its conditions of use.

Q: Is it expensive? Do I need to change my main power supply at home? Can I convince my employer to install charging stations at work?
A: These questions are all related, since the charging station that you would install at work or at home would be 240 volts. Installation doesn't cost more than installing a new electric appliance that works on this type of current, such as a stove, dryer, pool heater, etc. If there is enough space in the electrical panel for a new appliance such as those, then, there's no reason to think it will cost very much. Moreover, since the 240-volt terminal is extremely practical and pretty affordable, the governments of many states and provinces will reimburse some of the cost of the purchase and installation of stations at home or the workplace. This gives you a great angle to use when convincing your employer to provide you with a charge!

Q: I live in a condo. Will the owners' association allow me to install a charging station?

A: It's possible to install a device called a power meter directly on the electrical circuit of the charging station. This allows you to calculate the electricity consumption needed to charge your vehicle. A certified electrician can easily do the job. The condo's owners' association can then charge the user of the station for the kilowatt-hours consumed.

Q: I live in an apartment and I have to park my car on the street. How do I charge my car overnight?

A: Unfortunately, that's a problem, since you won't be able to charge your car at night. If this is your situation, get some information *before* you buy an electric car. Are there public charging stations nearby? Does a neighbor have a private entrance and a station of their own? Maybe the owner of your building would be interested in installing stations on the property, which would increase its value. Try asking. And if there is a fast-charging station near you, you can charge your electric car once or twice a week (the car will charge to 80 percent in less than 25 minutes). I would advise you to get in touch with an owner of an electric car in your area: They will probably have some answers and know about their advantages and disadvantages.

Conclusion

Even if there is a lot to know about charging electric vehicles, it doesn't take long to figure out this new world, and it's actually quite a satisfying project. Let the valuable information I've provided here serve as your survival guide if you feel a little lost about the types of stations, standards, networks and apps. Remember that most buildings have at least one exterior outlet, and that you can always ask a good Samaritan to charge your car. Remember: It's child's play.

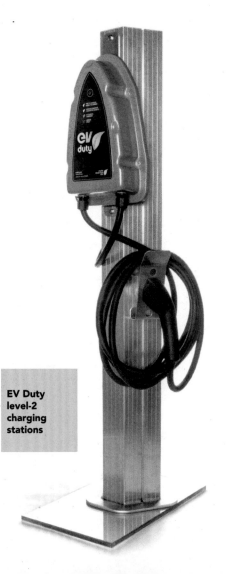

EV Duty level-2 charging stations

ARE ELECTRIC CARS REALLY MORE EXPENSIVE THAN GAS-POWERED CARS?

DANIEL BRETON

People often present the price of hybrid and electric cars as an argument to belittle their value. According to naysayers, partially- and 100-percent electric vehicles are not financially viable options since their return on investment isn't fast enough to come.

Let's have a closer look to see if they're right.

A matter of priorities

I find the argument that the purchase price of hybrid and electric vehicles makes them an unworthy investment nothing short of laughable.

To that I say the following: If the price tag alone is what determines whether you buy (or lease) a car, you'd be better off never purchasing one in the first place. Unless you're getting a car for business purposes, which could allow you to recoup your investment, you'd spend your money more wisely if you took public transit, rode your bike or got into a rideshare, especially if you live in the city. It doesn't matter what make or model of new car or light truck you buy, you are guaranteed to lose thousands of dollars in the first weeks you drive it.

So why don't we apply the argument of return on investment to every vehicle out there, why just EVs?

Not just a matter of price

If you ruled out every vehicle that could be considered "extra" or economically unfeasible, companies like Mercedes, Porsche, BMW, Lexus, Ferrari, Bentley and Audi wouldn't be able to get a single car off their lots. We'd all do better to roll in a Toyota Corolla, Ford Fiesta, Nissan Micra, Dodge Grand Caravan and other vehicles of the same caliber—cheap and Spartan!

In that same vein, why would we spend more to equip our cars with uneconomic options like:

- a leather interior
- a GPS
- a high-end sound system
- cruise control
- power mirrors
- AC
- Bluetooth connectivity...

The answer is simple: It's because we're prepared to pay for non-essentials.

Here's some evidence...

• The purchase price isn't that important

The average price of a vehicle is not $12,000 or $15,000. It's more than double that. According to Kelley Blue Book (kbb.com), the average price paid in 2015 for a car or light truck was $33,560 in the U.S. That's about $46,450 Canadian in 2016.

• Practicality is not all it's cracked up to be

An increasing number of automobile consumers are buying up SUVs and vans. 15 years ago, it was all about small and affordable cars. So more and more people are choosing to pay more for their vehicles, decidedly because they believe the extra cost is justified. Their enthusiasm is a passing fad. If people really wanted a practical vehicle, everyone would be buying minivans.

The problem with minivans? Most people think they're uncool. So what's in vogue right now? Small and medium-sized SUVs, vans and crossovers (whatever that means). Yet many SUVs and crossovers have less passenger room than minivans or even family cars!

• It's not all about fuel economy

Some automobile manufactures like Toyota sell traditional and hybrid vehicles (hybrids generally cost an extra $2,000, which you usually recoup pretty fast thanks to gas savings.) Lincoln sells its MKZ Hybrid for the same price as its traditional engine version! Nevertheless, many people prefer not to opt for the hybrid versions...

Lastly, though it's true that plug-in hybrid and electric vehicles cost more at the time of purchase than other gas and diesel vehicles in their class, once you've calculated...

- the thousands of dollars you save on gas
- tax incentives
- the thousands of dollars saved on maintenance and repair
- and the hundreds of dollars you save on insurance...

...electric cars often cost the same or *less* than their gas-powered competitors. For example, a new Nissan Leaf will run you about the same or less than a Honda Civic after three years of driving. After five years, you'll save thousands of dollars with the Leaf.

That's why, at the end of the day, the famous "rational" purchase price argument used to disparage hybrid and electric cars is anything but rational. In the end, it really comes down to you, the consumer, to define your priorities when it comes to your own vehicle.

Are electric cars really more expensive than gas-powered cars?

ELECTRIC CAR MAINTENANCE: NO REPAIRS, REALLY?

JACQUES DUVAL

No oil to check, no exhaust pipe to replace, no complex transmission, no spark plugs to change—I could keep going. I will not, however, feed into the myth that electric cars require no maintenance whatsoever.

Journalists and gurus are pleased as punch to tout the almost-no-repair virtues of electric cars and fuel-efficient vehicles. For the layman, let's just say that a certain accessory, the range extender, is really a conventional engine that's on standby and kicks into gear when the battery is low. It's an effective remedy to the stress you might encounter when eyeing a diminishing distance on the range meter for your electric battery. For that reason and more, electric cars still require a bit of maintenance.

An expert opinion

To get to the bottom of this question, we contacted Charles Rivard, manager of the Montréal Tesla service center located on Ferrier Street.

"Electric cars definitely require service—at least once a year or every 20,000 kilometers (12,000 miles)—whichever comes first," says Rivard, right off the bat.

According to this expert, you need to start with the car's security features first, and that goes for purely electric cars, as well as hybrids. You'll need to have the suspension inspected, which involves getting the shocks, all suspension components and bearings checked. It's an important inspection to carry out when dealing with a 1,950-kilogram (4,300-pound) Tesla Model S driving on imperfect roads.

Although Tesla drivers generally believe that the only maintenance their car needs is a brake-pad change, which is actually rare for a car that uses regenerative breaking, the whole system needs to be checked and so do the brake calipers.

Tires should be rotated, too, and you need to make sure that the alignment is on point. You also need to check for leaks or abnormal wear and tear everywhere.

Our Tesla expert, Charles Rivard, also adds that, at Tesla, you can receive service bulletins that advise you to change or improve certain parts so you can optimize your ride. In addition, after one year or 20,000 kilometers (12,000 miles), it's wise to replace the Tesla's cabin air filter.

Proper maintenance also includes new windshield wipers, brake fluids and coolant, every 40,000 kilometers/25,000 miles maximum.

Weight in salt

Lastly, mechanics worth their weight in salt will use diagnostic equipment to take the car out for a test-drive and make sure that everything's in proper working order. A bit of lube on the latches and hinges won't hurt either. I'd opt for a manufacturer-trained electric or plug-in hybrid specialist for your car. Don't trust just anyone, they might not be in the know when it comes to cutting-edge EV technology.

Tesla Model S's central control panel

Electric car maintenance: no repairs, really?

駆動用バッテリー
Battery

Lithium-ion battery

ALL BATTERIES ARE NOT CREATED EQUAL

PIERRE LANGLOIS

A rechargeable battery is technically a secondary battery, but that expression isn't used often in everyday speech. For simplicity's sake, we'll use the word "battery" and leave out the qualifier "rechargeable," since all batteries used in cars must be rechargeable.

Here we'll look at the main characteristics of different batteries found on the vehicle market.

IMPORTANT: When we describe the lifespan of a battery in terms of the number of charge cycles, we're referring to a deep discharge (at least 80 percent of the storage capacity); the life-cycle limit is the battery having lost 20 percent of its initial capacity.

Lead batteries

Lead batteries first entered the market at the end of the 19th century, and they are still used today in cars and trucks to start combustion engines. These heavy batteries can store 30 to 50 watt hours (Wh) of electrical energy per kilogram. Their lifetime is approximately 300 deep discharge cycles. The number of cycles increases if only 30 to 40 percent of the energy is depleted before charging.

Nickel-metal hydride (NiMH) batteries

NiMH batteries were made available in the 1990s and are used today in all of Toyota's hybrid vehicles. They can store about 60 to 120 Wh/kg and survive 500 discharges to an 80-percent depth. But by oversizing the battery and using only 10-percent electrical energy as you would in a normal (i.e., non-plug-in) hybrid car, the battery's lifespan can be extended considerably. That's why NiMH batteries in Toyota's Prius last about as long as the vehicles themselves; a Toyota Prius can chalk up more than 400,000 kilometers (249,000 miles) with its original battery.

Lithium-ion (Li-ion) batteries

An ion is an atom that has fewer or more electrons than a neutral atom, giving it an electrical charge. The coming and going of lithium ions between the positive and negative terminals of a Li-ion battery (depending on whether the battery is being charged or discharged) takes place via an electrolyte, usually liquid but sometimes solid (polymer film). A gel is often added to make the polymer film more conductive; this results in a Li-ion polymer battery. Usually, the negative section of the battery (the anode, connected to the negative terminal) is made of graphite (a form of carbon) while the positive section (the cathode) is made of one or more metal oxides.

The pioneering work of then Oxford professor John Goodenough led to the first functioning Li-ion battery in 1980. His brainchild was a cathode made of cobalt oxide. Sony was the first to market it, in 1991. This type of Li-ion battery is handy for portable devices (cameras, laptops, telephones) that use low currents, but the chemical reaction involved can too easily cause thermal runaway when used for strong currents. This can cause fires, therefore for safety reasons, they aren't used in electric vehicles.

Lithium-ion battery for a plug-in hybrid vehicle

All batteries are not created equal

Hyundai Ioniq hybrid

Lithium iron phosphate (LFP) batteries

Professor Goodenough, when at the University of Texas in 1996, made another innovation by adding iron phosphate to the cathodes of Li-ion batteries. Not long after, researchers at Hydro-Québec's research institute (IREQ) and the Université de Montréal made major improvements to LFP batteries, allowing them to produce stronger currents and significantly increasing their longevity.

LFP batteries use a very safe chemistry that prevents thermal runaway and the fire that could result from a short circuit. This type of battery can store 90 to 120 Wh/kg of electrical energy—three times more than a lead battery—and can withstand 1,000 to 4,000 deep discharges.

These batteries are sold by companies like China's BYD, which uses them in its electric cars and buses, and by A123 Systems in the U.S., which sells 12V batteries to replace lead batteries in micro-hybrid cars with a start-stop system.

Lithium nickel cobalt aluminum oxide (NCA) batteries

NCA oxide batteries are the batteries used by Tesla Motors in its vehicles; they source their batteries from Panasonic. The main advantage of NCA batteries is that they're light and can store 200 to 260 Wh/kg of electrical energy—twice as much as LFP batteries of the same weight. Their lifespan, however, is limited to about 500 deep discharge/charge cycles. This disadvantage is compensated for by the large size of the battery, like the ones used in Tesla vehicles (which have a 425-kilometer/265-mile range). A large battery requires much less frequent charging than a smaller one, and it can be partially charged to replace the power that has been used during the day—commonly about 20 percent of its full charge. Partial charges greatly increase the number of charge cycles.

One major motivation behind Tesla's choice of these batteries is that they're less expensive, since they're manufactured in vast quantities for the electronics industry. But this advantage is gradually slipping away with increased production of other kinds of Li-ion batteries for vehicles.

Lithium-ion nickel manganese cobalt oxide (NMC) batteries

NMC batteries currently offer the greatest potential for electric vehicles. These batteries were developed in the U.S. at the end of the 20th century by Argonne National Laboratory and 3M Company. The mass density of energy they can store is impressive: from 130 to 220 Wh/kg. The batteries have a much higher lifespan than NCA batteries—two to four times more—and can withstand 1,000 to 2,000 deep charges.

Samsung SDI, which supplies batteries to BMW for its electric vehicles, uses NMC technology. Samsung SDI will also be supplying NMC batteries for the electric SUV iEV6S made by Chinese car company JAC Motors.

LG Chem, a company that provides batteries for electric vehicles and plug-in hybrids for GM, Ford, Chrysler, Renault, Mercedes/Smart and Volvo, has made deals with Argonne Lab (2011) and 3M (2015) to license NMC batteries. LG Chem has always described its batteries as "manganese-rich," implying the presence of other metals in the cathode, but the company is very unforthcoming with the specifics. Their

licensing of NMC batteries suggests that LG Chem will be following other companies in using this battery chemistry for electric vehicles. Because they use a polymer for the electrolyte, their batteries are lithium polymer batteries.

Anticipating significant increases in sales of their vehicles, Tesla is also in talks with LG Chem and Samsung SDI to source batteries. That means Tesla plans to also use NMC batteries.

Lithium titanate (LTO) batteries

Titanate started being used in place of carbon in the anode of Li-ion batteries in the 1980s. Major developments were made to these batteries (called LTO in the literature) by the IREQ near the end of the millennium. By using iron phosphate for the cathode, IREQ lab researchers showed that this type of battery can be charged from 0 to 100 percent in just six minutes—more than 30,000 times, without losing capacity! Its heat stability is outstanding, and the battery is therefore very safe. Its performance at temperatures as low as -30°C (-22°F) is remarkable. Still, the disadvantage of these batteries for electric cars is that they are heavier. The density of energy stored is only 57 Wh/kg.

A version using a different formula for the cathode (not iron phosphate) was sold by Toshiba as the SCiB battery. It has a mass-based energy density of 90 Wh/kg and an announced lifespan of 10,000 cycles. The Proterra company uses these batteries in electric buses with ultra-fast charging (less than 10 minutes from empty to full). For this type of use, the bus's range doesn't need to be more than 50 kilometers (31 miles), because

All batteries are not created equal

TM4 electric motor.

the battery can be charged repeatedly during the day; a small battery is therefore enough.

Lithium metal polymer (LMP) battery

In the 1990s, the IREQ together with the Université de Montréal developed an entirely solid lithium metal polymer (LMP) battery. The anode in this battery is made of a thin sheet of lithium metal, and the electrolyte is made of a thin sheet of polymer with no gel or paste: thus it's completely solid. The technology was purchased by Bolloré, which was also working on the LMP battery, in the 2000s. Blue Solution, a subsidiary of Bolloré, currently makes a version of the LMP battery at its Bathium plant in Montréal for use in Bolloré's Bluecar electric city-cars in France and elsewhere: mainly for car-sharing organizations and in the Bolloré minibus (the Bluetram or Bluebus).

The only official specifications that we've been able to find on the LMP battery are on the Bluecar site (bluecar.fr). It tells us that the battery has a mass of 300 kilograms and a storage capacity of 30 kWh, making a specific energy density of 100 Wh/kg for the full-battery pack. We can deduce that the energy density at the level of individual cells should be in the range of 120 to 140 Wh/kg. The site also says that the Bluecar can travel almost 250 kilometers (155 miles) on a full charge in an urban environment, and that the battery's lifespan should be able to last for 400,000 kilometers (248,548 miles). The number of charge cycles should therefore be somewhere around 2,000 to 3,000. On top of that, the fact that the LMP is completely solid, makes it a very safe battery.

However, this kind of battery has two major limitations. The first is that it must be constantly heated to keep it around 80°C (176°F), even when the car is stationary and parked, if you hope to start it quickly anytime you want. To achieve this, the car must always be plugged in when not being used; if not, the battery empties in about three days in a country like France, and in less time in the winter in Nordic countries.

If the car is driven only two hours per day, you use as much electricity keeping the battery warm as you do driving the car. The second limitation is the low battery power, which is five to 10 times less than that of Li-ion batteries of an equal weight. That means it's impossible to charge quickly and to accelerate the car adequately; the electrical currents are too low. For this reason, the battery is used in low-power city cars. The peak power of the Bluecar is only 50 kW (for only 30 seconds), compared to the engine in the forthcoming Chevrolet Bolt, which will be 150 kW.

Moreover, because the 30 kWh LMP can't provide the Bluecar's 50 kW of power all by itself, an ultra capacitor is required that provides stronger currents for 30 seconds, the time it takes to accelerate. Then the battery slowly charges the ultra capacitor until the next time its power is needed. That means mountainous areas and sporty driving are off limits.

Cell with lithium plating

Chevrolet Volt's "Voltec" system

BATTERY POWER: THE KEY TO THE EV

PIERRE LANGLOIS

The only thing preventing electric vehicles from traveling longer distances is battery life. Where the technology is today, you need a 700-kilogram (1,500-pound) lithium-ion battery to travel 500 kilometers (310 miles). That comes out to 10 adults who each weigh 70 kilograms (155 pounds).

Though low weight is absolutely essential, a good battery must meet six principal criteria:

- Low weight and volume
- Excellent safety record
- Low manufacturing cost
- Resistance to extreme temperatures (-30°C to +60°C/-22°F to +140°F)
- Longevity (more than 1,500 charges)
- Fast-charge capability

Criteria 1: Low weight and volume

Experts expect lithium-ion batteries to weigh 30 to 50 percent less by 2020, with the addition of silicone. But the results from Paraclete Energy (paracleteenergy.com) suggest that Li-ion batteries—almost twice as light—will be available by 2017 for electric vehicles. In the longer term, lithium-air batteries could be five times lighter than they are today.

Criteria 2: Excellent safety record

Electric car manufacturers use a high-performance battery management system that lets them quickly identify potentially problematic cells and isolate them to prevent further damage. Up until now, statistics have shown that these batteries are safe: Over one million electric vehicles have been on the road since September 2015 without any major incidents.

Criteria 3: Low manufacturing cost

Batteries are now cheaper and faster to make than we could have ever imagined, as evidenced by a meta-study published in 2015. Average battery cost nosedived from $1,200/kWh in 2007 to $410/kWh in 2015. That means that the price of batteries has decreased by 14 percent on average every year. These numbers are only the average—the highest performance batteries, such as Tesla's, currently sell below $300/kWh.

Global lithium-ion battery production is set to triple by 2020. Tesla's mega-factory in Nevada, which was built in partnership with Panasonic, should double worldwide production (over 2014 levels) within a few years. We can expect to see a gradual decrease in lithium-ion battery prices until 2020, when they should settle below $200/kWh and possibly even reach $125/kWh by 2025.

Criteria 4: Resistance to extreme temperatures

Electric cars need to be able to drive in all kinds of weather, from -30°C to +50°C (-22°F to +140°F). In extreme conditions, batteries lose storage capacity and can even start to deteriorate. To lengthen battery life and boost performance, you can install heat management systems that warm batteries up and cool them down when necessary. You can even program the time you need your car to be ready to go—the system will keep the battery at just the right temperature while it's charging.

Floor of the Chevrolet Volt, with battery

Battery power: the key to the EV

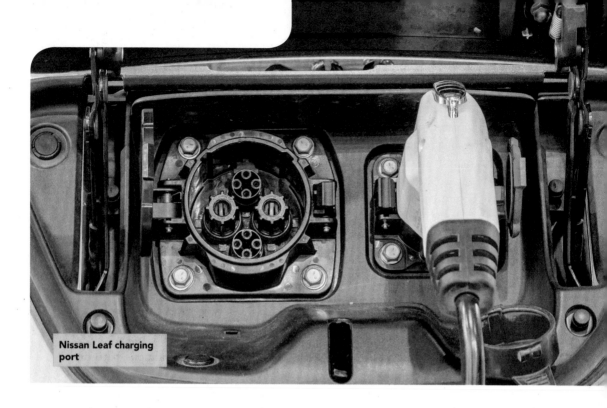

Criteria 5: Longevity

In real life, an electric car that drives 130 kilometers (80 miles) on a full charge needs to be recharged around 200 times a year if you want to drive it 20,000 kilometers (12,000 miles). That means 2,000 charges over 10 years. If the battery is two times larger and you travel the same distance, you'll only need to charge it 1,000 times. Hence the reason Tesla Motors offers their Infinite Mile Warranty for their batteries, which are three times bigger than those of other commercial electric vehicles. In general, other manufacturers offer up a 160,000-kilometer (100,000-mile) warranty, specifying that the battery might lose somewhere between 20 and 30 percent of its storage capacity afterward.

Criteria 6: Fast-charge capability

Good batteries will extend a fast charge that can extend the EV range about 250 kilometers (160 miles) in 30 minutes at future 150 kW level-3 charging stations. These more powerful charging stations will start popping up around 2020.

Second life and recycling

Many manufacturers have already started thinking about recycling used batteries to give them a second life. They could be used to store energy from the Sun or from the power grid. The marketing opportunities there are huge.

After powering a car for 200,000 kilometers (125,000 miles) or more, batteries are still good; they may simply lose about 25 percent of their storage capacity. If this percentage is critical when you are driving a vehicle, that battery can still serve other purposes, in buildings, for example. That's why you only need to recycle most used batteries every 20 years or so. In North America, the leader in the field is Retriev Technologies (retrievtech.com).

The company received $9.5 million from the U.S. Department of Energy to build a lithium-ion battery recycling plant for the American automobile industry.

In principle, you can recycle over 80 percent of a lithium-ion battery. Nowadays, it's profitable to recycle the cobalt and nickel, but not necessarily the manganese and iron found in some lithium-ion batteries. There isn't much to gain from recycling the lithium or graphite (a form of carbon) found in the most majority of lithium-ion batteries either—it's actually cheaper to mine these minerals.

That's why we need to put regulatory measures in place to incentivize recycling, which shouldn't entail greater costs, since they will have a resale value for their second life.

Tailor battery to your needs

That said, one thing is certain, environmentally speaking: You should purchase an electric vehicle whose battery is tailored to your needs. Buying an electric car with a range of 500 kilometers (310 miles) makes absolutely no sense if 90 percent of your day-to-day travel falls below 50 kilometers (31 miles) and you can recharge your car every day.

Maybe we'll come to the conclusion that a plugged-in hybrid vehicle—equipped with a battery and gas engine—with a 100-kilometer (62-mile) range is more environmentally viable than a 100 percent electric car with a big, 500-kilometer battery. With a 100-kilometer battery, you can drive 90 percent of the distance you need to travel using only electricity. For the remaining 10 percent, you could rely on second-generation biofuels produced from refuse and residue.

Nissan Leaf's batteries

Battery power: the key to the EV

Toyota Mirai

HYDROGEN
OR ELECTRIC?

PIERRE LANGLOIS

Hydrogen vehicles will finally hit markets in 2016. You won't see too many of them at first, likely only a few hundred units, since a hydrogen service infrastructure has yet to be fully developed.

Simply put, a hydrogen car is a fuel cell vehicle (FCV), which is powered by a hydrogen fuel cell as opposed to a battery. Fuel cells produce the electricity that electric car engines need, as long as they have enough hydrogen. That's why you need to fill them up at hydrogen stations where they can give the car the high-pressure injection it needs. It takes only five minutes to fill the tank, which gets you anywhere between 400 and 500 kilometers (250 to 310 miles), depending on

the vehicle. Inside the fuel cell, when the hydrogen reacts with oxygen, water forms, which is then discharged in the exhaust. That means hydrogen vehicles don't emit pollutants or greenhouse gases (GHG) on the road—just a little H_2O.

Selling points for FCVs

The main selling points for FCVs are their short refueling time and long range—again, five minutes gets you 500 kilometers (310 miles)—as opposed to a battery electric vehicle (BEV), which has a more limited range and requires several hours to recharge.

At first glance, hydrogen technology seems wonderful. When you take a closer look, however, you'll see that there are problems related to hydrogen production and distribution. There are also extra costs associated with FCVs.

Pruducing hydrogen from fossil fuels

One problem is that 95 percent of hydrogen is currently produced from fossil fuels, mainly by reforming natural gas. That's why the hydrogen sector is, in a way, an extension of the fossil fuel industry. Even though FCVs do not emit toxic or greenhouse gases on the road, the plants that produce the hydrogen do.

Studies on the hydrogen life cycle show that an FCV emits as much greenhouse gas as a hybrid-electric car that uses about five liters of gas for every 100 kilometers (47 miles per gallon). Unlike BEVs, which are becoming increasingly green with the uptick in renewable energy, FCVs will continue to indirectly contribute to greenhouse emissions stemming from hydrogen production. It will only get worse, environmentally speaking, since a lot of the natural gas used to produce hydrogen will start coming from fracking, meaning that the gas's ecological footprint will come closer to that of coal.

Producing hydrogen from renewable energy

Hydrogen can be produced by way of electrolysis using electricity from renewable energy sources, which translates into almost zero greenhouse gas emissions. Electrolysis, however, entails production costs that are 40 to 80 percent higher than those related to reforming natural gas.

Also, using electricity in this way to get from point A to point B in your car is not very efficient. An FCV needs three times more electricity than a BEV to travel the same distance. It's much simpler, more efficient and cheaper for a BEV to get electricity directly from the power grid.

FCVs vs. extended-range EVs

So we know the main draw for hydrogen-powered cars, after zero-emission driving, is

Hydrogen port

A Chevrolet Volt plugged in to a level-2 charging station

their range of 500 kilometers (310 miles)—but what about an extended-range electric vehicle (EREV) such as the Chevrolet Volt?

The Volt can drive 90 percent on electricity and refill on gas in five minutes as needed, and it boasts a total range (electricity plus gas) of 670 kilometers (416 miles). Not to mention that gas infrastructure is already in place. No extra cost is called for. Ten percent of the traveling you'll do with this car, using gas, will be outside the city, especially for longer trips, since the Volt's electric range is 85 kilometers (53 miles). In places where electric energy is clean, including Québec, Ontario, Vermont and Washington State, a car like the Chevy Volt is responsible for far fewer greenhouse gas emissions than an FCV. Elsewhere in the U.S. and Canada, it comes out to about the same for most of the population.

Hydrogen fuel cells trail behind constantly evolving batteries

At the dawn of the 21st century, it was predicted that FCVs would grace our markets by 2008. That means that today they're 10 years behind schedule. In the meantime, lithium-ion batteries have improved faster than ever—prices have dropped consistently and performance has increased. When BEVS, such as the Tesla Model S, with its 425-kilometer (265-mile) range, came on the scene, the recharging infrastructure for all EVs grew rapidly. With Tesla's Superchargers, you can now get 200 kilometers (125 miles) of extra range in 20 minutes—for free.

The people behind FCVs sure didn't see that coming.

All-around expensive technology

It's time to talk money. Today FCVs cost you about $60,000, which is $20,000 to $25,000 more than the majority of other EVs. And in 2017, there will be another two or three BEVs with 300 kilometers (186 miles) of range at a price tag under $40,000: for example, the Chevrolet Bolt and the Tesla Model 3.

At the 2014 J.P. Morgan Auto Conference in New York City, Toyota vice president Bob Carter stated that it would cost about $50 to fill up the Mirai (FCV) to travel 500 kilometers (310 miles). BEVs, however, only cost 10¢/kWh to operate in many places, which translates into a mere $10 to travel the same distance. That means the cost of hydrogen is five times higher than the cost of electricity and about the same as a full tank of gas.

As a result, if you want to recoup the purchase price of an electric car by saving on fuel, you'd be hard-pressed to do so with an FCV, especially with its high-ticket price.

When it comes to hydrogen filling stations, an in-depth 2013 National Renewable Energy Laboratory study in the U.S. showed that it would cost $2.8 million in 2016 for a station to provide 333 kilograms (734 pounds) of hydrogen per day. That amounts to only 60-odd tanks of hydrogen fuel for a car like the Mirai. A fast-charging station only costs $70,000 and can fully recharge vehicles up to 30 times a day. Plus, don't forget that EVs are mostly recharged at home or at work, not at service stations.

Conclusion

It makes perfect sense to ask why someone would even want an expensive FCV over a much cheaper EV. Who would want to pay five times more at a small number of service stations without reaping any environmental benefits?

Hydrogen or electric?

BMW's hybrid system

WHAT'S YOUR BEST OPTION: HYBRID, PLUG-IN HYBRID OR ELECTRIC?

DANIEL BRETON

When people ask me if I'd recommend one electric car over another other, I inevitably need to ask them certain questions to determine their *needs* (which should not be confused with wants). It's only once we've identified these needs that we can come to a decision on which car or cars can meet them.

For starters, people need to realize that there's no perfect vehicle. As the saying goes, a choice involves a loss. Each person must therefore determine what's important and what's less important. Here's a list of six questions to consider when shopping for an energy-efficient car:

Question 1: How much are you willing to pay?

Know that, unlike when choosing a traditional vehicle, you need to make the following short calculation: cost of buying the vehicle plus fuel cost (gasoline and/or electricity) plus maintenance costs plus insurance costs. The reason for this calculation is simple: If you don't account for the purchase or rental cost, you will most likely think that a partially or entirely electric vehicle is very (too) expensive. *However*, when you consider all the ownership costs, such as fuel plus maintenance, it changes the game, and a hybrid or electric car often turns out to be less expensive than a gas-powered one.

Question 2: What's your maximum daily and/or weekly mileage?

Nearly 90 percent of North Americans drive fewer than 60 kilometers (40 miles) a day to work and back. However, the vast majority of people feel that the range of a 100-percent electric car is insufficient even though *all these cars* can easily run for 75 kilometers (47 miles) a day. This can partially be explained by the fact that drivers know they sometimes cover greater distances during vacations or long weekends.

If you only need to travel longer distances for two weeks a year while you're on vacation, for instance, consider renting a car or exchanging yours. For these short periods, opt for a vehicle adapted to your trips rather than purchasing a car that you will use too little, or badly, during the other 50 weeks of the year.

Question 3: Where in North America do you live?

Where you live will *also* help you determine what car to buy. In some areas, electricity production still pollutes too much for people to switch to 100-percent electric cars. In those cases, environmental gains would be almost nil.

Therefore, if you live in:

- Kansas City, where 82 percent of electricity is from coal, it's better to buy a hybrid car instead of a plug-in or 100-percent electric car, since environmental gains will be better.
- Denver, where 65 percent of electricity comes from coal, the choice isn't as clear. Find out if your area is making strides to leave coal behind for renewable energy. If that's the case, you could choose so-called plug-in vehicles.

- Washington, DC, where 53 percent of electricity is from coal, you're at the tipping point. You can go for a pluggable car.
- Los Angeles, where 33 percent of electricity is from coal or in Miami where 60 percent of electricity is from natural gas, you can easily go the electric route.
- New York City, where 36 percent of electricity is from natural gas, opt for an electric or plug-in hybrid car.

And if you live in Portland, Oregon, where 63 percent of the energy is from hydroelectricity, in Seattle where this number climbs to 71 percent, or in the province of Québec where electricity is 99-percent renewable, what are you waiting for to make the jump to electric?

Question 4: Does your household have one or several vehicles?

If you own more than one vehicle, there's a strong chance that at least one of them could be entirely electric. The odds of having to drive long distances in *all* your vehicles are probably quite slim. If you only own one vehicle and sometimes cover more than 80 kilometers (50 miles), I suggest you go for a plug-in hybrid or an energy-efficient model.

Question 5: Can you plug your car in at home or close to home?

If you live in a downtown area, a residential building, on the top floor of a triplex or in any other location where you won't be able to conveniently plug in your vehicle, you should opt for carpooling, car sharing, public transit or...a non-pluggable vehicle like a hybrid or energy-efficient model.

Question 6: Got a big family?

We're obviously not talking about the big families of the past. Nowadays, all households with three or more children are considered to be large families. If that's the case, you're better off getting an energy-efficient minivan or SUV if it's your only vehicle. Some models with six or seven seats could meet your needs. Here are a few suggestions: the Toyota Highlander hybrid (the most energy-efficient and most expensive on this list), the Nissan Quest, Honda Odyssey, Toyota Sienna and even the Dodge Grand Caravan (less expensive to purchase, but poorer fuel economy than the others).

Once you've answered all these questions, I invite you to read the texts about the various vehicles we've tested so you can decide what the best choice is for *you*.

Thirty-six percent of New York's electricity comes from natural gas.

What's your best option: hybrid, plug-in hybrid or electric?

BEWARE OF SALESPERSONS

DANIEL BRETON

Think I'm being a tad harsh?

Well you're right. But I have my reasons. A little over 15 years ago, I was shopping around for a hybrid car. At the time, there were only two models available: the Toyota Prius and the Honda Insight, both first generation.

I started by searching the Web for information, then I headed to a dealership to see the cars up close. The salesman told me he didn't stock either of the hybrid models. I went to a second and then a third dealership. Same letdown every time. It ended up taking me more than three months to find a dealership that sold hybrids and then take them for a test drive.

Every time I met with a salesman, I was fed the same lines: "We don't have any in stock" or "They're on order" or "It'll take months." And, of course, there was the inevitable "You know, we don't know much about that model."

The funny thing is, 15 years later, dealerships still feed me similar lines.

And that's why, at the time, I scoured the Web for information to educate myself before heading to a dealership to negotiate.

In the end, I went with the Honda Insight... and 15 years later, I still sometimes take her out for a spin.

In short, it's not thanks to the dealerships that I finally bought my car, but *in spite of* them. If such a situation could be considered "normal" 15 years ago, what with the hybrid technology being so new and unknown at the time, it definitely shouldn't be today. And yet it is.

The question is: Why?

And the reasons for such a sad state of affairs are many:

Reason 1: Dealerships lack interest

These new products—hybrids, plug-in hybrids and electric cars—are only distributed in small numbers in most of North America. And small numbers mean marginal sales. And marginal sales mean marginal profits. So, most dealerships don't want to lose time, energy and money trying to sell a handful of these cars. They would rather sell the loads of models they have in stock. It's more profitable and a lot less complicated…

Reason 2: Dealerships face additional costs and losses

New technologies like these require investing in equipment (we're talking equipment costing six figures!) to be able to carry out maintenance and repairs. Mechanics need special training before they can work on hybrid and electric cars. Because of this, it's pretty common to have only one mechanic per establishment qualified to work on such vehicles. And finally, plug-in hybrids and all-electric cars take a slice out of profits usually generated from maintenance. For example, maintenance costs for my spouse's Smart Electric Drive are less than half of those of a fuel-powered Smart.

Keep in mind that most mechanics aren't too thrilled when they see an electric car pull up; they know that cars running on this kind of new technology require very little maintenance and repairs, and might even end up costing some of them their jobs.

Reason 3: The "knows-what's-right-for-you" salesperson

Such a salesperson will come up with plenty of reasons why you shouldn't buy a hybrid or electric vehicle: "It's not for you," "You don't drive enough," "It's not worth it if you do highway driving," "It's not worth what it costs," "You'll save just as much with this or that fuel/diesel model," etc. Germans, especially at Volkswagen, are great at this—they really want to sell you their super diesel cars!

In short, instead of trying to understand your *needs* (not to be confused with your wants), and instead of seeing how it's possible you might actually want to switch to an electric or semi-electric car, these salespersons will do everything in their power to dissuade you. And then they'll try to sell you one of the vehicles they have in stock.

IMPORTANT: Do not confuse serious salespersons, those who actually take the time to listen, with these others who try manipulating you with arguments that at first glance appear legit, but which are really anything but.

Reason 4: Lack of product knowledge

More than 15 years have passed since I first went shopping for a hybrid car, but I'm still floored by the fact that so many salespersons still seem to know so little about hybrid technology. Either they haven't read up on it or they simply don't get it. They might even be a little scared—cars built on this kind of technology may appear more complex than traditional cars. And don't forget: The majority of hybrid vehicle buyers are what we call "early adopters," meaning they're usually better informed than the salespersons themselves.

More often than not, they're engineers, scientists, environmentalists, people who closely follow the latest in technological innovations, for salespeople, dealing with such clientele can be stressful because they obviously want to come across as competent and knowledgeable about their products.

Reason 5: Lack of economic incentive for sales staff

Selling hybrid vehicles is time-consuming. Having to explain this new technology, and *especially* having to explain this new way of getting around, requires more time and effort than selling a traditional car. And for salespeople, time is money. Because they don't usually make more money selling hybrid or electric cars, even making less in commission than when they sell a similarly priced SUV, salespersons really aren't that interested in selling hybrids. Except the ones who have come to realize that the future lies in these smart little cars, of course.

Reason 6: Ill-informed about government incentives

Surprisingly, some dealers aren't aware of the government tax breaks offered when you buy or lease a hybrid, plug-in hybrid or electric car. On several occasions, friends of mine have had to take it upon themselves to explain to salespersons that such incentives are available after been informed they no longer were. In some cases, salespeople have simply admitted not knowing about their existence. As recently as 2014, I myself witnessed such a lack of knowledge at some dealerships.

Reason 7: Dishonesty

Some dealerships, rather than subtracting the tax break from the price of the car, charge the full price to the customer instead, letting the customers go through the hassle of claiming the credit themselves. This way, the dealership washes its hands of any effort and avoids having to finance the credit amount up-front and wait for the government to issue them a check. Some dealerships go so far as to tell their customers they don't stock hybrid or electric vehicles and that they won't be ordering them anytime soon.

I have no respect for dealerships that act like this. They don't want to know that if they didn't have these smart cars in their inventory, they wouldn't be able to sell their big SUVs and other gas-guzzling monsters because of the standards imposed by CAFE: (nhtsa.gov/fuel-economy).

Reason 8: Machismo

Some of the sales staff say they don't "believe" in these newer technologies, sometimes backing up their claims with the most ridiculous and condescending arguments, such as:

- "Nothing beats a good old internal combustion engine."
- "Electric cars aren't real cars. They're just fancy golf carts."
- "They don't make noise like a good old V8."
- "They're odorless. You don't get to enjoy the sweet smell of gasoline..." (I'm not kidding!)
- "They lack high-speed performance!" (This one's a little less common since the arrival of the Tesla.)

Any excuse is good when it comes to ridiculing the smart car and making it out to be the laughing stock of the road. I guess you could say it's the Elvis impersonator syndrome of the automobile world.

Don't give up!

I know that after reading this article, some of you might have lost the desire to go out and buy a hybrid, plug-in hybrid or electric car.

Yes, even 15 years after my first try at it, I can still honestly tell you that you should really and truly know what you're getting yourself into before you go out shopping for a partially or full-on electric vehicle.

That said, the advent of social media, websites and electric transport support groups have helped create a community that people can turn to for information on these new modes of transportation. This makes the act of going electric a much smoother ride. Plus, it's important to mention that some dealerships

and salespeople actually do care about developing and promoting the hybrid and electric car market. They believe in it. And they work hard at providing customers with information and offering excellent customer service. They're leaders who have chosen to do their job, all while contributing in their own way to the reduction of greenhouse gases and other harmful emissions, even helping to diminish our society's dependence on oil. They deserve our respect.

But they're few and far between, so buyer beware and get informed *before* heading to the dealership, and make sure your salesperson knows what they're talking about. If they try to sell you anything other than a hybrid, plug-in hybrid or electric car (which happens often), walk out the door and head to another dealership, one that'll sell you what you're actually looking for.

Beware of salespersons

WHAT DOES THE FUTURE HOLD FOR ELECTRIC CARS?

PIERRE LANGLOIS

What does the future of electric cars look like? At first sight, the future seems bright. Nonetheless, some would argue that recharging an EV with electricity from a coal or natural gas-powered plant makes for no real improvement as far as reducing greenhouse gas emissions is concerned. It's no secret that manufacturing an electric car produces more greenhouse gases than assembling a gasoline car due to the former's large battery. That's why you need to understand the true environmental impact of electric vehicles before understanding their future.

EVs also face marketing obstacles: purchase price, limited range and an underdeveloped recharging infrastructure are just a few that come to mind. To address these legitimate concerns, people have to do their research and be a little proactive based on the knowledge that's out there now.

In addition, the future of electric cars is inextricably linked to artificial intelligence, a theme that will be expanded upon in the following pages.

EVs and greenhouse gases

The American Union of Concerned Scientists published a report in November 2015 that compares battery-electric vehicles (BEVs) with similar gas-powered cars by examining their greenhouse gas emissions, both from the road and manufacturing, from cradle to grave. Here's what they concluded:

"On average, BEVs representative of those sold today produce less than half the global warming emissions of comparable gasoline-powered vehicles, even when the higher emissions associated with BEV manufacturing are taken into consideration."

It's important to note that two-thirds of U.S. electricity is derived from burning coal and natural gas. There are exceptions, however, like Québec, where 99 percent of electricity comes from renewables and is responsible for almost zero greenhouse gas emissions. Over the life cycle, Québec BEVs emit almost six times fewer global warming emissions (8 tons of CO_2e [carbon dioxide equivalent]) than BEVs elsewhere, mainly due to how the cars and batteries are manufactured outside the province. Emissions from electricity generation in Québec used to recharge EV batteries fall below one ton of CO_2e over their life cycle.

In places where electricity is less green, the prevailing trend is to move toward renewables and energy-efficiency to cut emissions. That's how Ontario, which shut down its coal-fired plants over the course of the last decade, saw emissions from electricity generation drop from 35 million tons in 2005 to just 5 million in 2015. In the U.S., solar energy has been experiencing exponential growth: a 77 percent annual rate of increase from 2010 to 2014. The 2015 Clean Power Plan enables the U.S.

Toyota Fun Vii prototype

Toyota prototype
presented at the
2016 New York
Auto Show

Environmental Protection Agency (EPA) to enforce a 32-percent greenhouse gas emissions reduction by 2030 (based on 2005 levels).

You can see that while electric cars become increasingly green, gas-powered vehicles are becoming worse and worse for the environment. That's especially true in North America, where non-conventional sources such as the tar sands and shale gas have gained a lot of ground. It's worth mentioning that these two resources are responsible for much more pollution and greenhouse gas emissions than conventional oil.

Purchase price, recharging infrastructure and range

People often find the ticket prices of EVs at local dealerships too high. What they don't consider, though, are the savings. Over an EV's lifetime, an owner can save $15,000 to $20,000 on fuel and $4,000 to $5,000 on maintenance. These figures don't even take tax incentives into account. In effect, owners will save during the entire life of the vehicle.

Despite the aforementioned facts, a $35,000 price tag might scare off a potential customer who could otherwise get into a gas-powered vehicle for $20,000. So let's have a look at how EV prices are set to change over the next decade. In the U.S., let's say an electric car with 300 kilometers (186 miles) of range will set you back around $37,500 in 2017, not counting any tax rebates you might enjoy. That's the price GM announced for its upcoming Chevrolet Bolt, which Tesla aims to beat with its Model 3 with over 300 kilometers (186 miles) of autonomy. Both cars will hit dealerships in 2017. Now, the decline of battery prices between today and 2025 (see Battery power: the key to the EV, p. 52) means that a similar vehicle in 2025 could run you below $25,000 excluding any tax incentives. Plus, you could even save over $20,000 in fuel and maintenance over the car's lifetime.

In 2025, fast-charging stations will be faster and more widespread than ever. Level 3 fast-charging stations currently run on 50 kW and can get an EV some 100 kilometers (62 miles) in range in under 30 minutes. The next generation will boast 150 kW, juicing batteries up with nearly 300 kilometers (186 miles) in range in 30 minutes. A consortium of European car companies called the CharIN e. V. initiative is working on establishing a standard and stimulating the development of these super stations, which should be installed by 2025 or even before.

All that to say, range won't be a problem in a few years. As it stands now, current EV ranges are sufficient for many consumers, all they have to do is purchase the right vehicle for their needs. Range extenders are an excellent solution in the interim; they're affordable and their electric range is good, just look at the Chevrolet Volt 2016 (85 kilometers/53 miles, EPA) and the BMW i3 REX (115 kilometers/71 miles, EPA). You can drive electric 90 percent of the time with these cars, then you can drive off into the sunset if you like—as long as you fill up your gas tank first.

Robotic, networked and shared cars

Back in April 2014, Google had already driven a million kilometers (621,371 miles) in its self-driving cars, which use sensors, cameras and artificial intelligence.

Though you most likely won't see too many driverless cars on the road before 2020, governments have started legalizing their use on highways and for automatic parking. A revolution is nigh.

Today, even though EVs can be a big part of the solution to noise and air pollution in the city, traffic and parking will remain problematic. To counter these problems, public and active transit should be promoted. Self-service carshares will also gain in popularity, each car in such services taking about 10 private vehicles off the road.

Better modes of public transport supported by long-range electric carshares will totally redefine urban travel, potentially resulting in four to five times fewer cars in big cities. Smartphones will allow for easy and effective ridesharing. Consumers will pay less without having to own a private set of wheels. They will also enjoy door-to-door service without all the fuss of finding parking or mechanics for maintenance and repair.

What does this mean for tomorrow's cities? Far fewer vehicles, less noise and toxic pollution, more green spaces, more bike paths and pedestrian streets—all thanks to a smart, networked electric car!

Porsche Mission E

CONCEPT CAR: THE ANTI-TESLA FROM PORSCHE

JACQUES DUVAL

Which automobile manufacturer might be able to compete with Tesla, and even usurp its throne? Porsche would be a good guess. A case in point is the prototype currently known as the Mission E, unveiled at the Frankfurt Motor Show in the fall of 2015.

The news is cause for celebration, but it doesn't change the criticisms that these exceptional models of technology—which can go 500 kilometers (310 miles) without the owner panicking about making it to another charging point—do nothing to democratize the electric car. That said, Porsche's design combines almost all the knowledge we have acquired (as of May 2016) in the field of automobile technology.

Make yourself comfortable, because the list of the Mission E's features is a long one. It is the first totally electric four-seater sports car. It has all-wheel drive; all-wheel steering; over 600 horsepower; more than 500 kilometers (310 miles) of range; an 80-percent recharge capacity in 15 minutes; and a set of revolutionary "intuitively operated" instruments, controlled by eye-tracking and gestures, and even some by holograms.

Racing technology

Winner of the 24 Hours of Le Mans Race in 2015 with the 919 Hybrid, Porsche has clearly accumulated extraordinary expertise, as shown by the performances of this champion, starting with its very debut. It seems likely that the German company got its hands on a number of Teslas in order to orient its own approach. The Mission E's motors are entirely new and have already been tested in competition. This is probably the time to mention the two permanent magnet synchronous motors that power the car and recover braking energy.

These two motors catapult the Mission E to 100 kph (62 mph) in 3 ½ seconds and to 200 kph (125 mph) in less than 12 seconds. Unlike existing electric motors, those of the Porsche are designed to withstand multiple accelerations in quick succession. Anyone who has driven a Tesla Model S on a track knows that the car slows considerably after two or three laps so the motors can cool.

Fast-and-easy recharging

Porsche is ushering in 800-volt technology. Doubling the voltage of existing electric vehicles (which have 400 V) has advantages, such as shorter charging time and lighter copper cables. The Mission E can also be powered by induction: Stop the car above a coil embedded in the ground, and the power is restored to a second coil in the vehicle's floor.

As in Tesla cars, the lighter design (aluminum, carbon fiber and plastic) and very low center of gravity (thanks to lithium-ion batteries installed in the floor) ensure a sporty ride consistent with Porsche's credo. Basically, we're talking about a sports limousine whose body panels are packed with aerodynamic features. Foregoing Tesla's bold design (falcon-wing doors), the Mission E offers two rear suicide doors for easy access to the cockpit.

A good look, inside and out

For safety, the driver uses discreet cameras instead of conventional mirrors. Inside, occupants enjoy top-quality bucket seats. If the undercarriage and the engines are not enough, the interior space is just as innovative. In front of the driver is an amazing new world of visual display. Using organic light emitting diode (OLED) technology, the instrument cluster shows five dials, each for a group of functions. Eye-tracking technology by camera identifies which instrument the driver is viewing. The driver simply touches the steering wheel to activate and navigate the corresponding menu. Even more impressive is that the display adapts to the seat position, based on the parallax effect. The 3-D display moves instantly to prevent the steering wheel from blocking any information. Thus the entire dashboard is packed with sensors and new ideas. The Mission E design can be configured via tablet, which makes it possible to add features remotely.

The question this impressive list of specifications prompts can be boiled down to two words: how much? The brand has a profit-hungry reputation, so it is probably safe to assume that it will be over $200,000. The Mission E is far from being the car for the general public, but the technological advancements it makes may have a positive impact on the electric car of the future.

Concept car: the anti-Tesla from Porsche

THE ELECTRIC ROAD TRIP

BY SYLVAIN JUTEAU

The road trip seems to be a vanishing phenomenon. Our grandparents, who were lucky enough to enjoy gasoline at 10 cents a gallon, could set out for carefree voyages in their vehicles whenever they had the opportunity. But with today's gas prices and our growing awareness of the environmental impact of car travel, the mythic road trip seems a thing of the past. How many travelers out there canceled their plans to do the famous Gaspésie Tour during their summer vacation in Québec, when they saw a sudden 20-percent spike in prices at the pump? Better to opt for an all-inclusive week in the Caribbean, with food, drink, lodging, round-trip transportation covered, and no unpleasant surprises. With the new style of travel, the destination is the only goal; the trip itself is considered a tedious intermediate step. The result is that our carbon impact is even worse—planes use a lot of kerosene—and we contribute more to another country's economy than our own.

And what about the beautiful scenic roads that crisscross the continent? Roads like the Trans-Canada Highway, the famous Route 66, and countless others to discover. Is there a way to explore them without breaking the bank?

The Solution: the electric car!

I know what you're thinking: "He's totally lost it. How can you do a long road trip with an electric car that has a shorter range per charge than a full tank with a conventional car?"

It's not the range per charge that matters, but the cost per kilometer/mile driven—and the cost is 10 times less with an electric car! Got your attention? I thought so.

I've owned an electric car (a Tesla Model S) for almost three years now. I've driven from Trois-Rivières (a city 150 kilometers/93 miles northeast of Montréal) to Florida a total of three times now—once was with my wife and my three kids. I had never done the trip before that. The journey takes no longer than in a conventional car, but costs zero dollars in fuel. Yes, you read that right: At Tesla charging stations, all charges are free—for life! We absolutely loved the experience. I urge you to try it yourself.

I drove to Ontario and even to Detroit, in the depths of winter and with temperatures averaging -25°C/-14°F. I drove to New York, twice. My electric car has almost 200,000 kilometers (124,274 miles) on the odometer—in just three years!

Talk to any owner of an electric car, no matter the model: they'll tell you they drive a greater distance per year since they went electric—typically an increase of 30 percent or more.

So what explains this fact?

Gliding on a cloud

The answer is our love of the open road: We have a passion for road trips and the freedom they symbolize. With an electric car, the cost is 10 times lower, and no oil or filter changes are necessary, before or after the trip. The brake disks and pads last much longer (I still have the original brakes on my Tesla!). Electric cars are also a lot more enjoyable to drive: silent, no vibration, etc. It's like gliding on a cloud. The experience is so different that you end up really surprised at how good you feel at the end of a trip.

The relative ease of travel often tempts you to take the scenic route: the comfort means you get to enjoy the countryside, shops and local artisans. I've noticed that the maxim is absolutely true: It's about the journey, not the destination. And, equally important, your carbon footprint is a lot smaller than it is when traveling by plane or gas-powered car.

In mere months, the long trips that now seem possible only in Teslas will be possible in Chevrolets, Nissans, Fords, etc., thanks to new models with greatly increased autonomy. If you're worried about charging stations, you can rest easy knowing that they're popping up across North America

Worth the investment

To be sure, a longer trip takes some planning before you set out, but it's worth the investment. If you're uninitiated in electric-vehicle road trips, talk to an electric-vehicle convert in your social circle—or, if there is none, come talk to me. I encourage you to experience it for yourself by renting an electric vehicle for a longer trip. But be warned: Electric vehicles are highly addictive!

"GREEN CARS": A DISGRACEFUL TOP 10

JACQUES DUVAL AND DANIEL BRETON

People who know anything about the automobile industry are aware that the expression "green car" has become very trendy... and hackneyed. If you listened to certain manufacturers, you might think that buying a car puts us on the track to saving the planet!

Let's be up-front about this: NO car is green!

Instead, we should talk in terms of varying degrees of ecological impact, meaning that some cars pollute, while others pollute *a lot* and some a bit less.

This review aims to expose green models that are or have been on the market and have failed to lived up to their promises.

Failure 1: Volkswagen Jetta, Golf, Passat TDI/Audi A3 TDI

Sold by the German manufacturer as some of the greenest cars on the market, and even winning the Green Car of the Year prize in 2009, these cars with two-liter (122-cubic-inch) diesel engines have proven to be real mobile pollution bombs. Occupying the top spot of our disgraceful list, the manufacturer cheated by putting especially polluting vehicles on the market (up to 40 times more than what is accepted by the EPA!). What this company did is scandalous on a rarely-before-seen scale.

Volkswagen should be ashamed. They have since given back their famous Green Car of the Year prize.

Failure 2: BMW ActiveHybrid X6

To set themselves apart, car manufacturers seem ready to commit the greatest follies, as illustrated by the big, good-for-nothing BMW X6 that wins the second spot on our disgraceful top 10. Here we have a model bogged down by more flaws than qualities, which earns it a key plot in this cemetery of electric and energy-efficient cars.

We're willing to accept the peculiar styles of some vehicles that set themselves apart with their efficiency, but before fawning over the BMW ActiveHybrid X6, there's a deep ditch in which we will bury this amazingly illogical SUV. With non-standard emissions, unremarkable spaciousness and poor visibility, it's a flop from A to Z.

This strange cross between a traditional SUV and a sports coupe struck a chord at Mercedes-Benz.

Failure 3: Mercedes-Benz GLE D

Viewing the BMW X6 as competition, Mercedes-Benz had the upsetting idea of creating an equivalent called the GLE D. It may be less terrible than its Bavarian rival, but it still sports questionable aesthetic. While trying to bring together an SUV's qualities and a coupe look, they completely forgot the virtues of both in the process. In short, this Mercedes is not a good SUV, an elegant coupe or even an energy-efficient vehicle.

Failure 4: Subaru Crosstrek Hybrid

Let's continue our quest for failure and hope for the funeral of a hybrid that never should have seen the light of day: the Subaru Crosstrek. This car brings nothing to its market segment and actually contributes only to tarnishing the hybrid name. Subaru usually offers acceptable (a well-chosen adjective) vehicles that are nothing to write home about. If you want to see for yourself, get behind the wheel of the small Crosstrek SUV and you'll soon understand.

Volkswagen Golf TDI

Mercedes-Benz GLE D

BMW X6 ActiveHybrid

Subaru Crosstrek Hybrid

ZENN

Second-Generation Honda Insight

Lexus HS 250h

Toyota Prius Plug-in Hybrid

Failure 5: ZENN

Launched in 2006, this Canadian electric adaptation of a small European diesel vehicle seemed promising, but it was much closer to a golf cart than a 100-percent electric car. If we told you that it's not even allowed to drive on highways due to its slowness (a maximum speed of 40 kmh/25 mph), you would understand that it doesn't really represent a leap forward for electric cars.

Failure 6: Second-Generation Honda Insight

While the first Honda Insight was critically successful despite weak sales, the model's second generation was a total flop across the board in the U.S. The first generation that was launched in 1999 as a quirky little coupe was the choice of this book's co-author, Daniel Breton. He has continued to drive it from time to time for many years, between jaunts in his Smart or Volt. After being driven long distances over 16 years, the car's batteries are still alive, even though we doubted their longevity.

This condemnation of Honda isn't so much a criticism of the Insight as of the manufacturer itself, as it takes its distance from hybrid and electric cars.

In the end, we expected better from Honda after their excellent start.

Failure 7: Lexus HS 250h

Now for the Toyota/Lexus group to come and fill out this list of painful failures in the short history of electric cars. Among the loads of vehicles released under the hybrid banner, we expected more from this banal HS 250h whose twin sister, the CT 200h, is one of our recommendations. In short, we say yes to the CT 200h, but no to the HS 250h.

Failure 8: Toyota Prius Plug-in Hybrid

More expensive than its non-pluggable counterpart, this derivative of the Prius icon has proven to be rather disappointing. Equipped with 100-percent electric range of 20 kilometers (!) (12.4 miles), and with only a trickle of them available, this Prius hasn't changed anything. A completely forgettable model.

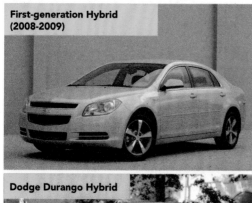

First-generation Hybrid (2008-2009)

Dodge Durango Hybrid

Failure 9: First-Generation Chevrolet Malibu (2008-2009)

With the Malibu, we're light-years away from the Volt. Promises of the future Bolt are interesting, but what about one of the most popular cars on the road, the Chevrolet Malibu? It takes pride in using hybrid technology, but barely gets anything out of it. Pointless.

Failure 10: Dodge Durango Hybrid/ Chrysler Aspen Hybrid (2009)

When a car manufacturer with NO experience with partially or entirely electric cars launches a hybrid version of one of its big SUVs the very year they're going bankrupt, doubts are bound to be raised to say the least. Sold in small quantities for only one year, this SUV hybrid— the product of a business known for reliability issues—is anything but recommendation material.

Seven other incredibly forgettable models also deserve a dishonorable mention:

- Mercedes S400 Hybrid (2009–2014)
- BMW 7 ActiveHybrid series (2012)
- Saturn VUE Hybrid (2007–2009)
- Honda Accord Hybrid (2005–2007)
- Volkswagen Touareg Hybrid (2011–2015)
- Nissan Pathfinder Hybrid (2014)
- Infiniti QX60 Hybrid (2014)
- And a whole whack of German diesel cars!

Nissan Leaf for Communauto.

CAR SHARING AND CARPOOLING

DANIEL BRETON

I recall a conversation I had over a decade ago with a young American couple I met on vacation. I told them I worked in environment and we got talking for hours. Then I brought up car sharing.

The couple's reaction was brutal: "Sounds like communism to me!" exclaimed the gentleman. "I would never share my car with strangers!" added his wife. Since then, however, things seem to have changed in the country where cars are king.

A slow start

The first car-sharing service ever was called Sefage and it started in Zurich, Switzerland back in 1948. More than two decades later, the Minicar Transit System was founded in Philadelphia, followed by Witkar in Amsterdam, Procotip in Montpelier and Short-term Auto Rental (STAR) in San Francisco.

That said, the oldest North American car-sharing service that's still in operation to this day is Communauto, which was founded in 1994 in Québec City by Benoît Robert. Twenty-two years later, Communauto serves cities in Canada (Montréal, Québec City, Gatineau, Sherbrooke, Ottawa, Kingston, Halifax) and Paris, France as of 2012.

Ever since, a bevvy of organizations, companies and coops have jumped feet first into car sharing, seeing that this particular form of public transit is a promising niche for economic development.

Car manufacturers have also gotten in on the action: Mercedes with Car2Go ; BMW with

DriveNow; Ford in partnership with Getaround; and GM with Let's Drive NYC.

These companies have understood that the upcoming generation (so-called Millennials) think less and less of owning a car as absolutely essential or a status symbol, especially in cities. Young people find that idea old-school. It's much more important for them to own a smartphone.

This is where carpooling and car-sharing services come in. Even though these young people don't exactly love the idea of owning a car, they definitely don't want to stay in one place! This generation is more mobile than ever—Millennials are set to become the most well-traveled generation in the history of humanity.

In the city, young people prefer to invest in smart transit rather than:

- dump thousands of dollars into a car that will be used 10 percent of the time and spends 90 percent of the time parked.
- pay for costly parking and/or tickets in urban areas.
- shell out hundreds or sometimes thousands of dollars a year for insurance, maintenance and repairs.
- make payments for several years to pay for something whose value decreases the moment it rolls off the dealership's lot.
- have to leave their car at home, in cities where traffic is restricted.
- get stuck in traffic jams when biking, walking, taking the subway, the streetcar or the bus is much more efficient.

When you see all of the downsides that car ownership entails, you must admit that it's not very practical! Plus, the advent of smartphones and apps has been revolutionary for innovative

transport—without them and all the possibilities they provide, the transit revolution would never have taken place at all.

Electric car sharing and driverless vehicles around the world

Reduce your ecological footprint by using public self-service electric vehicles.

- **Autolib'** (France). If you're not local, get an international license *before* you land. Autolib' doesn't accept foreign driving credentials. autolib.eu/en/
- **BlueIndy** (Indianapolis). blue-indy.com
- **City Car Share.** Located in several West Coast cities: citycarshare.org
- **Communauto** (Montréal). Electric car sharing without reservations (auto-mobile service). communauto.com/auto-mobile/
- **DriveNow** (San Francisco). drive-nowusa.com.
- **Enterprise CarShare.** Located in almost every major city in the U.S. enterprisecarshare.com/us/en/home.html
- **Téo** (Montréal). 100-percent electric taxi service. teomtl.com
- **Zipcar.** Located in several American cities and some Canadian ones, too. zipcar.com

Driverless cars are not far off the horizon, either. It's clear that smart transport is the way of the future.

However, far away from city centers, such services will continue to be scarce since they require densely populated areas to be economically feasible. Rural populations would not be able to support the likes of Zipcar, Communauto and Autolib'.

THE VOLKSWAGEN SCANDAL: DIESEL AND EMISSION TESTING ON TRIAL

DANIEL BRETON

The Volkswagen scandal has shocked the automobile world by revealing a darker side of the industry.

A look back on the events

It was the International Council on Clean Transportation (ICCT) that first exposed Volkswagen's diesel deception. The ICCT is an independent non-profit organization dedicated to technical and scientific analysis for the benefit of environmental regulators.

The ICCT revealed that Volkswagen cars were being sold with a "defeat device" that could detect when they were being tested for harmful emissions. These devices were then able to activate a system that reduced emissions, fooling experts everywhere. Once the test was over, the system would cease to filter nitrogen oxide (NOx) emissions, including nitrogen dioxide, which are held to very strict regulations in the U.S. The result? The diesel Jetta was emitting 15 to 35 times more NOx than the amount permitted by law, while the diesel Passat was emitting 5 to 20 times more than what is legally allowed.

Gases that cause illness

NOx emissions are pollutants that can penetrate deep into sensitive lung tissue, causing respiratory problems and bronchial hyperactivity, increasing the chances of bronchial infections in children.

IMPORTANT: Nitrogen dioxide is the most harmful air pollutant known to humans.

Vehicles account for the majority of NOx emissions (60 percent). Introduced in 1993, the catalytic converter has helped diminish the pollutants emitted by fuel-powered vehicles, but its effects still remain relatively negligible given the considerable increase in the vehicles worldwide and high turnover.

The lab vs. the road

There is a huge discrepancy between the results of emissions testing on diesel vehicles in laboratories versus those done under normal, real-life conditions in Europe and the U.S. In fact, a growing disparity between the two sets of results has been observed. This raises questions in regards to the credibility of official testing done by government bodies. In Europe, as in the U.S., these tests need to be more rigorous. A new method of calculating fuel consumption—one much truer to reality—was adopted on March 12, 2014, in Geneva by the United Nations Economic Commission for Europe (UNECE).

This new standard, known as WLTP (Worldwide Harmonized Light Vehicles Test Procedures), will replace the current system, which dates back to 1996: NEDC (New European Driving Cycle). It will serve to measure levels of fuel consumption, that is the CO_2 emissions generated by cars, vans and passenger vehicles weighing less than 3.5 tons (categories M1 and N1). The WLTP standard has been adopted by Australia, China, the European Union, India, Japan, Moldova, Norway, Russia, South Africa, South Korea and Turkey. Both Canada and the U.S. have chosen to continue using their own methods. The European Commission hopes to apply the WLTP cycle in 2017.

In conclusion

The Volkswagen scandal reveals:

- that Volkswagen consciously cheated by selling vehicles they knew were big polluters. Why did they do it? Probably not to suffer the consequences of a better-performing system: higher fuel consumption rates, poorer performance, higher selling prices and higher maintenance costs.
- that European automakers *do not want* to invest in hybrid, plug-in hybrid and electric technology, believing instead that the future lies in "clean" diesel. The truth is, it costs them much less to purify diesel than to invest in these new technologies.
- And yet, Volkswagen executives confirmed back in 2011 that they would invest $85.5 million (USD) between 2012 and 2016 in green technology. The company was supposed to focus primarily on "technologies for energy-efficient, hybrid and electric cars[1]."
- that although the World Health Organization clearly identified diesel exhaust as a carcinogen for humans[2] back in 2012, some automobile manufacturers have persisted in their diesel ways.

I'm of the opinion that diesel, which is already losing popularity in Europe after the adoption of the new anti-pollution standards and since people buying diesel vehicles no longer receive cash incentives, will disappear entirely from automakers' catalogues within a few years.

In any case, people who understand the laws of physics and thermodynamics know that diesel technology has run its course.

Conclusion: It's time to go electric.

1. http://collections.banq.qc.ca:81/lapresse/src/cahiers/2011/09/17/D/82812_20110917D.pdf
2. http://www.liberation.fr/societe/2012/06/14/le-diesel-est-cancerogene-c-est-officiel-et-il-se-passe-quoi-maintenant_826081

PART TWO

ROAD TESTS

RLX

HYB

PRICE: $65,490 (CAD) – $59,950 (USD)
FUEL CONSUMPTION: 7.8 L/100 km (30 mpg)
GREENHOUSE EMISSIONS:
185 g/km (297 g/mi)
GHG EMISSIONS RATING: 7/10
CALIFORNIA SMOG RATING: 8/10

Too much, not enough

DANIEL BRETON

Out of all the cars I got to test-drive for this book, I must say the one that intrigued me most was the Acura RLX Hybrid.

Compared to Lexus, which has a long track record when it comes to hybrid cars, Acura only has two models under its belt: the ILX and the RLX.

Since the ILX is derived from the Honda Civic Hybrid, I was really hoping to see what the RLX was made of as an all-wheel drive luxury hybrid. With a starting price above CAD 65,000 (USD 60,000) and fierce competition, expectations for this more environmentally friendly automobile are high.

After taking it out on the road, I can tell you that the RLX is a classic example of too much and not enough.

Too powerful?

With a 377-horsepower engine and all-wheel drive, this car is extremely powerful and remarkably agile on straight or winding roadways. As a result, you might be tempted to put the pedal to the metal...which, of course, leads to burning through a lot of extra gas.

Not economical enough

Official figures place fuel consumption at 7.8 L/100 km (30 mpg): 8.4 L/100 km (28 mpg) in the city and 7.4 L/100 km (32 mpg) for highways. Warning: Such results are only achieved with an extremely light right foot. Driving "normally," I ended up using

Specifications

SEATING CAPACITY: 5
CARGO SPACE: 311 L (11.6 ft³)
WEIGHT: 1,956 kg (4,312 lb)
ENGINES (GAS/ELECTRIC):
  Combined power: 377 hp (277 kW)
  Torque: 341 lb-ft (462 Nm)
BATTERY:
  Material: lithium-ion
  Storage capacity: 1.3 kWh
  Warranty: 8 years/160,000 km (96 months/100,000 mi)

8.8 L/100 km (27 mpg) when I took this luxurious all-wheel drive vehicle out for a spin. Not bad, but not good enough.

Kingly comforts

The RLX is obviously built for the highway. Quiet, powerful and extremely comfortable, this Acura makes long distances seem short and the ride is so smooth that you won't want to get out from behind the wheel. The opulent interior was designed in good taste, exuding discretion and refinement. It has everything you need, right down to the push-button transmission and the dashboard display. It feels like you're in a living room, a sensation enhanced by the curtains at the back of the car. Really good...

That being said, when you spend that much for a "greener" car, you might ask yourself how environmentally friendly it really is. The answer: not enough.

For the price of an Acura RLX Hybrid, you could get a Cadillac ELR, the prince of which has dropped. The latter is becoming less expensive and it boasts an engine that gets it 100-percent electric travel over 50 kilometers (30 miles). Also, the Cadillac's design is breathtaking. Then there's the Tesla Model S 70D with all-wheel drive which, at the end of the day, costs about the same as an RLX Hybrid once you factor in gas, maintenance and tax incentives. The Tesla Model S 70D is a luxury car, too, with electric range that totals nearly 400 kilometers (250 miles).

The Acura RLX Hybrid is definitely a good ride. That doesn't mean, however, that it is the right choice for the environment, nor does it necessarily stand out from the rest.

- High-quality interior
- Very powerful engine
- Excellent highway handling
- All-wheel drive

- High-fuel consumption
- Lower-quality hybrid system

Acura RLX

A3 e-tron

HYBR

PRICE: $39,200 (CAD) – $37,900 (USD)
FUEL CONSUMPTION: (gas/electric): 2.8 L/
100 km (84 mpg); gas: 6.7 L/100 km (35 mpg)
ELECTRIC RANGE: 25 km (16 mi)
CHARGE TIME: 120 V: 8 h; 240 V: 2.2 h
GREENHOUSE EMISSIONS: 98.7 g/km (158 g/mi)
GHG EMISSIONS RATING: 10/10
CALIFORNIA SMOG RATING: 9/10

For those who want sporty

DANIEL BRETON

The Audi brand has long been associated with sportiness, all-wheel drive, timeless design and world-class handling, but not with electric power. But that was before the arrival of the A3 e-tron.

While the diesel scandal centered on VW, Audi, which is part of the large conglomerate, was tarnished as well, particularly the Audi A3 TDI. That's why the arrival of this plug-in hybrid vehicle is timely. But does it reach the heights of other Audi products?

A true Audi

Hitting the road in this small family car is a real pleasure. In the mountains, in cities or on the highway, this car feels comfortable in any situation, with its elegance, classic design and driving pleasure. It perfectly represents the spirit of this manufacturer.

With its small 1.4-liter turbocharged engine combined with a 75 kW electric motor, it has 204 horsepower and 258 pound-feet of torque, giving it respectable takeoff and acceleration. Road handling is exceptional: Rock solid under all conditions, it provides a sense of safety.

A pretty ordinary plug-in hybrid

Even though there aren't many plug-in hybrids on the market, the A3 e-tron doesn't really stand out in terms of range or fuel consumption. Having tried it in winter conditions, the best 100-percent electric range I could get at 100 km/h (62 mph) on the highway, while being

Specifications

SEATING CAPACITY: 5

CARGO SPACE (MIN – MAX): 280 – 1,120 L
(9.9 – 39.5 ft³)

WEIGHT: 1,640 kg (3,616 lb)

ENGINES (GAS/ELECTRIC):
Power: 204 hp (150 kW)
Combined torque: 258 lb-ft (350 Nm)

BATTERY:
Type: lithium-ion
Capacity: 8.8 kWh

careful not to use the heating, was 23 kilometers (14 miles). When I did use the heating, the range dropped to 17 kilometers (10.5 miles). That's a far cry from the 50 kilometers (31 miles) touted by Audi. With a battery of just 8.8 kWh, you can hardly expect anything more. On the bright side, it does charge in just 2½ hours at a 240-volt station.

An average hybrid

When testing the car on the longest distances, I used Hybrid Auto mode to see whether fuel economy proved to be as good as the best hybrids out there. The results were so-so.

Using eco-driving, I was able to achieve a fuel efficiency of 5.5 L/100 km (42.8 mpg). Driving normally, that rises to about 6.7 L/100 km (35 mpg), which is in the high-average range for hybrid cars.

A comfortable interior

Sitting in an Audi means entering a world of comfort, style and ergonomics. The A3 e-tron is no exception. Everything is carefully thought out (except for the GPS) and well placed. The front seats are very comfortable. In the rear, adults would feel cramped. Cargo space is okay, but nothing more, even though the vehicle is shaped like a wagon. But in reality, it's a *very small* wagon. To illustrate the point, cargo space in the Chevrolet Volt is 50 percent greater.

Conclusion

The Audi A3 e-tron is the plug-in hybrid for those who want to drive a solid car with sporty handling, a somewhat preppy design and decent fuel economy. But if you're looking for maximum electric range and excellent fuel economy, you should probably look elsewhere.

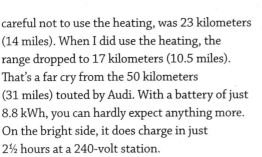

- Excellent road handling
- Fun to drive

- Limited electric range
- Disappointing fuel economy

Audi A3 e-tron

ELEC HYBR

Allergic to winter

JACQUES DUVAL

The first time I saw the BMW i3 at the Los Angeles Auto Show, I wondered if the company was trying to pull a fast one on me. Could the Bavarian manufacturer really hope to sell such a horror of an electric vehicle?

It's official—after one year on the market, people aren't busting through the dealership's doors to buy this car. The i3 isn't all bad, but its merits are questionable. Note that BMW had first placed its bets on hydrogen power, even going as far as to build expensive infrastructure to build FCVs before it decided to go electric. General Motors did the same thing with its High Wire project. Now that you know my opinion, let's take a look at the cold hard facts.

A horror show

The horror begins when you get behind the wheel and take sight of the plywood-looking dashboard—it's actually eucalyptus wood. To be totally honest, I have to say that, compared to the first i3s I tried in LA, the look of the latest models I've seen on the East Coast is much improved.

The desired effect—a modern look—has been pulled off a little better. The seats are comfortable and the spacious (height and width), window-lined interior makes for good

Specifications

SEATING CAPACITY: 4
CARGO SPACE (MIN – MAX): 260 – 1,100 L (9.2 – 39.2 ft³)
WEIGHT: 1,195 kg (2,634 lb)
ENGINE:
  Power: 170 hp (125 kW)
  Torque: 184 lb-ft (250 Nm)
  i3 REx: 650 cc 34 hp
BATTERY:
  Material: lithium-ion
  Storage capacity: 26.6 kWh
  Warranty: 8 years/160,000 km (96 months/100,000 mi)

all-around visibility. Quarters are close behind the driver, though, so your backseat passengers are bound to get to know one another fast. The trunk isn't very spacious either. At the wheel, the motor is as quiet as a whisper.

The i3's motor is activated by way of a knob, while a discreet lever allows for backward and forward motion, as well as parking. It's a bit confusing in the beginning, but you get used to it.

Winter? Yeah, right.

There are two different BMW i3s: one with a 100-percent electric motor and another with a combustion range-extending engine that gets you around 100 kilometers (62 miles) of extra travel. The latter is closer to the Chevrolet Volt, but with a BMW motorcycle twin engine with a 7-liter (2-gallon) tank, which limits range.

Here's how it all adds up range-wise: 170 kilometers (105 miles) in electric mode plus 100 kilometers (62 miles) from the range extender equals 270 kilometers (167 miles).

Buyer beware: The i3 is not a fan of chillier North American climates! When I took one for a spin, I lost a lot of range from high winds and cold weather that would make a polar bear's teeth chatter. After 30 kilometers (18 miles) behind the wheel, the range meter dropped like the mercury outside the car, spiraling from 117 kilometers (73 miles) to 37 kilometers (23 miles). When my colleague Daniel Breton tried the car in winter conditions at -20°C (-4°F), he experienced even more severe range loss. He also observed that the vehicle's thin wheels make for unstable driving in the snow.

That said, there are some nice features on the i3. One is how it handles the road, a trait

➕	➖
• Handling for city driving	• Allergic to winter
• Good range	• Expensive
• Great visibility	• Not comfortable enough
• True to the brand	• Questionable body design

that makes up the very fiber of the BMW brand. Its short wheelbase, however, has a negative impact on comfort: You'll feel just about any bump in the road in this car. The braking and steering do well for themselves. The regenerative braking, though, makes for a noticeable slowdown that can take a few days to get used to. According to one i3 owner I met during a test-drive, "At the wheel, you get the feeling that the car is solid."

Conclusion: There are things to like about the BMW i3, but given the big price tag and BMW's reputation, this car does not live up to expectations.

An owner's opinion

Fellow EV-owner Gad drives an i3 and a Tesla Model S. Here's what he thinks:

"I've driven the BMW i3 REx for almost two years now. It's a fantastic electric car for city driving—its range is perfect for that. The car's turning radius is tight, it turns on a dime and it's fun to drive. I also enjoy the large windows. The smart technology behind the

BMW i3 Rex makes it a safe ride and I really like the materials chosen for the interior.

On the other hand, if you want to open a back door, you'll need to open the one in front first, which I find annoying. The GPS and the main screen are poorly designed and it's difficult to display the information you need. I also find that the range extender makes a lot of noise when it kicks in. It would be better if drivers were allowed to start it themselves when the battery drops to five percent.

All in all, it's a great car for the city, but there's room for improvement for future models."

HYBRID

PRICE: $74,045 (CAD) – $65,995 (USD)

ELECTRIC RANGE: 62 km (39 mi)

CHARGE TIME: 120 V = 13 – 18.5 h, 240 V = 5 h

FUEL CONSUMPTION: gas/electric: 2.8 L/ 100 km (84 mpg); gas: 7.4 L/100 km (32 mpg)

GREENHOUSE EMISSIONS: 57 g/km (91 g/mi)

GHG EMISSIONS RATING: 10/10

CALIFORNIA SMOG RATING: 8/10

Beauty is as beauty does . . .

JACQUES DUVAL

Its career was short-lived. Indeed, the Volt's younger (prettier) cousin, the Cadillac ELR, began its public life starring in the showrooms, lauded by all. But in the space of a few months, the General Motors Cadillac group began to realize the truth behind the maxim, "Beauty is as beauty does." The problem was that Cadillac had overestimated the importance of appearance as a selling point. GM believed that people would buy this little Cadillac with a range extender at any price. So, while praising its divine lines, the public soon turned its back on the ELR in search of more realistic prices. To keep the gorgeous design from going into early retirement, they canceled its production for many months in order to modify it in ways that would make it more affordable—while remaining just as sporty.

A more assertive attitude

Among the 2017 modifications, if GM keeps this model in their catalogue, enhanced power and torque are the first attention-grabbers with a 25-percent increase that pushes the combined power of the gas engine and gasoline counter-part to 233 horsepower (174 kW). Of course, the extra peformance results in a loss of 4.5 kilometers (2.8 miles) in driving range, while boosting acceleration, since going from 0 to 100 km/h (0 to 62 mph) takes 6.5 seconds.

Specifications

SEATING CAPACITY: 2 + 2
CARGO SPACE: 297 L (10.5 ft³)
WEIGHT: 1,844 kg (4,065 lb)
ENGINES (GAS/ELECTRIC):
 Combined power: 233 hp (171 kW)
 Torque: 373 lb-ft (506 Nm)
BATTERY:
 Material: lithium-ion
 Storage capacity: 17.1 kWh
 Warranty: 8 years/160,000 km (96 months/100,000 mi)

In terms of range, much like the Volt, the ELR completely eliminates concern about power failure. Once you've maxed out the electric range, the gas engine will take over for the rest of your trip without you even noticing.

To make sure you leave the next day with as many electric miles on the range meter as possible, you just need to plug into 240 volts for five hours or a 120 socket (not recommended), for about 18 hours. Yearly fuel consumption could clock in at about 2.8 L/100 km (84 mpg), which is nothing short of remarkable.

The body revisited

The updated ELR's body has front high-performance-strength struts and showcases various touch-ups, as well as 20-inch tires with the optional performance package. The results are striking, notably with the steering, which acts on the handling. It's hard to find fault in the braking with its heftier disks and Brembo calipers. Stopping distances have been shortened by 12 percent. Braking doesn't just stop the car. It can also be used to generate electricity from decelerating brakes.

The sporty style is confirmed by visual elements: sport steering wheel, new grille, modernized logo and a whole range of accessories including the On Star 4G LTE system (which doesn't always measure up), adaptive cruise control and pedestrian detection.

Despite having backseats, the ELR is basically a two-seater that can occasionally welcome kids. The space is best used as an addition to the small trunk. With all the aforementioned improvements, the Cadillac ELR becomes a pretty irresistible car for lovers of eco-friendly transport, much like this writer.

- Improved handling
- Increased power and range
- Sleek design
- Meticulous finish

- Symbolic backseat
- Poor side visibility
- Still-unrealistic price

Cadillac ELR

Bolt EV

ELEC

WINNING ALL CATEGORIES

PRICE: n/a (CAD) – $37,500 (USD)
ELECTRIC RANGE: 321 km (200 mi) (approx)
CHARGE TIME: n/a
GREENHOUSE EMISSIONS: 0 g/km (0 g/mi)
GHG EMISSIONS RATING: n/a
CALIFORNIA SMOG RATING: n/a

The car that will change the world?

JACQUES DUVAL AND DANIEL BRETON

In Jacques Duval's opinion:

If there's one car that is most likely to pave the way for the electric car, it's definitely the Chevrolet Bolt EV, the small family car that General Motors will be offering at the end of 2016 or in early 2017. If I sound optimistic, it's because this newcomer meets all the elements that drivers have reported needing in the car they intend to buy.

When it comes to purely electric cars, there are two criteria that must be met for people to consider purchasing: an affordable price and a range of 320 kilometers (200 miles). The Bolt checks both of these boxes.

Make it or break it

I've predicted that the Bolt EV will change the world. But I should add a caveat: I think it will be either a huge success or an empty one. It will either mark a decisive victory for the future of the electric car, or it will be merely a critical success without leading to skyrocketing sales and GM stock prices.

What won me over to the Bolt most of all, I think, was its behavior on the road. Its electric engine delivers 200 horsepower, providing acceleration (0 to 100 km/h / 62 mph in 6.9 seconds) that doesn't quite catch up to the Tesla Model S70, but comes close. With four people on board, the car propels itself forward with an astonishing velocity. The engineer accompanying us even scolded me for speeding—twice. But its acceleration and passing are so lively that you can't help but have fun with them.

Specifications

SEATING CAPACITY: 5
CARGO SPACE: n/a
WEIGHT: n/a
MOTOR:
  Power: 200 hp
  Torque: 266 lb-ft
BATTERY:
  Material: lithium-ion
  Storage capacity: 60 kWh
  Warranty: 8 years/160,000 km (96 months/100,000 mi)

When it came to braking, I took a more reserved approach, out of respect for my passengers. It's safe to presume it is top-notch, though, and it also allows for energy regeneration, which the driver can adjust to higher or lower levels.

Tesla's cousin

As for the handling, the feel is similar to a Tesla. Its low center of gravity, a result of the battery being placed in the floor, allows for flat cornering. A slight roll can be detected, if you really provoke it: After all, this is a front-wheel drive. The tires have the Michelin signature.

The car is reasonably comfortable. The fifth seat, in the center-rear, seemed more accommodating than that of the Volt, despite the fact that the vehicles are pretty similar in terms of dimensions. However, the Bolt's trunk provides no less than 478 liters (17 cubic feet) of cargo space.

The only downside has to do with the steering, which is a bit imprecise in the middle. The steering thickness may also be too big for those with smaller hands. However, the turning circle gives the car some maneuverability in the city. Visibility can be enhanced with the optional accessory of a camera mounted to the rearview mirror, which offers a flawless view of what's behind you. The range analysis function, which estimates range according to route, topography, weather and even time of day, is also worth mentioning.

Another noteworthy feature is the 10.2-inch screen, with a more readable display than that of many other models.

My personal assessment of the Bolt EV would have to acknowledge that it offers consumers exactly what they want: a reasonable price, engaging drivability, good interior space and a reassuring range. But it may be worth considering some numbers: My

- Great range
- Satisfactory performance (*Jacques*)
- Thrilling to drive (*Daniel*)
- Practical
- Affordable

- Unknown reliability
- Steering is a bit imprecise (*Jacques*)
- Fast-charging port optional (*Daniel*)

Chevrolet Bolt EV

$130,000 Tesla Model P85D gives me a daily range of 365 kilometers (227 miles), compared with the Bolt's 320 kilometers (200 miles). The 45-kilometer (28-mile) difference could be cause for some serious thinking.

In Daniel Breton's opinion:
After years of discussion, speculation, disappointment and anticipation, here we are: welcoming the first electric car that's truly designed for the general public. As Jacques rightly says, this car stands a good chance of changing the game for individual transportation, since its range will reach and even exceed 320 kilometers (200 miles).

High-strength steel and aluminum
According to the Bolt's chief development engineer, the crossover's range could easily exceed 320 kilometers (200 miles) when driven reasonably. Our own experience driving the Bolt EV led us to think that that will prove true in the real world. Moreover, considering the range of a Tesla Model S70—377 kilometers (234 miles), according to the EPA, with a battery that's only 10 kWh more than the Bolt's, but which also weighs more—GM's claims seem altogether credible. Of course, the Bolt EV isn't made entirely from aluminum like the Tesla Model S, but from high-strength steel and aluminum. On the other hand, keep in mind that the Bolt EV costs half less than the most affordable Tesla Model S.

Amazing handling
With its weight distribution split 50:50 between the front and the rear, the Bolt EV is very well balanced, even more so since the batteries are located in the floor, making the center of gravity lower than a gasoline-powered

vehicle can go. That results in impressive road handling.

With 200 horsepower and 266 pound-feet of torque, acceleration and passing are at the level they should be for an electric vehicle worthy of the name.

Don't forget, we're talking about a crossover here: It is therefore taller and shorter than the Volt. And, of special note, the interior space is larger, making it a practical vehicle for everyday life. Families would do well to travel in a Bolt EV—particularly with numerous fast-charging stations popping up in different regions of North America.

GM offers the fast-charging port for the Bolt EV, but as an option. I presume the reason for this is to keep the initial price very competitive, but a Bolt without a fast-charging port wouldn't seem to have a lot of appeal.

An American car

After more than 500,000 kilometers (310,686 miles) of testing on the roads of North America, Europe and South Korea, this crossover will be built in Michigan, which bodes well. GM's experience with the Chevrolet Volt has shown that the company can build excellent cars, as reliable as the best of Japanese cars.

The Tesla Model 3, recently unveiled to the public, is sure to offer fierce competition to this Bolt EV in the market for "affordable" and practical 100-percent electric cars. But one thing's for sure: The competition we're about to see is a good thing for those who care about reducing our dependence on fossil fuel. That's why I tip my hat to Chevrolet: a job well done.

Chevrolet Bolt EV

CHEVROLET

ECO

Silverado

PRICE: $27,950 (CAD) – $26,895 (USD)
FUEL CONSUMPTION: 2.8 L/100 km (29 mpg) (4 x 2)
GREENHOUSE EMISSIONS: 281 g/km (449 g/mi)
GHG EMISSIONS RATING: 4/10
CALIFORNIA SMOG RATING: 6/10

Still in the running

JEAN-FRANÇOIS GUAY

There's a real battle going on between U.S. auto manufacturers in the race to reduce fuel consumption in their pickup trucks. In the wake of the unveiling of Ford's EcoBoost technology and a V6 turbo diesel engine from FCA (Fiat Chrysler Automobiles), General Motors took the initiative of updating its V6 and V8 engines, whose valves are still operated by rocker arms.

This choice seems a little outdated when judged against the double overhead camshafts used by GM's rivals. Nevertheless, it's a proven mechanism that ensures a degree of reliability compared with new engines from Ford and FCA.

Since 2014, the Silverado 1500 and the Sierra 1500 have been powered by three new EcoTec3 engines: a 4.3-liter V6 (285 horse-power, 305 pound-feet of torque); a 5.3-liter V8 (355 horsepower, 383 pound-feet of torque); and a 6.2-liter V8 (420 horse-power, 460 pound-feet of torque). All three engines have direct injection, active fuel management (cylinder deactivation) and continuous variable valve timing, a combination not offered by competitors. Among other updates, these overhead valve engines are made of lightweight components: For instance, their blocks and cylinder heads are aluminum, which reduces the weight and therefore fuel consumption.

V6 or V8

For low fuel consumption, the 4.3-liter V6 can save you about five percent on gas over the 5.3-liter V8. The question, though, is whether

Specifications

SEATING CAPACITY: 3 (single cab)
CARGO SPACE: 1,728 L (61 ft³) (6½ ft skip)
WEIGHT: 2,049 kg (4,517 lb)
ENGINE:
  Power: 285 hp (210 kW)
  Torque: 305 lb-ft (413 Nm) (V6 with 4.3 L)

Silverado

choosing the V6 over the V8 ultimately makes sense. For one, the V6 costs slightly less than the V8—a difference of CAD $1,225 (USD $1,095). However, a 5.3-liter V8 is clearly superior in terms of power: The towing capacity of a 4.3-liter V6 is 3,357 kilograms (7,400 pounds), while that of the 5.3-liter V8 is 5,035 kilograms (11,000 pounds). The 6.2-liter V8 pushes the limit to 5,443 kilograms (12,000 pounds).

As for transmission, both the 4.3-liter V6 and the 5.3-liter V8 are mated to a six-speed automatic transmission. The deluxe versions of the 5.3-liter V8 and the 6.2-liter V8 have an eight-speed automatic transmission.

For better fuel economy in its pickups, GM announced the arrival of the light hybridization technology e-Assist in 700 pickups (500 Silverado and 200 Sierra) sold only in California. GM will increase production in 2017 if there is high demand.

A midsize pickup?

In spite of the cosmetic and mechanical overhaul, General Motors full-size pickup trucks have lost market share to the Ford F-150 and the Ram 1500. And despite the step forward, they are not on par with the Ford F-150 EcoBoost or the Ram 1500 EcoDiesel in terms of fuel consumption.

It's only a temporary setback, however, since the upcoming Silverado, Sierra and large SUVs (Yukon, Tahoe and Escalade) from General Motors should have an aluminum body by the end of 2018.

In the end, the Silverado and Sierra consume a little more than Colorado and Canyon. Large GM pickups, however— although more cumbersome on the road—are more versatile on a construction site or towing a trailer.

- Updated V6 and V8 engines
- Eight-speed automatic transmission (5.3-liter V8)

- Lack of a truly energy-efficient engine (Silverado/Sierra)
- No eight-speed gearbox (4.3-liter V6)
- Unnecessary 6.2-liter V8

Chevrolet Silverado 1500/GMC Sierra 1500

ELEC

PRICE: $29,995 (CAD) – $25,120 (USD))
ELECTRIC RANGE: 132 km (82 mi)
CHARGE TIME: 120 V = 20 h, 240 V = 7h,
fast-charge = 80% in ½ h
GREENHOUSE EMISSIONS: 0 g/km (0 g/mi)
GHG EMISSIONS RATING: 10/10
CALIFORNIA SMOG RATING: 10/10

A real pocket rocket

DANIEL BRETON

The Chevrolet Spark has no doubt been the biggest surprise for EV enthusiasts. This little Chevy basically came out of nowhere and it's been a real eye-opener. The gas-powered Spark is nothing special, but its EV counterpart can be described as, well, electrifying.

Handle with care

This small vehicle is equipped with an electric 140-horsepower motor with no fewer than 327 pound-feet of torque. It goes from 0 to 100 km/h (0 to 62 mph) in about 7.5 seconds, but power and control are off-balance. With sudden acceleration, the steering wheel becomes difficult to handle due to torque—proceed with caution.

That said, the Spark is extremely efficient at weaving in and out of just about anywhere due to its smaller proportions and snug turning radius. Its height, however, makes it pretty sensitive to side winds.

Surprising range

Starting in 2015, Chevrolet started using a new kind of lithium-ion battery cell from LG Chem, the company that makes batteries for the Volt and Cadillac ELR. Battery storage capacity has dipped from 20 to 19 kWh in this case, but GM says that that has had no impact on energy consumption or range.

According to the US Environmental Protection Agency (EPA), the Spark has a total range of 132 kilometers (82 miles). Personally, I drove a bit under 125 kilometers (77 miles) in

Specifications

SEATING CAPACITY: 4
CARGO SPACE (MIN–MAX): 272 – 667 L (9.6 – 23.4 ft³)
WEIGHT: 1,300 kg (2,866 lb)
MOTOR:
  Power: 140 hp (103 kW)
  Torque: 327 lb-ft (444 Nm)
BATTERY:
  Type: lithium-ion
  Storage capacity: 19 kWh
  Warranty: 8 years/160,000 km (96 months/100,000 mi)

it in -20°C (-4°F) winter weather—which is rather impressive. Obviously, to get that kind of range, I needed to drive between 85 and 95 km/h (50 to 60 mph) and keep the heat off most of the time. I turned on the seat warmers as an alternative.

When I tested this little car with high speed (105 to 115 km/h or 65 to 70 mph), I was amazed by the range I got at -10°C (14°F)—almost 110 kilometers (68 miles) on one charge.

In springtime, the Spark's total range can easily top 150 kilometers (93 miles).

Charging

You can charge the Spark EV in seven hours with a 240-volt connection. You can also use a level 3 quick-charger if your car is equipped with a CCS plug, like the one I tested. When you're working with a 120-volt charge, you're in for about 20 hours of waiting...

Imperfect form

The interior finish is unremarkable and the materials used are not the best, even for the Spark's category. It's spacious enough, however, for four adults.

I'm not a huge fan of the look—okay, I'm not even close to a fan of it. I found the exterior lines of the car to be incongruous,

while my wife found that the color scheme inside and the interior finish left a lot to be desired.

The Chevy Spark EV is a robust vehicle that's fun to drive, boasts great range and given the cost, it's definitely worth considering if you want an electric...pocket rocket.

Another problem is availability. In fact, the Chevrolet Spark EV are notoriously hard to obtain. These cars are assembled in South Korea, and the wait for one can be very, very long. Some people wait up to a year! That's totally unacceptable.

That is why I strongly suggest that you determine the availability of this car from dealers in your area before choosing to order.

- Very efficient compact car
- Agile
- Good mileage
- Reliable

- Bottom-line interior finish
- Availability issues

Chevrolet Spark EV

PRICE: $19,495 (CAD) – $20,300 (USD)
FUEL CONSUMPTION: 8.1 L/100 km (29 mpg)
GREENHOUSE EMISSIONS: 191 g/km (306 g/mi)
GHG EMISSIONS RATING: 7/10
CALIFORNIA SMOG RATING: 6/10

Slow and steady

JEAN-FRANÇOIS GUAY

In downtown areas, where space is at a real premium, urban SUVs are in their element. These small vehicles, most of which measure less than 4.3 meters (14 feet) long, have a great appeal for city dwellers thanks to their elevated seat position, cargo space and all-wheel drive option.

In cities with poor snow removal, the four-wheel drive allows drivers to get out of snowbanks in no time. Also, thanks to their slightly higher ground clearance, the SUVs can venture into places that would be inaccessible to compacts or subcompacts.

The Chevrolet Trax isn't new, having been unveiled in Canada in 2013, when small, energy-efficient cars were all the rage due to high gas prices. General Motors decided to market it in the U.S. in 2015 to counter the breakthrough of rival brands in this growing sector. The Trax is part of a class that includes the Kia Soul, the Mitsubishi RVR, the Nissan Juke, the Subaru Crosstrek hybrid, as well as newcomers Fiat 500X, Honda HR-V, Jeep Renegade and Mazda CX-3. Competition is fierce, and the Trax, due to its age, may seem a little outdated compared to its more modern rivals.

Familiar mechanics

The Trax shares mechanical components with the Buick Encore, an almost identical twin that distinguishes itself with a more luxurious appearance and a quieter ride thanks to its QuietTuning system (exclusive to Buick), designed to block or absorb ambient noise and dampen or eliminate vibrations. It has a turbocharged 1.4-liter four-cylinder engine with 138 horsepower and 148 pound-feet of

Specifications

SEATING CAPACITY: 5
CARGO SPACE (MIN – MAX): 530 – 1,371 L
  (18.7 – 48.4 ft³)
WEIGHT: 1,293 kg (2,850 lb)
ENGINE:
  Power: 138 hp (101 kW)
  Torque: 148 lb-ft (201 Nm)

torque. In Canada, the entry-level version has a six-speed manual transmission and front-wheel drive. The six-speed automatic transmission is standard on more deluxe models, and all-wheel drive is optional. On the U.S. side of the border, the automatic transmission and all-wheel drive are also standard. The power-to-weight ratio doesn't provide strong acceleration—evidenced by its 0-100 km (62-mile) sprint in 11.5 seconds—which leaves the Trax at the back of the pack. On the other hand, the powertrain compensates for its relative torpor with a good fuel economy of 8.1 L/100 km (29 mpg)—among the best in its category.

Room to spare

Despite its tiny dimensions, it's easy to get in and out of the Trax, thanks to the large door openings and the ceiling of the vehicle. The range of storage spaces inside is astonishing: two glove compartments, storage space in the four doors, seatback pockets, bins under the cargo floor and a hidden drawer under the front passenger seat.

Trunk space goes up to 530 liters (18.7 cubic feet) and 1,371 liters (48.4 cubic feet) when the 60/40 split-folding seats are folded down. Even the front passenger seat folds forward to expand the loading area, so you can transport items measuring up to eight feet long.

If you're not in a hurry to buy, the Trax will be revamped in 2017 with a style similar to the new Malibu, Cruze and Volt. It will sport a redesigned grille, headlights and taillights. Inside, the dashboard will be fitted with higher quality materials. In terms of the mechanics, it will be almost identical.

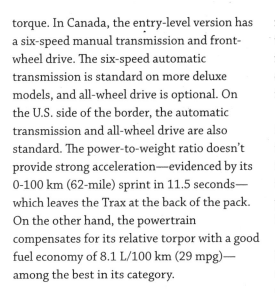

- Smart storage spaces
- Spacious cabin for tall people
- Folding backrest on front passenger seat

- Poor interior finish
- Disappointing acceleration
- All-wheel drive slow to respond

Chevrolet Trax

Volt 2017

HYBRID

PRICE: $38,390 (CAD) – $33,170 (USD)

FUEL CONSUMPTION: 5.6 L/100 km (42 mpg);
2.2 L/100 km (gas/electric)

ELECTRIC RANGE: 85 km (53 mi)

CHARGE TIME: 120 V: 13 h, 240 V: 4.5 h

GREENHOUSE EMISSIONS: 32 g/km (51 g/mi)

GHG EMISSIONS RATING: 10/10

CALIFORNIA SMOG RATING: 8/10

The pride
of Chevrolet

DANIEL BRETON AND JACQUES DUVAL

In Daniel Breton's opinion:

I know the Chevrolet Volt pretty well. The first time I heard about the project, now eight years in, I was as curious as I was skeptical. How could a company like GM, which had scrapped its EV1 to throw itself into the mass production of the Hummer H2, manufacture an efficient and reliable electric car?

Sure enough, Chevrolet managed to surprise the skeptics. The first-generation Volt proved to be a remarkably efficient, reliable car and a pleasure to drive. I bought one almost four years ago, and after 70,000 kilometers (43,500 miles), I have no complaints. The car has needed only a single oil change and requires fewer than four gas fill-ups per year. I'd say that 95 percent of the time I drive on electricity, except for long distances. And now the second-generation Volt has come along; it turns out to be a little better in every respect.

Better range

Under ideal conditions, I can do 95 kilometers (59 miles) in 100-percent electric mode with the first-generation Volt; with the new model, I'm able to drive up to 120 kilometers (75 miles).

In very cold temperatures (-30°C/-22°F), this range can drop to 50 kilometers (31 miles) for the first-generation Volt. Not having tested the second-generation Volt in extreme cold, I'm

Specifications

SEATING CAPACITY: 5
CARGO SPACE: 301 L (10.6 ft³)
WEIGHT: 1,607 kg (3,543 lb)
ENGINES (GAS/ELECTRIC):
  Combined power: 149 hp (171 kW)
  Torque: 294 lb-ft (398 Nm)
BATTERY:
  Material: lithium-ion
  Storage capacity: 18.4 kWh
  Warranty: 8 years/160,000 km (96 months/100,000 mi)

assuming its range drops proportionally, so it would be about 65 kilometers (40 miles).

Greater power and more savings

Another welcome change is that the new 1.5-liter engine, which replaces the previous 1.4-liter engine, runs on regular gas. According to GM, the drive unit is now 12 percent more efficient, which also makes the gas engine more economical. Accelerations are livelier—close to two seconds faster for going from 0 to 100 kilometers/hour (0 to 62 miles)—and the Volt has shed 100 kilograms (220 pounds).

The weight loss, combined with two higher-performing engines, makes this car even more agile and enjoyable to drive than the first-generation Volt on curves and in the city as well as on the highway, while maintaining the earlier version's stability.

A more discreet look

If the first-generation Volt stands out with its unique look, this model is a lot more mainstream in feel, if not somewhat generic. I can't help but see some resemblance to the Honda Civic Coupe.

The interior finish is a bit too "plasticky" for my taste. That said, the dashboard is very intuitive and provides a lot of information for efficient electric driving.

For more aggressive regenerative braking, there's now a paddle that allows you to recharge the battery while barely using the brakes.

A disappointment in terms of size: The onboard charger is only 3.6 kWh, which means charging is still too slow for many consumers, and obviously no fast-charging port is available.

Ultimately, this Chevrolet Volt is a success from almost every perspective. Thus far, no other manufacturer on the planet has been able to build such a winning combination.

➕
- Improved electric range
- No longer needs premium unleaded gas
- Better fuel economy
- Agility on the road

➖
- Onboard charger just 3.6 kWh
- Plastic-feeling interior finish
- Caution required when entering the rear (*Jacques*)
- The fifth seat isn't worth mentioning (*Jacques*)

Chevrolet Volt 2017

In Jacques Duval's opinion:

I own a first-edition Chevrolet Volt as well. It was therefore with high expectations that Daniel Breton and I waited for the follow-up to that fairly revolutionary automobile. To date, I have logged an overall average of 2.7 L/100 km (87 mpg), which is better than the Toyota Prius. The $750 (CAD) I spent on gas over two years was quite reasonable, and the new developments only make that fuel economy even better. My wife, who uses the Volt most, enjoys its comfort and ease of driving. Her two main complaints are the size of the A-column, which really makes diagonal visibility problematic, and the unpopular headlights of the 2012 Volt. The LED headlights in the 2017 version, however, should make an improvement in that area.

A second generation underway

At first sight, the new Chevrolet Volt didn't bowl me over with its reworked and adjusted silhouette. I found it pretty generic and less distinctive than that of its predecessor. Its profile, however, evokes the superb Tesla to some extent.

By all appearances, the major development for the year is the four-cylinder 1.5-liter engine, replacing the 1.4-liter engine used until now, and adding an extra 17 horsepower. Even better, though, is its 87-kilometer (54-mile) range, which exceeds the previous version's 67 kilometers (42 miles). That makes a difference behind the wheel—even if acceleration hasn't changed much, with a nine-second time for the 0—100 km/h (62 mph) sprint. A full charge takes only 4½ hours on a 240-volt outlet. Further good news is that the car is perfectly happy with regular gasoline.

Quiet, more comfortable and tied soundly to the road, the new Volt is the first GM vehicle to use the Delta platform, which is more solid and uses high-strength steel.

Five seats: really?

Inside, the enormous dashboard is not in the best of taste, but the instrument cluster facing the driver is colorful and offers an array of applications. I was most impressed with the one that lets you determine the moment you want to drive in electric mode. Simply put the

system into charge-sustaining mode and you conserve electric energy to use later—in the city, for example, where fuel economy tends to matter more than on the highway.

It's a little audacious to claim that the most recent Volt is a five seater. The middle spot in the rear looks more like a torture device than a comfortable seat. Also, to get to it you have to bend over to avoid hitting your head on the roof, as with many cars that slope in the back.

Does it beat 2.7 L/100 km (87 mpg)?

The extraordinary fluidity between the electric motor and its gasoline alter ego is still there. It requires a sharp ear to detect when the car is shifting from one mode to the other. In my time driving the 2012 Volt, I reached an overall average of 2.7 L/100 km (87 mpg), and I was ready to see an even better result with the new model. If you're the type of person who wants the numbers to speak for themselves, consider that the latest Volt is 12 percent more effective overall, and its powertrain was lightened by 45 kilograms (99 pounds), which, combined with other reductions in weight, makes it 100 kilograms (220 pounds) lighter, as Daniel Breton wrote above. And if the regenerative braking bothers you, you can modify its effects using paddles behind the steering wheel.

The new Chevrolet Volt made its impressive and much-buzzed appearance amid the spectacular foliage of fall. This is clearly GM's best product, a fact that quickly became universally known among motorists. With all its improvements, it has surpassed its rival, the Nissan Leaf.

ELEC⚡

PRICE: NA (CAD) – $31,800 (USD)

ELECTRIC RANGE: 135 km (84 mi)

CHARGE TIME:
   120 V: 24 h, 240 V: 4 h, fast-charge: ½ h at 80%

GREENHOUSE EMISSIONS: 0 g/km (0 g/mi)

GHG EMISSIONS RATING: 10/10

CALIFORNIA SMOG RATING: ZEV 10/10

All too rare

DANIEL BRETON

I'm not normally a big fan of the Fiat 500—far from it. The gas-powered Fiat 500 is not economical from a fuel-consumption perspective, and it proved to be somewhat unreliable.

Well, similar to my experience in discovering the Smart Fortwo Electric Drive, the electrification of the Fiat 500 has transformed this stylish little car into a highly desirable item.

Big heart, small body

The Fiat 500e is equipped with a 24 kWh battery, like the basic Nissan Leaf, but weighs 270 kilograms less than the latter. And the Fiat's motor is more or less as powerful as that of the Leaf: this little Fiat gives big performance.

Much more consideration was given to performance than to the environment in terms of the car's design. Witness the lack of leaf icons or others like it on the dashboard, which are meant to encourage you to save energy. There's no B-mode or Eco mode. The vehicle has even been calibrated so that the tires squeal a little to emphasize its lively acceleration.

Also, to highlight the sporty side of the 500e, Fiat is offering the e-Sport package—which is nothing more than a few visual features to give the car a sportier look. That said, its acceleration is as quick as that of the gas-powered Abarth model (a high-performance car); and the Fiat is more balanced.

Specifications

SEATING CAPACITY: 4
CARGO SPACE (MIN – MAX): 199 – 745 L (7.0 – 26.3 ft³)
WEIGHT: 1,355 kg (2,987 lb)
MOTOR:
 Power: 111 hp (82 kW)
 Torque: 147 lb-ft (199 Nm)
BATTERY:
 Material: lithium-ion
 Storage capacity: 24 kWh
 Warranty: 8 years/160,000 km (96 months/100,000 mi)

Acceptable range

With a 24 kWh battery in a vehicle that's this light, it would be reasonable to expect superior range to that of the Leaf, wouldn't you think? But that's not the case. According to the EPA, the two vehicles have the same range: 135 kilometers (84 miles). That said, when you drive the Fiat 500e in an energy-efficient way, you'll find that you can push the range to 160 kilometers (99 miles) or more.

No fast-charging

Charging this small car takes less than four hours, thanks to an onboard 6.6 kWh charger for use with a home charging-station rated at 30 amps. As opposed to the vast majority of 100-percent electric cars on the market, however, there is no way to obtain a fast-charging port, either CHAdeMO or CCS; in my view, that's a drawback.

Inside

The Fiat 500e is indeed a very small car, but the battery was installed in the floor of the vehicle in the rear, which makes its small cargo space more acceptable (proportionally) than that of the Ford Focus EV. Still, although this car is officially a four-seater, only shorter adults or kids will be comfortable in the back.

You have to hand it to the designers at Fiat: They have created a small car with a ton of style, comparable to no other electric car. With its color combinations, interior design and comfortable seats, this little machine is really a treat for the eyes.

Unfortunately, few will have the chance to try this little wonder, as it is sold only in California and Oregon.

Offering it across the continent would make a lot of people very happy.

- A sporty, small electric car
- Decent range
- Amazing look

- Is it as reliable as its gas-powered sibling?
- Available only in two states

ECO

PRICE: 22,995 (CAD) – $20,000 (USD)
FUEL CONSUMPTION: 8.4 L/100 km (28 mpg)
GREENHOUSE EMISSIONS: 195 g/km (313 g/mi)
GHG EMISSIONS RATING: 7/10
CALIFORNIA SMOG RATING: 6/10

From the same manufacturer as the Ferrari 488 GTB

JACQUES DUVAL

It's hard to imagine that the unimpressive little Fiat 500X comes from the same automobile group as the Ferrari 488 GTB. But it's true: This mini Italian car, which usually ends up on the bottom rung in reliability tests, comes from a conglomerate that includes such esteemed brands as Alfa Romeo, Lancia, Maserati and, of course, Ferrari. In a different class, you could

also add Chrysler, since the Fiat group is a major shareholder for this U.S. manufacturer, which distributes Fiat in the vast U.S. market.

Basically, then, the Italian auto industry revolves around a single manufacturer, and the products it creates are not equal. Hence the Fiat 500X is pretty much the antithesis of the Ferrari 488 GTB, a vehicle that embodies the genius of a small group of engineers devoted to having the Italian flag fly around the world via the F1 World Championship.

Dubious quality

In contrast with the Ferrari, Fiat is still stuck marketing a "people's car" of dubious quality. So why include the Fiat 500X in this book? Mainly to deliver a warning: Don't be taken in by the darling little Fiat 500 and its many gas-driven descendants that the company hoped to raise to brand-new sales heights.

In fact, Chrysler managed to sell a decent number of its original Fiat 500 in the convertible version, mainly to a female clientele. The success is owing to the car's sassy

Specifications

SEATING CAPACITY: 5

CARGO SPACE (MIN – MAX): 634 – 1,268 L
(22.4 – 44.8 ft³)

WEIGHT: 1,457 kg (3,212 lb)

ENGINE: 1.4 L TURBO
Power: 160 hp (118 kW)
Torque: 184 lb-ft (249 Nm)

look; but the satisfaction rate certainly doesn't make it a classic. It should be added that the fuel economy ratings for the 500X model that I tried are much higher than they should be for a vehicle of this format. And the all-wheel drive option, so popular in some markets, results in 10 to 15 percent higher fuel consumption than front-wheel drive.

Anemic engines

With engines that are far from robust, neither the performance nor the fuel economy will put a smile on your face, despite what some of our colleagues might say. Expect an average of 9 L/100 km (26 mpg) for the Fiat 500X, which has a 2.4-liter 180-horsepower engine; that's significantly worse than the fuel economy of a Toyota RAV4, which is, don't forget, an SUV.

The 1.4-liter turbocharged engine offered is a little more reasonable, but is paired with a six-speed manual transmission that works abysmally, which means that the only semi-interesting choice is the nine-speed dual-clutch automatic transmission paired with a 2.4-liter engine.

Finally, I could tell you the Fiat 500X is relatively more spacious than the other versions in the same line, and that its hatchback trunk is roomier—but that probably wouldn't affect your buying intentions.

The idea of reviving the iconic car from the Fiat group was an excellent one, and it deserved better quality of execution. Whichever version you choose, reliability is at the same level it has been: inferior to that of its rivals.

+
- Attractive shape
- Original interior
- Models X and L are the most appealing

−
- Durability is a concern
- Poor transmission
- Disappointing performance and fuel economy

Fiat 500X

C-MAX/Energi

HYB HYBR

PRICE: Hybrid: $25,999 (CAD) – $24,170 (USD)
Energi: $31 999 (CAD) – $31,170 (USD)
FUEL CONSUMPTION:
Hybrid: 5.9 L/100km (40 mpg)
Energi: (gas/electric): 2.7 L/100 km (87 mpg);
gas: 6.2 L/100 km (38 mpg)
ELECTRIC RANGE: Energi: 30 km (19 mi)
CHARGE TIME: Energi: 120 V: 7 h, 240 V: 2.5 h
GREENHOUSE EMISSIONS:
Hybrid: 141 g/km (225 g/mi)
Energi: 81 g/km (129 g/mi)
GHG EMISSIONS RATING: Hybrid: 9/10,
Energi: 10/10
CALIFORNIA SMOG RATING: 9/10

Two options worth considering

DANIEL BRETON

If there's one category of vehicle in which energy-efficient vehicles do not abound, it's in SUVs/crossovers. Indeed, for mysterious reasons, most manufacturers insist on not offering any of their vehicles in hybrid, plug-in hybrid or electric versions, even though these versions are becoming more and more popular.

This is not the case with Ford, which offers the C-MAX in hybrid and plug-in hybrid versions as well as the Energi plug-in hybrid.

The C-MAX crossover definitely isn't huge in size, but for an average-sized family (with one or two kids), it can certainly meet your daily needs handily, as long as you aren't too demanding in terms of cargo space. With the same powertrain as the Ford Fusion hybrid, you'll definitely have enough power to drive your brood from place to place. The main competitor, the Toyota Prius V, is far from being as fast and powerful, which makes the C-MAX Hybrid rather sporty by comparison.

In addition, its short, high format makes it easy to maneuver in city traffic, and its European suspension makes this vehicle very enjoyable to drive—for a crossover.

Specifications

SEATING CAPACITY: 5

CARGO SPACE (MIN – MAX):
Hybrid: 679 – 1472 L (24.5 – 52,6 ft³)
Energi: 538 – 1,189 L (19.2 – 42.8 ft³)

WEIGHT: 1,651 – 1,768 kg (3,640 – 3,899 lb)

ENGINES (GAS/ELECTRIC):
Power: 188 hp (138 kW)
Torque combined: 196 lb-ft (266 Nm)

BATTERY:
Material: lithium-ion
Capacity: Hybrid: 1.4 kWh
Energi: 7.6 kWh
Warranty: 8 years/160,000 km (96 months/100,000 mi)

The interior is very well designed, but is not the most spacious you can find. The cargo space is even smaller than that of most competitors' crossovers and compact SUVs, in large part thanks to the location of the battery for the hybrid and plug-in hybrid powertrain systems. The cargo space is barely larger than that of a Ford Focus. On the other hand, the quality of the interior finish is good, and this C-MAX is equipped with several up-to-date gadgets, even in its standard version.

True fuel-efficiency

The hybrid version of the C-MAX is the most energy-efficient in its category after the Prius V. The average combined fuel consumption of this crossover—5.9 L/100 km (40 mpg)—makes it a practical vehicle, more enjoyable to drive than the Prius V, and better than average in terms of reliability.

As for the Energi version (a plug-in hybrid), its 100-percent electric range is about 30 kilometers (19 miles), under ideal conditions. During my test-drive, I had an average fuel economy of 2.9 L/100 km (81 mpg) after driving more than 450 kilometers (280 miles), 40 percent of which was highway driving and 60 percent city driving. One useful feature of this version is that even when the battery's electric range is depleted, the hybrid system still works effectively.

In summary, these two vehicles remain very good choices for practical and energy-efficient vehicles. The option of plugging it in or not should determine your final choice.

- Well-designed vehicle
- Enjoyable to drive
- Good fuel consumption
- Reliable

- Limited cargo space
- Availability issues

Ford C-MAX / Energi

F-150 EcoBoost

ECO

PRICE: $25,299 (CAD) – $26,315 (USD)
FUEL CONSUMPTION: 11.2 L/100 km (21 mpg)
GREENHOUSE EMISSIONS: 264 g/km (423 g/mi)
GHG EMISSIONS RATING: 5/10
CALIFORNIA SMOG RATING: 7/10

An aluminum-bodied pickup

JEAN-FRANÇOIS GUAY

There aren't really that many ways you can improve the fuel economy of a pickup truck. While FCA (Fiat Chrysler Automobiles) decided to put a diesel engine in the Ram 1500, General Motors opted to go smaller, reviving its Chevrolet Colorado and GMC Canyon. For its part, Ford made a more pragmatic move, reducing both the weight of the F-150 and the engine capacity.

The F-150's aluminum body is revolutionary in the fairly conservative pickup segment, since this manufacturing process is primarily used by luxury brands like BMW, Mercedes-Benz, Porsche and Tesla, to name a few. The aluminum shell is a risky choice, since pickups tend to be used at construction sites where impacts frequently occur. The material is more expensive and harder to patch up than steel, so repairs have to be done by qualified personnel in shops with specific tools—it all means higher costs.

The good news is that aluminum is fully recyclable. That means 90 percent of the energy can be saved by recycling the aluminum instead of extracting it from the soil (in the form of bauxite), and the quality of the recycled aluminum is actually identical to that of primary aluminum. And because aluminum doesn't rust, the body of the F-150 presumably has a longer than average lifespan.

Lighter and more powerful

The F-150 was lightened by 318 kilograms (700 pounds), allowing it to outclass the

Specifications

SEATING CAPACITY: 3 or 6
CARGO SPACE: na
WEIGHT: 1,877 kg (4,138 lb)
ENGINE:
  Power: 325 hp (239 kW)
  Torque: 375 lb-ft (508 Nm) (V6 EcoBoost 2.7 L)

competition by increasing the maximum payload to 1,497 kilograms (3,300 pounds)—the weight the load body can support .

With the 3.5-liter EcoBoost V6, towing capacity can reach up to 5,539 kilograms (12,200 pounds). Its turbocharged engine can produce 365 horsepower and 420 pound-feet of torque.

To improve fuel economy, Ford also offers another V6 with EcoBoost technology: With a fuel consumption of 11.2 liters, the 2.7-liter EcoBoost produces 325 horsepower and 375 pound-feet of torque. More energy efficient than the 3.5-liter EcoBoost, the 2.7-liter version uses about 15 percent less gas: 11.2 L/100 km (21 mpg), city and highway combined, which is excellent. Payload capacity for an F-150 with a 2.7-liter EcoBoost V6, however, is just 1,021 kilograms (2,250 pounds), and the towing capacity tops out at

3,855 kilograms (8,500 pounds). If they aren't pushed too hard, these two EcoBoost engines offer good energy performance. When a F-150 is secured to a heavy load, a V6 EcoBoost can have better fuel economy than a 5.0-liter Ford V8. As for the naturally aspirated Ford 5.0-liter V8 (385 horsepower, 387 pound-feet of torque), it's less powerful and environmentally friendly than the 2.7-liter EcoBoost, but it's also less expensive to buy.

On the road, the F-150's shedding of weight translates into better agility and sharper braking.

Other changes to come

So as not to frighten its customers who tend to be rather cautious with any radical moves, Ford is proceeding incrementally and holding off on further changes (such as a 10-speed transmission) to the F-150, to ensure that it remains the best-selling vehicle on the planet.

- Lighter body
- Increased payload capacity
- Good fuel economy for the 2.7-liter EcoBoost V6

- Cost of repairs (aluminum body)
- Poor fuel economy with a heavy load
- No eight-speed transmission

Ford F-150 EcoBoost

FORD

ECO

Fiesta 1 L

PRICE:

Fiesta: $18,694 (CAD) – $16,315 (USD)

Focus: $19,599 (CAD) – $19,010 (USD)

FUEL CONSUMPTION: Fiesta: 6 L/100km (36 mpg)

Focus: 7.4 L/100 km (38 mpg)

GREENHOUSE EMISSIONS:

Fiesta: 153 g/km (247 g/mi)

Focus: 170 g/km (272 g/mi)

GHG EMISSIONS RANGE: 8/10

CALIFORNIA SMOG RATING: 6/10

Frugal, but a bit expensive

DANIEL BRETON

The small Ford Fiesta has been a success ever since it hit the market. Quick, fun to drive and a high-quality ride, this little sub-compact has proven to be a good bet since its arrival.

Available in many versions, it's even offered as a sports option. It actually has a small 1.6-liter turbo engine that can get you 197 horsepower and has no less than 202 pound-feet of torque, which means it can go from 0 to 100 km/h (0 to 62 mph) in under seven seconds.

It has earned "pocket rocket" status.

But let's stay on track...

One liter!

Ford's 1-liter (0.26 gallon) EcoBoost engine received the title of best engine in its class in 2014. The small three-cylinder engine has great fuel efficiency, making this car one of the most efficient gas-powered sub-compacts out there. Plus, the turbo manages to make the little engine high performance enough for the drive not to be too dull.

A rather unique counterweight system also ensures that the three-liter (0.79-gallon) engine (meaning unbalanced fuel) removes the vast majority of vibrations inherent to a three-cylinder engine.

Specifications

SEATING CAPACITY: 5
CARGO SPACE (MIN-MAX):
Fiesta: 423 – 720 L (14.9–25.4 ft³) (hatchback); 362 L (12.7 ft³) (sedan)/(hatchback), (sedan)
Focus: 659 – 1,242 L (23.3–43.8 ft³) (hatchback), 374 L (13.2 ft³) (sedan)
WEIGHT: Fiesta: 1,151 kg (2,537 lb)
Focus: 1,337 kg (2,948 lb)
ENGINE:
Power: 123 hp (90 kW)
Torque: 125 lb-ft (169 Nm)

Focus 1 L

The quality of the interior finish is acceptable but some competing models like the Honda Fit are ahead of the Fiesta.

Available room in the passenger compartment is rather limited, notably when it comes to the backseats and trunk space.

Given the engine's reduced weight, it's particularly quick, weaving effortlessly through the city and easily gobbling up miles of winding country road.

In short, it's a true pleasure to drive.

And its big sister...

If the Focus 1-Liter EcoBoost is almost just as efficient, the weight surplus inherent in its larger size makes it sluggish and somewhat slower. That said, for those interested in a car roomier than the Fiesta, both in terms of interior and trunk, the Focus might prove to be an interesting option.

I'd say that the Fiesta 1-Liter EcoBoost is a very interesting city car, while the Focus 1-Liter EcoBoost is more at home on the highway. Indeed, thanks to the small engine, I was able to get fuel consumption down to under 5 L/100 km (47 mpg) by driving 100 km/h (62 mph), which is commendable.

As for the additional price of the EcoBoost option, it makes the Fiesta even more expensive than its competitors like the Toyota Prius C. The latter consumes even less, since it's equipped with a hybrid engine.

I recommend test-driving the Ford Fiesta 1-Liter and the Toyota Prius C. These two cars fall into the same urban-driving category, so your choice should be based on personal taste.

Focus 1 L

➕
- Frugal fuel consumption
- Interesting driving enjoyment

➖
- Somewhat high price
- Limited interior space (Fiesta)

FORD Fiesta / Focus 1 Liter

ELEC

PRICE: $31,999 (CAD) – $29,170 (USD)

ELECTRIC RANGE: 122 km (76 mi)

CHARGE TIME: 120 V = 20 h, 240 V = 3.6 h,
  Fast-charge (2017) = 80% in ½ h

GREENHOUSE EMISSIONS: 0 g/km (0 g/mi)

GHG EMISSIONS RATING: 10/10

CALIFORNIA SMOG RATING: 10/10

A slight improvement, but...

DANIEL BRETON

For those of you who think you haven't seen one yet, it might be because this car looks almost exactly like the gasoline-powered Focus. Besides the EV logo, there are very few differences between the electric and gas models.

Ford invited me to test-drive their brand new Focus EV in 2011. Even though I only took this car out for a quick spin, I must say it handled itself well.

Fast forward a few years and I'm back in the saddle.

The latest test-drive left me pensive. Rumors and testimonies about the Focus EV's technical problems are widespread, so much so that the car was shortlisted as one of the most potentially problematic electric cars on the market.

Then I got firsthand experience.

During a road-test that lasted a few days... I wasn't able to charge the car at a 240-volt station at all. I tried at home and at a public station. This EV doesn't have a fast-charging port—I had to charge the battery at 120 volts, which is—you got it—a slow ordeal.

I have to hand it to Ford, though—this car is a pretty good ride and it handles nicely. The battery is located in the trunk instead of the floor (like most electric cars), which causes the car to understeer. It also

Specifications

SEATING CAPACITY: 5
CARGO SPACE (MIN - MAX): 401 – 940 L
(14.2 – 33.2 ft³)
WEIGHT: 1,643 kg (3,622 lb)
MOTOR:
Power: 143 hp (106 kW)
Torque: 184 lb-ft (250 Nm)
BATTERY:
Material: lithium-ion
Storage capacity: 23 kWh
Warranty: 8 years/160,000 km (96 months/100,000 mi)

makes for a smaller trunk, which is less practical on the day-to-day front than other EVs like the Nissan Leaf. The difference in cargo space between Focus EV and the Leaf is considerable. That's what happens when a car is designed not to be electric from the very start.

That being said, the comfort and finish of this car rise above industry standards. Indeed, when you sit in the Ford Focus EV, you quickly realize that the interior is more opulent than what would typically be expected in a compact car. The seats are as comfortable as those in a European car, and instrumentation is more complete.

Plus, it comes fully loaded for a much lower cost than it used to.

For 2016...

The Ford Focus EV was slightly improved for 2016. Its new battery gives the EV more autonomy, up to 160 kilometers from 122 (76 to 100 miles). Also, you can now plug it into a fast-charging station—it was about time.

Despite the abovementioned upgrades for 2016, I wouldn't recommend this vehicle. It's riddled with too many problems and becomes increasingly less attractive when compared to the Nissan Leaf and Chevrolet Volt and their superior reliability—not to mention their upgrades.

- Very comfortable
- Lots of room for passengers
- High-quality finish

- Unreliable
- Tight cargo space

Ford Focus EV

Fusion Energi

PRICE: Hybrid: $28,699 (CAD), $25,185 (USD)
Energi: $36,399 (CAD), $33,900 (USD)
FUEL CONSUMPTION: 5.6 L/100 km (42 mpg)
(Hybrid)/(gas/electric): 2.7 L/100 km (87 mpg);
(gas): 6.2 L/100 km (38 mpg) (Energi)
ELECTRIC RANGE: 30 km (19 mi) (Energi)
CHARGE TIME: 120 V: 7 h, 240 V: 2.5 h (Energi)
GREENHOUSE EMISSIONS: 132 g/km (211 g/mi)
(Hybrid)/81 g/km (129 g/mi) (Energi)
GHG EMISSIONS RATING: 9/10 (Hybrid)/
10/10 (Energi)
CALIFORNIA SMOG RATING: 9/10

Looking
for solutions

DANIEL BRETON

Most auto manufacturers focus on just one technology in terms of energy efficiency in the compact and mid-size range. For example, Toyota and Kia are putting their money on the hybrid; Chevrolet on extended-range electric vehicles; Nissan on the 100-percent electric vehicle; Mazda on its SkyActiv technology; and Honda on the turbo.

Ford, however, is working on several technologies at once: the turbo, the electric, the hybrid and the plug-in hybrid. So how are they doing? Let's take a closer look.

Ford Fusion: a highway car at the front of the pack

Of all the cars in the midsize category, I'd say that the Ford Fusion Hybrid and Energi are at the top of the list in terms of passenger comfort.

Fully equipped, with very comfortable seats and a spacious cabin, the Ford Fusion is particularly generous with its offerings. Space and comfort for passengers in the rear is far superior to that of its competitors. Ford's improved Sync system makes the Fusion's dashboard functions easier to use for applications such as GPS, Bluetooth and vocal recognition, etc.

When it comes to cargo space, however, things aren't so rosy. The battery takes up a lot of

Specifications

SEATING CAPACITY: 5

CARGO SPACE: Hybrid: 340 L (12 ft³)
Energi: 226 L (8.2 ft³)

WEIGHT: Hybrid: 1,664 kg (3,668 lb)
Energi: 1,775 kg (3,913 lb)

ENGINES (GAS/ELECTRIC):
Power: 188 hp (138 kW)
Torque: 196 lb-ft (266 Nm)

BATTERY:
Type: lithium-ion
Storage capacity: 1.4 kWh (Hybrid)/7.6 kWh (Energi)
Warranty: 8 years/160,000 km (96 months/100,000 mi)

Fusion Hybrid

room in both the Hybrid and the Energi, limiting the cargo space in the trunk. In fact, the extreme shortage of space in the Energi is just short of ridiculous.

So, if you're looking for cargo space, these two cars are significantly less appealing than the competition's models, in which better ways to store the battery were found.

Excellent fuel consumption

I drove for hours with the Ford Fusion Hybrid and was able to maintain an average fuel consumption of 4.7 L/100 km (50 mpg), which is excellent. Obviously, you need to practice eco-driving to reach that average.

As for the plug-in hybrid version (the Energi), I managed to go an average of 30 kilometers (19 miles) in 100-percent electric mode, and I averaged a little under 3 L/100 km (78 mpg): Superb.

· This puts these two cars in the top rung for their category in terms of energy efficiency.

Driving pleasure

The Ford Fusion's accelerations are more laborious that those of the Chevrolet Volt or the Hyundai Sonata because of its transmission and its hybrid system. Still, the Ford Fusion is an enjoyable car to drive on the highway.

Solid and well-balanced, it covers mile after mile calmly and confidently, absorbing any bumps in the road. But I found the delay in acceleration rankled a little.

Ford's hybrid system has proven itself; It's reliable. That's why people who own them appreciate them and tend to hang on to them for a long time. If you cover a lot of miles and do a lot of highway driving, I recommend the Ford Fusion Hybrid. However, if you can maximize electric use by driving short distances between charges, the Ford Fusion Energi is for you—as long as you don't need much cargo space.

One thing for sure: You'll be satisfied with your purchase.

➕	➖
• Very comfortable	• Very little cargo
• Very reliable	space
• Secure road	• Limited 100-percent
handling	electric range
• Two very affordable	(Energi)
hybrids	

Ford Fusion Hybrid/Fusion Energi

Mustang EcoBoost

ECO

PRICE: $28,899 (CAD) – $25,395 (USD)
FUEL CONSUMPTION: 9.4 L/100 km (25 mpg)
GREENHOUSE EMISSIONS: 218 g/km (349 mpg)
GHG EMISSIONS RATING: 6/10
CALIFORNIA SMOG RATING: 7/10

A four-cylinder Mustang? Yes, please!

DANIEL BRETON

I have loved Mustangs since childhood.

When I was little, one of my cousins used take me for rides in his Fastback '67, and I have many cherished memories of wildly accelerating and speeding. My appetite for it speed was insatiable.

As the years went by, oil crises changed the landscape, and the Mustang changed with it.

The fire in my blood cooled.

The Mustang II era resulted in the first four-cylinder versions, and most Mustang enthusiasts have mixed feelings at best about that generation. It's fair to say that no one is jumping over great hurdles to get their hands on a Mustang II as a collector's item.

After this forgettable episode in Mustang's history, the four-cylinders disappeared, making way for six-cylinders and, obviously, eight-cylinders, in versions that were successively more powerful.

And now the four-cylinder Mustang is back.

A regrettable return to the past?

Definitely not.

A truly sporty ride...for a big American car

At the age of 25, I owned an eight-cylinder 1965 Mustang. So when driving the Mustang EcoBoost, I was taken aback to feel the same thrill I experienced in my younger days. Sitting in this heavy car with its long nose, I felt like I had jumped back in time to a true 1960s

Specifications

SEATING CAPACITY: 4
CARGO SPACE: 382 L (13.5 ft³)
WEIGHT: 1,602 kg (3,532 lb)
ENGINE:
  Power: 310 hp (228 kW)
  Torque: 320 lb-ft (434 Nm)

model—that is, until I had to negotiate a curve.

Under a firm grip, this Mustang and its four-wheel independent suspension (you can't stop progress!) took every curve with an ease that would have been unimaginable in the past. The brakes are powerful and reassuring, worthy of the best systems, despite the car's weight (which, however, is made somewhat lighter by the smaller engine).

The acceleration of the 310-horsepower, 2.3-liter turbocharged four-cylinder engine is impressive. You really feel like you're in an original *pony car*: it's an exhilarating feeling. All told, this four-cylinder stands its ground against many previous eight-cylinder versions.

Very reasonable fuel economy

Fuel consumption for the Mustang EcoBoost is extremely reasonable. I had fun accelerating—you know, in the spirit of the 60s—taking a number of curves with ease, and the average consumption remained under about 10 L/100 km (23.5 mpg), which is more than decent under the circumstances. I was even able to get an average of 7 L/100 km (33.5 mpg) while driving 100 km/h (62 mph) on the highway under ideal conditions.

This car has good breeding. The interior finish is high quality, its style strikes the right balance between classic and modern, and the Mustang feeling remains intact. It stands out from its competitors by virtue of the ensemble of its characteristics, making it superior to the Camaro or the Challenger, for instance.

So, unless you're a die-hard racing afficionado with a constant need to win—in other words, the prove-you're-a-real-man type, which would probably compel you to buy the eight-cylinder engine—this four-cylinder version is a worthy example of the best Mustangs in history.

- Real driving pleasure
- Reasonable fuel economy
- It's a real Mustang!
- Reliable
- The definition of good quality

- Less of that intoxicating Mustang engine sound (a drawback for purists only)

Ford Mustang EcoBoost

Civic

PRICE: $16,155 (CAD) – $18,640 (USD)

FUEL CONSUMPTION: 6.7 L/100 km (35 mpg)

GREENHOUSE EMISSIONS:
 157 g/km (252 g/mi)

GHG EMISSIONS RATING: 8/10

CALIFORNIA SMOG RATING: n/a

Back on top

DANIEL BRETON

After once ranking as the compact car world leader when it comes to quality, performance, fuel-efficiency and reliability, the Honda Civic has found itself trumped by other more competitive models in recent years.

But for its 10th-generation Civic, Honda pulled out all the stops. Not only is this compact now complete with two engines (one of which is a 1.5-liter/91-cubic-inch turbo), but you can also get one that uses CVT (continuously variable transmission). That

makes the 2016 Civic the most fuel-efficient gas-powered car in its category with a 6.7 L/100 km (33.5 mpg) city/highway combined fuel efficiency. I got an average of 5 L/100 km (47 mpg) on the highway and I noticed that the car gets astonishing fuel economy in the city. My driving resulted in using 6.4 L/100 km (39 mpg) over 400 kilometers (250 miles), half of which were driven in urban areas.

Drivability recaptured

The last two generations of Honda Civics were social climbers (read: more annoying to drive) and the 10th gives us back a bit of that drivability that characterized the first Civics. Let's cut to the chase—the newest generation is nothing like its predecessors. The 2016 version weighs less than 1,000 kilograms (2,200 pounds), but its new engine/transmission/streamlined design make it quicker on its feet and tighter on the road than ever before.

Specifications

SEATING CAPACITY: 5
CARGO SPACE (MIN–MAX): 428 L (15.1 ft³)
WEIGHT: 1,320 kg (2,900 lb)
ENGINE:
  Power: 174 hp (129 kW)
  Torque: 162 lb-ft (220 Nm)

Enhanced interior

The quality of the Civic's finish, which wasn't in step with the competition up until now, is also much improved. Adios low-end plastic coatings and shortsightedly anti-ergonomic buttons! This car is moving on up and it's more spacious than the generation before it. It makes you wonder when compacts will stop growing...

A look that's more...aggressive?

The 2016's look is much more pronounced than its predecessor's, which is sure to please those who don't care for anonymous grilles. That said, the tsunami of Civics that's about to hit roadways will make owning one far from unique. The interior, which is much more modern, boasts cutting-edge communications technology and fashionable displays. Now there's room for a smartphone that's CarPlay and Android Auto compatible.

For those interested in fuel economy, the dashboard is particularly well designed. It has both a very intuitive fuel-consumption meter and an average consumption indicator, which allows you to manage consumption and potentially change your driving habits.

As reliable as ever

Though it's been freshly engineered, now is not the time to question the reliability of the brand-new Honda Civic. Honda's manufacturing reputation is flawless, which leaves me no choice but to recommend this car, unless you've got your heart set on a hybrid or electric vehicle.

Speaking of which, I wonder if Honda is going to start selling a new hybrid or plug-in hybrid version of this Civic? No matter how you spin it, the new 2016 Civic still uses 30 percent more fuel and therefore emits 30 percent more CO_2 than the 2015 Civic Hybrid.

To be continued...

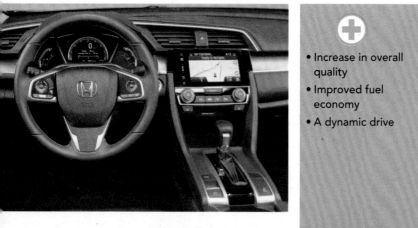

- Increase in overall quality
- Improved fuel economy
- A dynamic drive

- Hybrid no longer available

Honda Civic

HONDA

ECO

PRICE: $14,730 (CAD) – $15,790 (USD)
FUEL CONSUMPTION: 6,8 L/100 km (35 mpg)
GREENHOUSE EMISSIONS:
  154 g/km (247 g/mi)
GHG EMISSIONS RATING: 8/10
CALIFORNIA SMOG RATING: 6/10

Perfect for the city

DANIEL BRETON

There's a lot of variety when it comes to subcompact cars, but they're not all good buys, and it's not all about quality either. A combination of certain factors is what makes a subcompact worthwhile. But which ones, exactly? Let's take a closer look.

A surprising size

It's easier to get around urban areas behind the wheel of a smaller car that's easy to park. In this regard, the Honda Fit is perfect. Easily seating four people in a super-spacious cabin, the Fit is aptly named for its category. It all comes down to the car's famous lowered floor in the back (the gas tank is located under the front seats), allowing for more room in the backseat of this Honda than a Mazda3 or Ford Focus, both of which are compact cars.

Plus, you can move the seat base in the back up and down using the Magic Seat feature, allowing you to transport big objects that are difficult to lay flat. Pure ingenuity.

Continuously variable transmission is more economic

All four versions of the Fit enjoy the same engineering: a four-cylinder 1.5-liter 130-horsepower engine with 114 pound-feet of torque.

Specifications

SEATING CAPACITY: 5
CARGO SPACE (MIN-MAX):
470 – 1492 L (16.6 – 52.6 ft³)
WEIGHT: 1,131 kg (2,493 lb)
ENGINE:
Power: 130 hp (96 kW)
Torque: 114 lb-ft (154 Nm)

It's nothing to write home about, but when you take the vehicle's weight into account (barely 1,100 kg/2,400 lb), the structure doesn't hamper performance. Power can be routed from the wheels via a six-speed manual transmission or CVT (continuously variable transmission).

Though the Fit is more fun to drive in manual, CVT makes your life a whole lot easier in the city. Also, reported energy consumption in the city is much less with the CVT version (7.3 L/100 km or 32 mpg) than its manual counterpart (8.1 L/100 km or 29 mpg). When we tested it, median consumption totaled 6.8 L/100 km (35 mpg), but we drove a fair bit on rural roads, where cars tend to be more fuel-efficient.

No need to worry about reliability here—the Honda emblem is a worry-free guarantee.

Fun to drive in the city

The Fit is definitely fuel-efficient on big highways, but where it really shines is in heavy traffic. Maneuverable as ever, this car is fun to drive and lets you weave in and out of traffic where others wouldn't dare to venture. On the downside, it's loud when driven at highway speeds and its engine spins at 3,000 rpm. Longer trips are a bit of a snore. That being said, the latest generation of this Honda (2015) boasts improved comfort and stability, so no need to fret in that department.

The Fit in the city is a Yes. On the other hand, if you need to travel elsewhere, you might find a better fit for you...elsewhere.

- Very practical
- Well equipped
- Deceptively small

- Sensitive to wind

Honda Fit

HR-V

ECO

PRICE: $20,690 (CAD) – $19,115 (USD)

FUEL CONSUMPTION: 7.6 L/100 km (31 mpg)

GREENHOUSE EMISSIONS: 178 g/km (285 g/mi)

GHG EMISSIONS RATING: 7/10

CALIFORNIA SMOG RATING: 6/10

A small SUV worth considering

DANIEL BRETON

If there's one category that's increasing in popularity, it's compact SUVs. With an all-wheel-drive option, these high-riding vehicles have found their way into the hearts of many North Americans and even a growing number of Europeans.

While I'm not personally the biggest fan of these vehicles, I nonetheless recognize their good qualities, the principal one being their usefulness in regions suited for all-wheel drive.

What's more, they aren't overly large and can move easily in city traffic.

A small newcomer that's meant to be modern

You can definitely feel the Honda touch when you look at the HR-V. With its curved lines and its sporty nose, the HR-V is fully in line with current tastes, and will definitely appeal to fans of the class.

Like its siblings, the Civic and the Fit, its interior is decidedly modern. The highly effective and intuitive touch screen at the center of the dashboard provides a very nice effect. It's a satisfying choice for those of us who are tired of the overwhelming array of buttons that has been common in recent years.

The quality of the finish is first class; indeed, finish quality has improved for all Honda products in 2016, a much-needed change after years of over-reliance on cheap-looking plastic.

The cabin space is sufficient to seat four adults comfortably—and a little bit of luggage. Its cargo space is quite limited; but most

Specifications

SEATING CAPACITY: 5
CARGO SPACE (MIN – MAX):
 688 – 1,665 L (24.3 – 58.8 ft³)
WEIGHT: 1,314 kg (2,897 lb)
ENGINE:
 Power: 141 hp (104 kW)
 Torque: 127 lb-ft (172 Nm)

people don't go on trips every week, right? And the goal of purchasing a vehicle aimed at a certain level of energy efficiency (presumably a concern for those reading this book) should be sufficient motivation to buy a little smaller rather than larger.

You can easily put a box on the roof or use a small trailer when needed, rather than carrying unnecessary weight around all the time. Driving a vehicle that's heavier than it needs to be 90 percent of the time simply means a useless waste of gas.

On the road

This small and very agile SUV does very well under a range of circumstances. In cities, on the highway or during a full-on snowstorm, you'll never be caught unprepared with the HR-V. It does it all with a confidence and ease

that you wouldn't normally expect from a vehicle in this format.

Its fuel economy is decent. I was able to average about 7.6 L/100 km (31 mpg) on the highway, which is pretty respectable. However, that rose to almost 11 L/100 km (21 mpg) under winter conditions in the suburbs. The Subaru Impreza, another all-wheel drive compact, does better under the same conditions. If you value looking up-to-date, though, note that it's obviously not as modern looking as the HR-V.

If you're looking for a small SUV with all-wheel drive, the Honda HR-V will definitely meet your expectations. It's a reliable vehicle and a pleasure to drive, but it's not the most energy-efficient car you'll find.

✚	⊖
• Agile and assured driving in all conditions • Practical, despite its small format	• Unnecessary if you don't need an all-wheel-drive vehicle

Honda HR-V

HYB

PRICE: $29,649 (CAD) – $26,000 (USD)
FUEL CONSUMPTION: 5.7 L/100 km (41 mpg)
GREENHOUSE EMISSIONS: 137 g/km (220 g/mi)
GHG EMISSIONS RATING: 9/10
CALIFORNIA SMOG RATING: 6/10

Right on the edge of a real life

JACQUES DUVAL

The Korean brand Hyundai has joined the ranks of car manufacturers that offer their clients what Americans might call "the next best thing to an electric car": a hybrid that combines a gas engine (like in the good old days) with an electric motor.

The model with this combo is the Sonata. Some claim to be extremely disappointed, while others are satisfied.

The hybrid version does better when it comes to reliability. In any event, it's a car you'll buy after a heads-or-tails type of decision, especially since the Sonata has irresistible charm and makes a good first impression. This second-generation hybrid model (they've fixed the previous model's mistakes) is accompanied by a pretty interesting rechargeable version.

Among its most appealing characteristics, it offers the possibility of driving at 120 km/h (74.5 mph) in electric mode simply by disconnecting the gas engine from the drive shaft. This leads to the welcome fuel economy of merely 3.3 liters (0.87 gallons) every 100 kilometers (62 miles) according to our tests, while the non-rechargeable model requires 5.5 liters (1.5 gallons) for the same distance.

A more efficient battery

These numbers are attributable to an ordinary two-liter Atkinson cycle direct injection engine that works with a 38 kW electrical unit for a total of 193 horsepower. You gain nine

Specifications

SEATING CAPACITY: 5
CARGO SPACE: 376 L (13.3 ft³)
WEIGHT: 1,586 kg (3,497 lb)
ENGINES (GAS/ELECTRIC):
  Combined power: 193 hp (142 kW)
  Torque: gas: 140 lb-ft (190 Nm)
          electric: 151 lb-ft (205 Nm)
BATTERY:
  Material: lithium polymer
  Storage capacity: 1.6 kWh
  Warranty: 8 years/160,000 km (96 months/100,000 mi)

horsepower with the rechargeable battery, without forgetting the power added by the regenerative braking, which also must be taken into account. Another extra accessory is the stop/start system that stops the engine when the car is sitting in traffic and re-launches it as soon as you take your foot off the brake. This is mostly a gadget, and resulting savings are minimal. In this second-generation Sonata hybrid, the battery is noticeably lighter and more compact, allowing them to keep the backseat space that's often reduced by the presence of the lithium-ion polymer battery, now located in the trunk. Charging time at 240V is three hours rather than nine hours with a 120V outlet.

It accelerates quickly (0-100 km/h/0-62 mph in 7.5 seconds) without ever falling prey to the delay that's common in single-engine cars. Following in the footsteps of Mercedes, the Sonata hybrid also wears the Blue Drive moniker. Aside from the Genesis, which now goes it alone as Hyundai's only luxury brand, the Sonata is the South Korean group's best vehicle. All the usual high-end car accessories are on board: rearview camera, intelligent cruise control (the car goes at the speed of the car in front of you until coming to a full stop), blind spot sensors and a beep for lane changes. You can even throw in a heated steering wheel.

That is, in sum, Hyundai's answer to environmental issues. Its competence deserves to be highlighted, exceeding results of the Japanese manufacturers.

- Second-generation hybrid
- More compact battery
- Advanced aerodynamics
- Generous equipment

- Varying reliability
- No all-wheel drive
- Feedback-free steering

Hyundai Sonata Hybrid

133

Sonata PHEV

HYUNDAI

HYBRI

PRICE: $43,999 (CAD) – $34,600 (USD)
FUEL CONSUMPTION: 2.4 L/100 km (99 mpg)
(gas-electric); 5.9 L/100 km (40 mpg) (gas)
ELECTRIC RANGE: 43 km (27 mi)
CHARGE TIME: 120 V: 9 h – 240 V: 2.7 h
GREENHOUSE EMISSIONS: 63 g/km (101 g/mi)
GHG EMISSIONS RATING: 10/10
CALIFORNIA SMOG RATING: 9/10

A happy surprise

DANIEL BRETON

My first experience driving a Hyundai Sonata Hybrid wasn't great. While the Korean manufacturer claimed to have found the right balance between fuel economy and driving enjoyment, I found it next to impossible to deactivate the gas engine in the car while practicing eco-driving.

Thus the fuel economy I got in real life was 50 percent lower than the results of official tests. That was five years ago.

Since the all-new Hyundai Sonata Plug-in Electric Hybrid Vehicle (PHEV) hasn't received a lot of attention, I had a lot of questions as to whether its actual capabilities were equal to those advertised.

Good winter range

With its 9.8 kWh polymer lithium polymer battery, Hyundai claimed it had a battery range of 40 kilometers (25 miles). However, when I tested the car in winter conditions, I reached and even exceeded that range more than once—a very welcome surprise. It almost seems that cold temperatures (0 to -15°C/32 to 5°F) affect this battery less than others.

Incredible fuel economy

On short trips, I often achieved fuel consumption under 1.5 L/100 km (156 mpg). But during my week of tests, I often had to drive longer distances on the highway. During a 130-kilometer (80-mile) trip, my fuel consumption was 4.3 L/100 km (55 mpg), which is very good, particularly under snowy conditions. The week ended with an average

Specifications

SEATING CAPACITY: 5
CARGO SPACE: 280 L (9.9 ft³)
WEIGHT: 1,718 kg (3,787 lb)
ENGINES (GAS/ELECTRIC):
  Combined power: 202 hp (148 kW)
  Torque: 140 lb-ft (190 Nm) (gas); 151 lb-ft (205 Nm)
  (electric)
BATTERY:
  Material: lithium polymer
  Storage capacity: 9.8 kWh
  Warranty: 8 years/160,000 km (96 months/100,000 mi)

fuel consumption of 3.5 L/100 km (67 mpg): 712 kilometers (442 miles) driven and 6.6 gallons used equals 3.5 L/100 km (67 mpg).

A comfortable, luxurious car

The vehicle is spacious, comfortable and very well equipped. While the Chevrolet Volt can't seat five adults comfortably, the very spacious Sonata holds three adults comfortably in the rear.

The finish quality is impeccable. The interior design is tasteful and understated, but the conventional design will neither thrill nor offend.

The Sonata Plug-in Hybrid is replete with all the latest gadgets: a radar-based anti-collision system, lane departure warning, touchscreen and voice recognition, heated and cooled seats, heated steering wheel, etc. The only downside is that the trunk is hampered by the battery.

Still, its cargo space is much bigger than that of the Ford Fusion Energi.

The battery can be charged at a level 2 charging station in 2½ hours, which is totally acceptable.

A good highway car

Driving this car is an enjoyable, not to say transcendent, experience. It's solid, takes curves with assurance, and accelerates decently. It sits on the good side of average for highway cars in its category, but lacks the dynamism of a Volkswagen Jetta Turbo Hybrid or a Mazda 6.

The Sonata Plug-in Hybrid is one of the best surprises of 2016. Its higher price tag compared to that of competitors Fusion and Volt diminishes its appeal somewhat, but for those looking for a car that is well made, very well equipped, spacious and above all truly energy-efficient, it is definitely an option worth considering.

- Enjoyable to drive
- Soundproofed cabin
- Significant savings
- Surprising off-road capabilities

- Lifeless steering
- Performance could be improved
- Price is a deterrent

Hyundai Sonata PHEV

ELEC

KIA

PRICE: $34,995 (CAD) – $31,950 (USD)

ELECTRIC RANGE: 149 km (93 mi)

CHARGE TIME: 120 V = 24 h, 240 V = 4 – 5 h,
fast-charge = 80% in ½ h

GREENHOUSE EMISSIONS: 0 g/km (0 g/mi)

GHG EMISSIONS RATING: 10/10

CALIFORNIA SMOG RATING: 10/10

A most interesting prospect...if you can find one

DANIEL BRETON

A few years back, I tested the gas-powered version of the Kia Soul. This little crossover's most memorable feature? Its speakers. It's safe to say the gas engine Soul didn't provide the most memorable ride.

Its unique design wasn't enough to make me forget its modest performance, questionable handling and gas-guzzling tendencies. I wasn't even close to being a fan of this one.

I must say, however, that I am much more impressed with the Soul's electric sister.

A bit like how the Smart was transformed by an electric motor, the Soul became much more interesting when it went electric. That's not to say it's reached heaven.

Improved engine

Powered by a 109-horsepower electric motor with 210 pound-feet of torque, we don't have a racing car on our hands, but it's got everything you need for proper acceleration and easy maneuvering. So this EV's electric motor gets the job done. Note that the gas engine version of the Kia Soul only has 164 horsepower and 151 pound-feet of torque. In terms of performance, it's as if the Kia replaced its gas-engine with a diesel one...without the pollution.

Specifications

SEATING CAPACITY: 5
CARGO SPACE (MIN - MAX):
532 – 1,402 L (18.8-49.5 ft³)
WEIGHT: 1,492 kg (3,289 lb)
MOTOR:
Power: 109 hp (80 kW)
Torque: 210 lb-ft (285 Nm)
BATTERY:
Material: lithium-ion polymer
Storage capacity: 27 kWh
Warranty: 8 years/160,000 km (96 months/100,000 mi)

A battery that's up to snuff

The Kia Soul EV sports has a 27 kWh lithium-ion polymer battery, which delivers 90 kW. My winter trip from Montréal to Beaumont, the equivalent of Portland to Providence (263 kilometers or 163 miles) was therefore quite comfortable—I knew I had enough range to get there with just two 15- to 20-minute stops, where I recharged the battery to 80 percent at fast-charging stations. I could have driven farther south, however, with 40 kilometers (25 miles) left on the range meter. I got there in 3½ hours driving 90 to 100 km/h (56 to 62 mph) with an ambient temperature of nearly five degrees Celsius (41 Fahrenheit), which is quite good.

I'm of the opinion that you can drive the distance between Montréal and Kingston with a single stop at a level 3 charging station in the summer, or three stops in winter weather. The battery charges pretty quickly—under five hours with a 240-volt station and the 6.6 kW onboard charger. With a 120-volt outlet, it'll take 24 hours. Thanks to the car's fast-charge port, you can charge the battery up to 80-percent capacity in under 20 minutes. The range meter reads 115 kilometers (71 miles) when the battery is fully charged, but I

managed to squeak out 130 (81) in 5°C (41°F) weather. I bet that in optimal summer conditions, you could drive more than 180 kilometers (112 miles) on a full battery, which is excellent. Until the Chevrolet Bolt and Tesla Model 3 come out, that is.

Fully loaded

The Soul EV comes particularly well equipped with heated and air-conditioned front seats, a heated steering wheel, leather trim, GPS, rearview camera and more. In short, it's on par with the gas-powered Kia Soul SX Luxury. It's got that little something extra, though: a driver-controlled heating and air-conditioning feature that allows the person at the wheel to save battery power, which makes a whole lot of sense when you think about it.

- Great range
- Fast-charging
- Competitive pricing

- Availability issues
- Lousy GPS

KIA Soul EV

That being said, the GPS is average at best, *especially* the feature that helps you find charging stations on the road.

Cargo space in the Kia Soul EV 2015 is equal to that of the gas-engine version. That doesn't mean a lot, but it has 50 percent more loading space than the Nissan Leaf with its fold-down backseats. This Kia boasts 49.5 cubic feet while the Leaf comes in at only 30.

With tax incentives (where available), the Soul EV will run you about the same as a similarly equipped gas-powered Soul, making this crossover an extremely affordable choice, especially when you consider how much you'll save on gas and maintenance.

Smooth...or just soft?

The suspension is quite weak. For people who like a comfortable ride, you're in for a smooth drive in this car, but take it easy on turns. The button push to adjust the car's handling doesn't have much effect, except to make the steering wheel a bit more difficult to manage.

The car's soft suspension and imprecise steering make the Soul EV's handling nothing to write home about. Highway driving is fine, but on narrow winding roads, it's less relaxing, unless you drive really slowly. The seats are also pretty soft so you might feel like you're aboard an all-encompassing marshmallow. For drivers who love to have a slow go of it, however it can be kind of nice.

If only...

I can extol the virtues of this little crossover all I want, but that won't change the fact that it's almost impossible to find in Canada. In the U.S., you won't have a problem zeroing in on one in zero emissions jurisdictions. North of the border, a bunch of potential clients have put their names on a never-ending waiting list. Many of them have resigned themselves to opting for another manufacturer or scooping up the gas-powered Soul instead.

This crossover is surely one of the most interesting prospects in the EV world...if you can manage to find one.

Good luck!

LEXUS — CT 200h

HYB

PRICE: $31,650 (CAD) – $31,250 (USD)
FUEL CONSUMPTION: 5.6 L/100 km (42 mpg)
GREENHOUSE EMISSIONS:
  132 g/km (212 g/mi)
GHG EMISSIONS RATING: 9/10
CALIFORNIA SMOG RATING: 8/10

Nice as can be

JACQUES DUVAL

With its Mazda 3 look and Lexus logo stuck in the middle of the front grille, the CT 200h doesn't speak much to common mortals. However, it's actually a fun little car to take for a spin if you can put the somewhat daunting price tag out of your mind. I don't know another car in the hybrid camp with so much appeal. We're dealing here with a small luxury family car that's not cumbersome in the city and is both comfortable and quiet once you get on the highway.

The first piece of good news, for those who still aren't ready to move to a 100-percent electric vehicle, is about energy efficiency. Of all the models in the category, the CT 200h impressed me the most in this respect. Just think: During a 200-kilometer (124-mile) trip going between 100 and 115 km/h (62 and 71 mph), the new Prius-type model sipped only 4.8 L/100 km (49 mpg)—a remarkable feat.

This close cousin of Toyota's popular hybrid also shares its mechanical makeup with the Prius, including its 1.8-liter (110-cubic-inch) gas engine coupled with an electric motor and an NiMH battery, which provides the CT 200h with a combined power output of 134 horse-power (99 kW). The latter is carried to the front-wheel drive via an automatic trans-mission (CVT), which works smoothly without any noise.

Given its heaviness (batteries aren't featherweights), this car seems to drag its feet a bit, but proper adjustments will make up for any lag. You just need to shift into sports mode to see it come to life.

Specifications

SEATING CAPACITY: 5
CARGO SPACE (MIN – MAX): 405 – 700 L (14.3-24.7 ft³)
WEIGHT: 1,420 kg (3,130 lb)
ENGINES (GAS/ELECTRIC):
 Combined power: 134 hp (98 kW)
 Torque: gas: 105 lb-ft (142 Nm)
     electric: 142 lb-ft (192 Nm)
BATTERY:
 Material: nickel-metal hydride (NiMH)
 Storage capacity: 1.3 kWh
 Warranty: 8 years/160,000 km (96 months/100,000 mi)

In sports mode

If you choose not to act like a responsible citizen, and instead press your pedal to the metal, gas consumption will of course soar. Selecting the sports setting has a positive impact on road-handling abilities, making for a safer ride. This enhanced security can be felt through the steering, which allows for a strong connection with the pavement. One disappointing detail: The car's soundproofing in the city is less in evidence than on the road, harking back to the old days when that was the norm.

At the wheel, you'll be delighted by comfortable seats and, from the outset, confused by the onboard feeling provided by the novel instrumentation and unusual gearshift. However, this vehicle's most serious shortcoming is its substandard visibility. It's an annoying drawback brought to you by both the rearview window and right-hand blind spot.

On the plus side, the quality of interior workmanship is attention-grabbing due to the large dashboard packed with information highlighting this car's half-sport, half-environmental character.

In the backseat, your passengers won't feel crammed like sardines, but the batteries reduce trunk size, a weakness common to all hybrid cars derived from gas-powered models. The narrow trunk forces you to fold down the seats to save a bit of space.

Since it isn't very popular, the CT 200h could mean poor resale value. However, it's a car worth considering if you're looking for a vehicle that sets itself apart from the Prius and provides unexpected driving enjoyment.

- Low fuel consumption
- Modest power
- Comfortable seats

- Poor soundproofing
- Poor visibility
- Mini-size trunk
- Poor resell value

LEXUS CT 200h

LEXUS

HYB

PRICE: $41,400 (CAD) – $38,000 (USD)
FUEL CONSUMPTION: 5.9 L/100 km (40 mpg)
GREENHOUSE EMISSIONS: 139 g/km (223 g/mi)
GHG EMISSIONS RATING: 9/10
CALIFORNIA SMOG RATING: 9/10

Driving on a cloud

DANIEL BRETON

Lexus was the first auto manufacturer to take the plunge into luxury hybrid vehicles, and the gamble paid off: Getting an early start helped set Lexus apart from other luxury manufacturers that continued to charge blindly toward the dead end of high power and excessive fuel consumption.

Today, Lexus wants to show a sportier side, thereby adding cool factor to their image; but they are doing so without compromising on their vehicles, which are unmatched in the field of energy-efficient luxury vehicles.

The Lexus ES 300h is the perfect example of a successful balance of efficiency and luxury.

A discreet car

It doesn't turn heads; it doesn't inflame passions. Some night mistake it for a Toyota Camry or a Honda Accord. But for owners of a vehicle like this, it simply isn't a concern. Their preference is not to attract attention, but rather to be discreet.

It may seem incomprehensible to those who would rather flaunt their wealth, but car buyers who will gravitate to the ES 300h are the kind who feel that flashiness is just in bad taste. What Lexus enthusiasts especially value is comfort, classic luxury, good taste and above all, quality. A car like the Lexus ES 300h offers all that for a very reasonable starting price, which compares favorably against the competition.

The competition

While the Lincoln MKZ hybrid rivals the Lexus ES 300h in terms of fuel economy, the BMW 328d consumes more fuel, pollutes more and

Specifications

SEATING CAPACITY: 5

CARGO SPACE: 343 L (12.1 ft³)

WEIGHT: 1,660 kg (3,660 lb)

ENGINES (GAS/ELECTRIC):
Combined power: 200 hp (147 kW)
Torque: gas: 156 lb-ft (211 Nm)
electric: 199 lb-ft (270 Nm)

BATTERY:
Material: nickel-metal hydride (NiMH)
Storage capacity: 1.6 kWh
Warranty: 8 years/160,000 km (96 months/100,000 mi)

emits almost 30 percent more CO_2, which is still a lot. The Lincoln clearly has a bolder look, which will please some car buyers, but not necessarily Lexus-type buyers.

As for Cadillac, the ELR is quite attractive thanks to the technology it borrows from the Chevrolet Volt, which gives it over 60 kilometers (37 miles) of range, but it costs about $25,000 more than the Lexus, which is a hefty sum.

A warm, comfortable interior

Climbing into this car is like stepping into a friend's living room. The quality of the finish is impeccable, the seats are extremely comfortable in the front and the rear, it's completely quiet and, as should be the case, all the modern gadgets are incorporated: GPS, heated and cooled seats, Bluetooth, etc. In short, this car pampers you on the road.

A driving experience

Driving a Lexus ES 300h isn't supposed to be a thrilling experience. Quite the contrary, it is meant to make your life more Zen. You don't feel like you're flying around bends. You flow into them gently, like liquid, getting maximum pleasure from the stereo as you drive as fast as the speed limit allows (maybe just a touch faster) on the highway.

In the city, it drives silently and doesn't try to impress; it practically cradles you. Its combined fuel economy is less than 6 L/100 km (39 mpg), which is excellent for a car in this class.

Unmatched service and reliability

With Lexus, the icing on the cake is unequaled reliability and outstanding service. Once you experience that kind of service, it's hard to go back: Hence the great respect this brand commands today. German brands should take note and follow suit.

- A high-quality car
- Outstanding reliability
- Unparalleled service
- Very good fuel economy

- Suspension and driving feel may be a little soft for some

Lexus ES 300h

LEXUS

GS 450h

HYB

PRICE: $75,500 (CAD) – $63,080 (USD)
FUEL CONSUMPTION: 7.6 L/100 km (31 mpg)
GREENHOUSE EMISSIONS: 179 g/km (283 g/mi)
GHG EMISSIONS RATING: 7/10
CALIFORNIA SMOG RATING: 8/10

Not the most popular

JEAN-FRANÇOIS GUAY

When Toyota put the Prius its first hybrid vehicle in North America, on the market, few believed the technology would ever be used for luxury vehicles. At the time it was assumed that price and fuel economy would not be a major priority for affluent car-owners. But attitudes have changed, and Toyota has taken advantage of the opportunity that has opened up. Today, the Lexus line includes no less than six hybrid-powered models. Since the launch of its first hybrid model in 2006 (the RX 400h, now called the RX 450h), Lexus went on to produce more than 500,000 of the eight million hybrid vehicles that Toyota has sold around the world.

Although the car has a pretty much flawless track record, it's generally known that the GS 450 isn't the most popular Lexus model. Despite its many strengths, it competes with big names like the Mercedes-Benz E-Class and the BMW 5 Series. So, to boost GS sales in 2016, stylists have tweaked the bumper design and the trapezoidal grille for a touch of sportiness, adding LED headlights, daytime running lights and L-shaped rear lights.

This upgrade coincides with the arrival of the high-performance version of the GS F with a 5.0-liter V8 engine and 467 horsepower—showing that the Lexus is capable of the best and the worst in terms of energy-efficient driving. All joking aside, the "F" is basically the signifier from the brand to tell you that the GS is not merely comfortable and quiet, but provides some driving thrills as well. In any case, the GS F will have very limited distribution.

Specifications

SEATING CAPACITY: 5
CARGO SPACE: 450 L (15.9 ft³)
WEIGHT: 1,865 kg (4,112 lb)
ENGINES (GAS/ELECTRIC):
Combined power: 338 HP (249 kW)
Torque: 257 lb-ft (348 Nm) (gas), na (electric)
BATTERY:
Material: nickel-metal hydride (NiMH)
Storage capacity: 1.9 kWh
Warranty: 8 years/160,000 km (96 months/100,000 mi)

A hybrid with attitude

The GS 450h drivetrain combines a 3.5-liter V6 direct-injection Atkinson-cycle engine with an electric motor for a total output of 338 horsepower. This duo provides the acceleration of a V8, with a 0-100 km/h (0-62 mph) time of 5.6 seconds. If you prefer to prioritize energy-efficiency, you can use EV Mode to extend the fully electric range.

Depending on where you buy your vehicle, it may be possible to customize the look or the road handling by going for the F-Sport group (not to be confused with the GS F), which includes a more dynamic grille, a rear spoiler, 19-inch wheels, race-car-inspired instrumentation, more enveloping seats and adaptive suspension.

Rear-wheel drive

Unlike Lexus's RX 450h and LS 600h L, the GS 450h is equipped with rear-wheel drive, not all-wheel drive; this accentuates its sporty feel, but limits its distribution in markets where winter prevails for a large part of the year. To get all-wheel drive, you have to go for the GS 350, equipped with a 3.5-liter V6 rated for 311 horsepower. Also on offer is a 200t version with a 2.0-liter turbocharged four-cylinder engine with 241 horsepower, with propulsion mode (available in the U.S.).

In terms of accessories, all the embedded technology you could want is provided, and the various functions are accessible with a knob on the central console and a 31.2-centimeter (12.3-inch) screen.

The Lexus GS 450h is almost unrivaled. The only car that comes close is the Infiniti Q70 Hybrid, which is available in the U.S., but no longer in Canada. Compared to the Q70, the GS offers a more subdued and quiet ride.

- Reliable hybrid system
- A quiet, comfortable ride
- Good road handling

- No all-wheel drive with the hybrid
- Not the mostly lively brakes or steering
- Expensive

Lexus GS 450h

LS 600h L

HYB

PRICE: $147,200 (CAD) – $120,440 (USD)
FUEL CONSUMPTION: 11.7 L/100 km (20 mpg)
GREENHOUSE EMISSIONS:
  269 g/km (431 g/mi)
GHG EMISSIONS RATING: 4/10
CALIFORNIA SMOG RATING: 8/10

The Lexus of Lexuses

JACQUES DUVAL

The Lexus LS 600h L makes a first startling impression with its instruction manuals: three books and a whopping 1,292 pages. This will give you an idea of the range of systems and equipment found in this, the flagship of Toyota's luxury division.

If the name of the car is unfamiliar to you, the letters LS stand for the high-end model (luxury sedan), and the letter h stands for hydrid and L indicates long wheelbase. This model failed to cause much of a stir on the market, likely because it asked consumers to pay $40,000 more than the Lexus 460—a car that's more spacious in the back and slightly more economical thanks to its electric motor.

What about fuel economy?

The combined output of the 5.0-liter V8 engine and two electric motors is 438 horsepower, which gives the car real racing power, but at the cost of high fuel consumption. In the city, consumption is about 12 L/100 km (20 mpg), while more relaxed driving uses about 10 L/100 km (23.5 mpg).

That's nothing to boast about, since many automobiles of the same size can do as well or better with a conventional engine. And that's the crux of the problem, since the Lexus 600h L costs an arm and a leg. At the asking price, you could even buy a Tesla Model S and have enough money left for a Prius.

The Californian car offers neither the luxury nor the array of features found in the Japanese car, but it does have two baggage compart-

Specifications

SEATING CAPACITY: 4 or 5
CARGO SPACE: 283 L (10.1 ft³)
WEIGHT: 2,320 kg (5,115 lb)
ENGINES (GAS/ELECTRIC):
  Combined power: 438 hp (322 kW)
  Torque: gas: 385 lb-ft (522 Nm)
            electric: 221 lb-ft (300 Nm)
BATTERY:
  Type: nickel-metal hydride (NiMH)
  Capacity: 1.9 kWh
  Warranty: 8 years/160,000 km (96 months/100,000 mi)

ments, while the 600h L has only one, and a small one at that. But you can give a point to Lexus for its four-wheel drive.

More or less a limousine, the 600h L takes the best from each area, including an eight-speed automatic transmission with sequential mode and paddle shifters behind the steering wheel.

The driver can choose from four driving modes: Eco, Comfort, Sport S and even Sport S+. The last mode makes the vehicle most enjoyable to drive, in my opinion. The Lexus 600 does not drag its feet, with a six-second 0-100 km/h (0-62 mph) sprint time.

Outstanding reliability

Its build quality is nothing short of spectacular, and I wouldn't hesitate to say it is even equal

to, if not superior to, that of a Rolls or a Bentley. For proof, just look at the layout of the dashboard and all its accessories.

Before concluding the discussion, it is worth knowing that this Lexus has an environmental touch that offers unparalleled comfort and luxury. No less than 52 buttons for various functions are at your disposal, and no trendy accessory is missing.

It even has a work tablet in the back, and includes a system that detects pedestrians, inviting seats and a refrigerator. When do we open the champagne?

➕	➖
• Great luxury meets green strategies	• The control center
• Supreme comfort	• Sometimes hesitant transmission
• A substitute for Rolls-Royce	• Astronomical price for the hybrid version
• Careful craftsmanship	• Mixed driving enjoyment

Lexus LS 600h L

LEXUS

HYB

PRICE: $41,400 (CAD) – $38,000 (USD)
FUEL CONSUMPTION: 7.1 L/100 km (33 mpg)
GREENHOUSE EMISSIONS: 139 g/km (223 g/mi)
GHG EMISSIONS RATING: 9/10
CALIFORNIA SMOG RATING: 9/10

A frugal beauty

DANIEL BRETON

If there's one trend that keeps on growing, it's small luxury SUVs. Having already clogged up the streets and driveways of the planet, SUVs, each one bigger and more powerful than the next, are finally starting to give way to models with a more "reasonable" size—insofar as that's possible for an SUV.

Although I'm not a big fan of SUVs, I'll admit they have a certain appeal. Sitting so high up gives you a better perspective on what's around

you, which is a plus. All-wheel drive isn't something you need to avoid if you're living in a mountainous or snowy area. However, you can just as easily go without it, as evidenced by most people I know, who do indeed live in snowy, mountainous areas without SUVs.

So why might you be interested in a compact SUV like the Lexus NX 300h? Because if you just can't fight the craving for such an SUV, this one is particularly comfortable and energy-efficient. Of all the small luxury SUVs offered by Cadillac, BMW, Audi and other manufacturers around the world, the NX 300h is the most energy-efficient and least polluting—unless you move to a plug-in hybrid SUV, which would cost a good $20,000 more.

Well thought-out

In any luxury vehicle, you'll find some unneeded gadgets. That's not the case here. This vehicle was designed with care, for safety and a fully comfortable drive. Its road handling is among the best in the segment; its agility is incredible; its all-wheel drive is effective; its

Specifications

SEATING CAPACITY: 5
CARGO SPACE: 343 L (12.1 ft³)
WEIGHT: 1,660 kg (3,660 lb)
ENGINES (GAS/ELECTRIC):
  Power: 200 hp (147 kW)/ 156 (211 Nm) (gas)
  Torque: 199 lb-ft (270 Nm) (electric)
BATTERY:
  Material: nickel-metal hydride
  Storage capacity: 1.6 kWh
  Warranty: 8 years/160,000 km (96 months/100,000 mi)

fuel economy is truly commendable; and its acceleration is perfectly acceptable. Its cousin, the NX 200t outdoes it in terms of horsepower, but it uses 33 percent more gas than the NX 300h.

After several hundred kilometers, I had an average fuel economy of 7.4 L/100 km (32 mpg), and that was with winter driving in temperatures that sometimes verged on -15°C (5°F). That's an excellent result. When eco-driving, it's even possible to go below 6.5 L/100 km (36 mpg), which is exceptional for an all-wheel-drive SUV.

Comfort

The vehicle's interior is thoroughly inviting. When you sit down you're enveloped in very comfortable, high-quality seats. Even passengers in the rear will feel relaxed. The vehicle's ergonomics are thorough and the center-console display is, in my humble opinion, very intuitive—although apparently this view isn't held by everyone.

A stylish look

Everyone I've encountered who's had the chance to glimpse the face of the NX 300h has been impressed by its distinctly modern look, according to contemporary automotive beauty standards. I'm not sure I share that enthusiasm, but maybe it's best not to delve into questions of colors and tastes—still, note that those elements are a selling point.

Handsome, well-designed, energy-efficient and without a doubt as reliable as any product on the market, I expect the Lexus NX 300h to be quite a success.

➕
- Energy-efficient SUV
- Impeccable road handling
- Agile
- Great initial quality

➖
- A little pricey

Lexus NX 300h

RX 450h

HYB

PRICE: AWD: $68,550 (CAD) – $52,235 (USD)
  FDW: $54,575 (USD)
FUEL CONSUMPTION: AWD: 7.8 L/100 km (30 mpg)
GREENHOUSE EMISSIONS: 187 g/km (299 g/mi)
GHG EMISSIONS RATING: 7/10
CALIFORNIA SMOG RATING: 8/10

An indirect route

JACQUES DUVAL

It turned out Lexus kept the best for last when it unveiled the latest incarnation of its midsize SUV, the RX 450h. The event was held at Massif, a well-known ski resort 75 km (47 miles) from Québec City, and the moderate amount of real snow enhanced with its artificial equivalent made for a particularly treacherous route.

It presented a considerable challenge for a luxury SUV like the Lexus RX 450h, whose all-wheel drive system only activates in the back when needed. As with Toyota's RAV4, a small electric motor on the rear axle provides propulsion while charging the battery.

This four-wheel-drive vehicle bravely made its way through brush, bumps and sudden turns. The secret? Hold the accelerator down, despite the temptation to slow your speed in the dangerous terrain. An instructor was even on hand at the side of the track to remind us not to slow our pace in the most challenging spots. In the end, the tow truck never left its position while a good dozen of our machines maneuvered through the course without a hitch.

This shows that the RX 450h truly has joined the ranks of the most hardcore in the category, something that tends to be overlooked due to the vehicle's luxury and comfort. This is the SUV that comes closest to driving like a car, even though steering could be more engaging. Careful attention has been given to smooth running, comfort, flat cornering and a wealth of accessories that

Specifications

SEATING CAPACITY: 5

CARGO SPACE (MIN – MAX): 510 – 1557 L (18.0 – 55.9 ft³)

WEIGHT: 2,150 kg (4,740 lb)

ENGINES (GAS/ELECTRIC):
Combined power: 308 hp (227 kW)
Torque: 247 lb-ft (335 Nm) (gas); n/a (electric)

BATTERY:
Material: nickel-metal hydride (NiMH)
Storage capacity: 1.9 kWh
Warranty: 8 years/160,000 km (96 months/100,000 mi)

appeal to both your curiosity and your active safety. The RX is also more welcoming for occupants; there is more legroom in the rear, and heated seats as a bonus. The presence of a larger screen (31.2 cm/12.3 inches) on the undeniably stylish dashboard is welcome.

Thirty percent more economical

As for the hybrid powertrain, there's no major change over the previous model. The 3.5-liter Atkinson cycle V6 engine, however, has undergone countless minor updates aimed at making it more energy-efficient. Without electrical assistance, the Lexus RX consumes a good 12 L/100 km (24 mpg) on average; but if you add an "h" to make it a hybrid, those figures drop to 7.6 L/100 km (37 mpg) for city driving and 7.8 L/ 100 km (36 mpg) for

highway driving (according to the EPA). As for performance, it's decent if unspectacular. The eight-speed automatic transmission with paddle shifters gives this SUV a touch of sportiness. You can even order the F Sport version, which replaces the vehicle's "comfort mode" with "Sport plus," an option that comes with 20-inch wheels, which definitely give the RX a fiercer look.

After having driven the RX 450h over mountains and through valleys, it's clear why this model and its twin, the gas-powered RX 350, are the best-selling vehicles from Lexus. I've searched it for possible faults, and I've come up short. It's definitely the best buy in its category.

- Enjoyable to drive
- Soundproofed cabin
- Significant savings
- Surprising off-road capability

- Lifeless steering
- Performance could be improved
- Price is a deterrent

LEXUS RX 450h

MAZDA

ECO

PRICE: $15,550 (CAD) – $17,845 (USD)
FUEL CONSUMPTION: 6.9 L/100 km (34 mpg)
GREENHOUSE EMISSIONS:
  162 g/km (260 g/mi)
GHG EMISSIONS RATING: 8/10
CALIFORNIA SMOG RATING: 9/10

Small but mighty

DANIEL RUFIANGE

Automobile manufacturers are locked in competition, but they are not blessed with equal resources for the battle. Mazda, for example, has to manage its budget much more cautiously than a company like Toyota, which has almost unlimited means at its disposal. Like a sports team from a small town that goes up against rivals from megacities with infinite revenue, the company must innovate to deliver the goods.

That's what Mazda did at the end of the 20th century. Before that, its vehicles were handicapped by gaz-guzzling mechanics. Today, its engines are among the most frugal in the non-hybrid industry.

Mazda's approach can be summed up in one word: SkyActiv.

Like all vehicles in the line, the Mazda3 gains a lot from this concept. Before we go on, let's take a look at what SkyActiv entails.

Innovation

Knowing that it needed to modernize and make its machines more economical, Mazda leadership put out a call for innovation. It lacked the resources to launch long research and development studies, so it simply asked engineers to take a different tack, to think differently, to defy established conventions— basically, to reinvent the wheel.

The result was SkyActiv technology. In concrete terms, this technology affects the entire design of the vehicle, from the body to the chassis to the mechanics.

The engineers' first goal was to improve the performance of the gas engine by reducing loss (exhaust systems, cooling systems, etc.). Their

Specifications

SEATING CAPACITY: 5
CARGO SPACE (MIN – MAX):
hatchback: 572 – 1334 L (20.2 – 47.1 ft³)
sedan: 340 L (12.4 ft³)
WEIGHT: 1,300 kg (2,866 lb)
ENGINE:
Power: 155 hp (114 kW)
Torque: 150 lb-ft (203 Nm)

list of improvements was impressive and included increased compression ratio (13:1); smaller diameter of the combustion chamber and its pistons; and a newly designed exhaust system. The result was an engine that was 10-percent lighter. In the process, they also reduced friction by 30 percent and improved fuel economy and CO_2 emissions by 15 percent.

As for the transmission, priority was put on compactness and lightness. The chassis was also reimagined with a reduced weight, increased rigidity and a focus on stability.

That's the SkyActiv philosophy in a nutshell.

The car

The result? The Mazda3 is still a fun car to drive, but now its energy performance has reached the level of its competitors. With a two-liter, four-cylinder engine, I maintained an average fuel consumption of 6.2 L/100 km (38 mpg)—an excellent result for a car in its size and price range. To do better, you have to enter the world of hybrids or consider a Civic Turbo. The 2.5-liter, four-cylinder engine also gets good performance, but closer to 7 L/100 km (34 mpg). The difference is minimal whether you opt for manual or automatic transmission, but automatic can be somewhat lazy at times.

Beyond that, the Mazda3 needs no introduction: attractive, a well-crafted and versatile interior, sharp handling. As a bonus, the warranty lets you hit the road without worrying about mileage.

A solid purchase.

- Reasonable fuel economy
- Fun to drive

- Average reliability
- Rust in previous models

Mazda3

CX-3

ECO

PRICE: $20,695 (CAD) – $19,960 (USD)
FUEL CONSUMPTION: 7.6 L/100 km (31 mpg)
GREENHOUSE EMISSIONS:
 180 g/km (288 g/mi)
GHG EMISSIONS RATING: 7/10
CALIFORNIA SMOG RATING: 6/10

A sibling rivalry emerges

JEAN-FRANÇOIS GUAY

While Ford and Toyota have been slow to make their way into the mini SUV category, Mazda has finally decided to produce the CX-3 to compete with the Nissan Juke, the Honda HR-V and the Chevrolet Trax. With the CX-5's already small size, it isn't surprising that Mazda didn't rush to put the CX-3 on the market: Bad timing would mean that both models would end up competing against each

other. There is an unwritten law, however, that an urban SUV should not exceed 4.4 meters (14.4 feet) in length (the Subaru Crosstrek hybrid is at the limit). At 4.5 meters (14.8 feet), the CX-5 leaves the field open to the CX-3, which measures 4.2 meters (13.8 feet) from bumper to bumper.

In the tradition of Mazda models with a design inspired by Kodo principles, the CX-3 impresses with both its aesthetics and its features. In terms of technology, the CX-3 integrates the SkyActiv concept to optimize the powertrain and the vehicle weight, thus reducing fuel consumption while improving handling.

No manual transmission

Under the hood, the 2.0-liter four-cylinder engine features the latest advances in gasoline engines: direct injection, very high compression ratio (13:1), optimized cavity pistons, reduced internal friction in the engine and lighter weight. It all translates into better low- and mid-range torque and reduced fuel consumption and emissions. The six-speed

Specifications

SEATING CAPACITY: 5
CARGO SPACE (MIN – MAX): 452 – 1,528 L (16 – 54 ft³)
WEIGHT: 1,275 kg (2,811 lb)
ENGINE:
  Power: 146 hp (107 kW)
  Torque: 146 lb-ft (198 Nm)

automatic transmission actively lowers fuel consumption, thanks to a new type of torque converter that reduces slippage and power loss. The CX-3 has only automatic transmission, while its big brother, the CX-5, offers manual or automatic transmission with front-wheel drive and automatic transmission with all-wheel drive.

Despite all the technological bells and whistles, the CX-3's 2.0-liter engine is not the strongest in its category and is outclassed by the Nissan Juke and the Fiat 500 X. It develops 146 horsepower and 146 pound-feet of torque, which is comparable to the Honda HR-V and the Subaru Crosstrek hybrid, but it is faster than these in terms of acceleration, going from 0 to 100 km/h (0 to 62 mph) in 9.5 seconds. What's more, this engine is one of the most frugal in its category, using only 7.6 L/100 km (31 mpg) in two-wheel drive mode. Adding all-wheel drive increases consumption by about seven percent.

The *Jinba Ittai* concept

The cabin seats four adults comfortably, but it can fit five. Backseat passengers will appreciate the soft cushioning. In the front, the space is narrower due to the enveloping shape of the dashboard and the console, which is meant to create the feeling of being one with the vehicle—a concept known by the Japanese name *Jinba Ittai*. The GT version sits on 18-inch tires for sportier handling.

Because of the car's short chassis, the 452-liter (16-square-foot) trunk is smaller than that of the Mazda3 Sport (572 liters/20.2 square feet). When the seat is folded down, the cargo space is on par with its closest competitors.

There is no doubt that the CX-3 features the best design and the best road handling in its class. We can only hope that its makers will find a way to increase the engine power, without negatively affecting fuel economy.

- Successful design
- *Jinba Ittai* style cabin
- Sporty road handling

- No manual transmission
- Small trunk space
- Limited space in backseats

Mazda CX-3

MX-5

ECO

PRICE: $31,900 (CAD) – $24,915 (USD)
FUEL CONSUMPTION: 7.8 L/100 km (30 mpg)
GREENHOUSE EMISSIONS:
184 g/km (295 g/mi)
GHG EMISSIONS RATING: 7/10
CALIFORNIA SMOG RATING: 6/10

Fountain of youth

JACQUES DUVAL

What on Earth is a sports car doing in a guide to electric and more eco-friendly vehicles? Well, "fuel-efficient" is also blazoned across the front of this book, and the same label can be applied to certain sportier rides like the Mazda MX-5, a car more commonly referred to as *Miata*.

When I took it for a test-drive, something became clear right off the bat: this car is fuel-efficient. A sports car that only uses 7.8 L/100 km (30 mpg) deserves industry recognition for fuel economy. The term SkyActiv is plastered all over different Mazdas and it might not make sense to you right away. Nonetheless, this series of technologies produces results. By optimizing engine parts, the company has produced positive performance elsewhere in the car, including the suspension, brakes and body. Aluminum parts have lightened this car's load by a total of 60 kilograms (132 pounds).

Small appetite

A lighter car makes for less fuel consumption, but it also improves the performance of the two-liter engine which, with direct injection, puts 155 horsepower in the hands—and foot—of the driver. Though this Mazda posts a three-horsepower deficit compared to the previous generation, the MX-5 pushes the envelope in terms of drivability. Both automatic and manual versions get you from 0 to 100 km/h (0 to 60 mph) in seven short seconds. It's not a Ferrari, but on a narrow winding road with good company on a midsummer afternoon, it feels like one.

Specifications

SEATING CAPACITY: 2
CARGO SPACE: 130 L (4.6 ft³)
WEIGHT: 1,058 kg (2,332 lb)
ENGINE:
 Combined power: 155 hp (114 kW)
 Torque: 148 lb-ft (201 Nm)

Retract the top, which is child's play to operate, and multiply your fun by five.

Some say performance is key for sports cars, so handling is even more important for the simple reason that speed is not always welcome on the road. Without totally burning rubber, the MX-5 handles turns with ease by way of the beautiful balance provided by the central front location of the car's engine. As for parking, its size makes it easy to handle the necessary maneuver.

Anti-ageing

This Mazda is a veritable fountain of youth, hence all the gray hair behind the wheel. That said, you need to be young at heart and body to tolerate the MX-5's intolerance for potholed roadways in several North American regions.

When road quality dips, so does comfort aboard this vehicle. You also need some flexibility to get behind the wheel, and even more to slide back out. Mazda MX-5 owners are not usually afraid of such a challenge and even take to the wheel in the winter. You gotta try it!

I must tell you that the trunk volume totals a mere 130 liters (4.6 cubic feet). That means that you should purchase this car for the pleasure and low fuel costs it provides, not for day-to-day practicality.

P.S. Following an agreement with Fiat, the MX-5 will apply its designing principles to a Spider Fiat remains to be seen whether its different engine will be just as serious as the Japanese model.

- One of a kind
- Anti-ageing
- Easy as pie to drive
- Fun guaranteed

- Tight cabin space
- Imperfect soundproofing
- Minimal comfort
- Lack of storage space

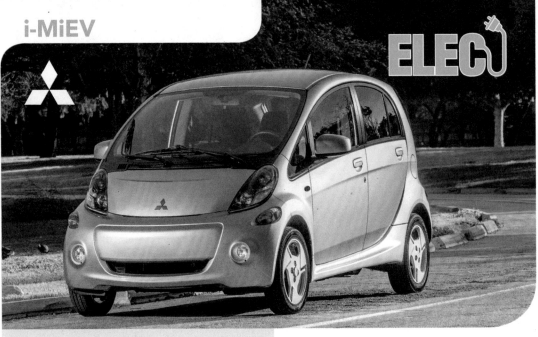

PRICE: $27,998 (CAD) – $22,995 (USD)

ELECTRIC RANGE: 100 km (60 mi)

CHARGE TIME: 120 V: 14 h (12A), 22 h (8A), 240 V: 7 h, fast-charge: 80% in ½ h

GREENHOUSE EMISSIONS: 0 g/km – 0 g/mi

GHG EMISSIONS RATING: 10/10

CALIFORNIA SMOG RATING: 10/10

A truly Spartan EV

DANIEL BRETON

While the Nissan Micra is the sparest gas-powered four-person vehicle on the market, the Mitsubishi i-MiEV wins in the 100-percent electric category. Learning to love this little car entails a bit of deprogramming on your part, however—you need to let go of deep-seated assumptions like:

- bigger and more powerful equals better
- gadgets are a necessity

- 500 kilometers (310 miles) of range are a must

This car isn't big, powerful, nor is it littered with gadgets...and it's for the better. Most people care about getting from here to there in a vehicle that's safe, is big enough to run daily errands with, and is affordable.

The Mitsubishi i-MiEV ticks all three boxes, easy.

Low autonomy on the road

It's a quiet drive. Acceleration doesn't happen in an instant—the i-MiEV isn't that powerful. You can't take turns at breakneck speeds, but who wants to burn rubber in an i-MiEV? It gets you from A to B at a steady pace without slowing down traffic.

The EV in question turns well, but its handling is a bit weak. Luckily, by housing its batteries in the floor, the i-MiEV's center of gravity is nice and low.

The car's range is nothing to brag about. The best I could do in ideal conditions was 125 kilometers (78 miles), far behind the

Specifications

SEATING CAPACITY: 4
CARGO SPACE (MIN – MAX): 377 – 1,430 L (13.3-50.5 ft³)
WEIGHT: 1,154 kg (2,545 lb)
MOTOR:
  Power: 66 hp (49 kW)
  Torque: 145 lb-ft (196 Nm)
BATTERY:
  Material: lithium-ion
  Storage capacity: 16 kWh
  Warranty: 8 years/160,000 km (96 months/100,000 mi)

Smart Fortwo Electric Drive's 145 kilometers (90 miles). That means the i-MiEV has the lowest range of any other 100-percent electric car on the market.

Plugged in

Its 16 kWh battery (about 12 kWh of which are usable) can be recharged in 14 hours with a 120-volt connection, so seven hours at 240 volts.

The car is equipped with a 3.3 kWh onboard charger. It must be said: An onboard charger under 6 kWh is *totally passé* for a 100-percent electric car in 2016.

That being said, you can use the car's CHAdeMO fast-charge port to get the i-MiEV up to 80-percent battery power in 20 minutes

(which is excellent) at a fast-charging station. It's only going to get better as Canada and the U.S. start deploying 400-volt stations across the continent.

Inside and outside

Both the body and the interior of this car can be described as sparse. The build-quality is solid, but nothing special. At rest, the windshield wipers are so poorly located it's *extraordinary*. Also, there's no cruise control.

Basically, this car couldn't care less about what people think a plug-in car should look like in 2016. To interested parties: The i-MiEV is the Spartan EV par excellence.

- Not expensive
- Reliable
- No gadgets

- Short range
- Mediocre handling at most
- Inferior inside fit and finish

Juke

ECO

PRICE: $20,698 (CAD) – $20,250 (USD)
FUEL CONSUMPTION: 7.8 L/100 km (30 mpg)
GREENHOUSE EMISSIONS: 184 g/km (295 g/mi)
GHG EMISSIONS RATING: 7/10
CALIFORNIA SMOG RATING: 6/10

Cutting-edge format and design

JEAN-FRANÇOIS GUAY

Wherever it goes, the Nissan Juke is sure to be noticed—and either loved or hated. Unveiled in 2011, the Juke opened the way for the urban SUV concept. Despite its age, it doesn't seem at all dated; that's how forward-thinking it was in terms of appearance.

The Juke can pride itself on being one of the two smallest SUVs on the market, the other being the Mini Countryman. Measuring 4.1 meters (13½ feet) in length on a 2.5-meter (8.3-foot) wheelbase, the Juke fits squarely in the SUV category. And unlike full-size SUVs (whose dimensions impose certain limits on stylists' imagination), the Juke, like the Smart Fortwo and similar vehicles, allows the stylists' imagination free rein. Thus the reduced dimensions of the Juke allow for some stylistic quirks, such as the sculpted hood, turn signals that are integrated into the front fenders, large round headlamps, boomerang-shaped rear lamps, rear-door handles hidden in the body and a high beltline and flowing roofline reminiscent of Nissan's GT-R and 370Z coupes.

A cramped cabin

The interior is less extravagant, and it would have been nice if the instrumentation had been designed with a little more inspiration from the sports car. However, given the Juke's measurements, it makes sense that the cabin and seats are tight.

Still, tall people can easily fit into the front seats with no complaints. In the rear, it is another story altogether, since the slope of the

Specifications

SEATING CAPACITY: 5
CARGO SPACE (MIN – MAX): 297 – 1,017 L
(10.5 – 35.9 ft³)
WEIGHT: 1,324 kg (2,918 lb)
ENGINE:
Power: 188 hp (138 kW)
Torque: 177 lb-ft (240 Nm)

roof and the wheel arches take up a lot of the space in the door openings.

Another disappointment is that there is little storage space, and the trunk space is the smallest in its class. Making things even more inconvenient, you have to remove the headrests from their base to fold down the 60/40 split rear seats, and rear visibility is problematic (the rearview camera is there for good reason).

Manual or CVT

The 1.6-liter turbo four-cylinder engine develops 188 horsepower and 177 pound-feet of torque. For sportier performance, there is a NISMO version with an engine that delivers 215 or 211 horsepower, depending on whether it has front-wheel or all-wheel drive. The extra power does not increase the average fuel consumption by much (0.3 L/100 km/1 mpg). Even though the stick shift is long and lacks precision, it's a shame that the manual six-speed transmission isn't offered with the all-wheel drive so that the full potential of the engine could be exploited. Accelerations are energetic, but the CVT transmission can sometimes lag.

Compared with its essentially utilitarian rivals, the Juke stands out with a more lively and agile handling. Even though its turning radius is long for vehicles of its size, the Juke moves easily in traffic. It stays level when cornering, and crosswinds and traveling on highways have little affect on stability. The short wheelbase and stiff shocks, however, are not very effective in mitigating imperfections in the road.

- Unique design
- A go-anywhere vehicle
- Powerful engine

- Sluggish CVT
- Tiny trunk
- Cramped rear-seat access
- Will never win a beauty contest

Nissan Juke

ELEC

🍃🍃🍃🍃🍃🍃🍃🍃🍃🍃

PRICE: $31,998 (CAD) – $29,010 (USD)

ELECTRIC RANGE: 135 km (84 mi) (24 kWh);
172 km (107 mi) (30 kWh)

CHARGE TIME: 120 V = 21 h, 240 V = 5 h,
fast-charge = 80% in ½ h (24 kWh), 120 V = 26 h,
240 V = 6 h, fast-charge = 80% in ½ h (30 kWh)

GREENHOUSE EMISSIONS: 0 g/km – 0 g/mi

GHG EMISSIONS RATING: 10/10

CALIFORNIA SMOG RATING: 10/10

Citius, Altius, Fortius[1]

DANIEL BRETON AND JACQUES DUVAL

In Daniel Breton's opinion:

Nearly five years ago today, I performed my first test of the Nissan Leaf. And, just recently, I test-drove the model's newest incarnation for 2016, which is already becoming an icon in its category.

A healthy understanding

Unlike many other models designed as vehicles with internal combustion engines, the Nissan Leaf was always designed to be an electric car, with its battery beneath the floor. And that's for the best.

Nissan's emphasis on practicality—generous interior and cargo space given the vehicle's size—and aspects unique to an electric car—such as plug location, GPS with charging stations, and *tutti quanti*—makes this one of the most enjoyable cars to drive on a daily basis.

Designed to keep you entertained, the NissanConnect system with mobile apps includes a Bluetooth phone system, continuous Bluetooth audio transmission, as well as hands-free texting and an iPod™ USB port that's compatible with other devices.

---

1. These three Latin words, which mean "faster, higher, stronger," have come to be the Olympics motto.

Specifications

SEATING CAPACITY: 5
CARGO SPACE (MIN-MAX): 668 – 849 L (23.6 - 30 ft³)
WEIGHT: 1,477 kg (3,256 lb) (24 kWh);
  1,515 kg (3,340 lb) (30 kWh)
MOTOR:
  Power: 107 hp (79 kW)
  Torque: 187 lb-ft (253 Nm)
BATTERY:
  Material: lithium-ion
  Storage capacity: 24 kWh (S); 30 kWh (SV, SL)
  Warranty: 8 years/160,000 km (96 months/100,000 mi)

Worthy performance

This car provides a tremendously smooth ride. It's especially silent, even when compared with other electric cars, its suspension is as supple as it is firm (taking turns with remarkable assurance), and it accelerates most convincingly. A true delight to drive.

Greatly improved freedom on the highway

While the previous model's weakness was the highway, the new version with a 30 kWh battery seems to have solved the problem: Driving at 100 km/h (62 mph) in an average temperature of 0°C (32°F), I was able to cover 180 kilometers (112 miles) without batting an eyelash. I was even able to push the car's range all the way to 200 kilometers (124 miles) when traffic was heavier.

I wouldn't be at all surprised to see the Leaf traveling over 250 kilometers (155 miles) in ideal summer conditions. The fast-charging port is now actually offered across all new versions. That means you can charge this car to 80-percent capacity in under half an hour at the fast-charge stations popping up all over North America.

Five years after first trying my first Nissan Leaf, I must conclude that this car's update is very timely. Persistent rumors lead us to believe that the 2017 version will be even more powerful. This would be a good idea given that the Chevrolet Bolt and Tesla Model 3 are set to be on the market very soon.

To sum up, the 2016 Nissan Leaf is an improvement on the 2015 model in many respects, which will make it a success, especially since its starting price hasn't gone up. That said, the 30 kWh battery only comes standard on the SV and SL versions, which cost thousands of dollars more than the basic one.

In the end, since Jacques appreciates the Leaf's driving attributes less than I do, it's up to you to decide.

Go and test it out!

- Greatly improved range
- Very fun to drive *(Daniel)*
- Fast standard-charging station

- Average interior finish
- Low-end feel
- Ordinary road behavior *(Jacques)*

In Jacques Duval's opinion

For starters, allow me not to share my esteemed colleague Daniel's enthusiasm for the Leaf. Not so much because it left me high and dry during my first test-drive five years ago, but mostly because the way it drives could be likened to an unrefined small car. For the asking price, it reminds me of a cheap set of wheels. Overly light handling, overlooked soundproofing and a low-end feel.

That said, I was very disappointed by its range claim during my first outing behind the wheel when, after 90 kilometers (56 miles) on the road, the promised 150 kilometers (93 miles) of electric battery life forced me to call a tow truck.

The 2016 Leaf claims 200 kilometers (124 miles) of range, and I had no problem getting exactly 204 kilometers (126 miles) out of it on a course identical to the one from my first test-drive. I'll add to its credit that its charge times were only seven to eight hours on a simple 120-volt socket. What this means in practical terms is that if you live in, say,

Concord, NH and work in Boston, you can drive round-trip without having to worry about plugging in your Leaf to a charging station. Of course, you'll have to drive hyper-economically knowing that this type of performance will only be possible in the summer. You need to take into account that every electric car loses about 20 percent of its range in the snow.

That can even go up to 30 percent with the Leaf if you drive without the slightest consideration for fuel economy.

Note that the same drawback applies to cars with gas-powered engines. However, since this car's range indicator isn't numbered in miles or kilometers, but is rather a needle with very approximate readings, you can't visualize what acceleration really costs on the fly. Also, what can be said of the 2016 Nissan Leaf's other innovations? If you exclude the higher-performing battery, changes are minimal and nothing allows you to distinguish the new model from the old one, unless you focus on tiny details.

The Leaf has two available driving modes: One that allows you to free up acceleration and shorten the 0 to 100 km/h (62 mph) sprint by half a second (at its range's expense, of course). As soon as this mode is engaged, the Leaf is powered forward without you even having to press down on the accelerator. Very useful for passing, but you'll need to get used to it. Much like the shifter that's a bit confusing at first with its dial, which allows you to activate forward or reverse motion, as well as the parking brake. At the wheel, visibility is excellent and the often-neglected windshield's size makes it very useful at sunset. However, I felt that the seats could have had better padding. The finish was flawless in the car I tested, though the abundance of plastic on the dashboard dulls your view.

You also need to practice restraint while driving, since it's easy to get distracted by the plethora of information displayed on the central display.

In the end, taking the Leaf out on the open road is what disappointed me most. Its wobbly suspension absorbs the pavement's unevenness with small, unpleasant shakes, while braking is accompanied by a skipping that prolongs the time it takes to stop. This is often the case with low-rolling resistance tires that favor range. Finally, its handling isn't very remarkable.

Although I was not terribly happy with the Nissan Leaf, buyers generally claim satisfaction. In my view, however, when it comes down to pure driving, this car demands some sacrifices.

Micra

ECO

PRICE: $9,998 (CAD) – n/a (USD)
FUEL CONSUMPTION: 7.8 L/100 km (36 mpg)
GREENHOUSE EMISSIONS:
  184 g/km (295 g/mi)
GHG EMISSIONS RATING: 8/10
CALIFORNIA SMOG RATING: n/a

A celebration of voluntary simplicity

DANIEL BRETON

I test-drive a different fuel-efficient vehicle every week. I can test electric, plug-in hybrid, regular hybrid and cars that are just plain fuel-efficient for their category. In 2016, however, no one is talking about totally eco-friendly cars that embrace voluntary simplicity.

Let me explain why.

Voluntary simplicity entails unburdening something of everything that isn't absolutely necessary. It's about questioning the needs that manufacturers create. That's where the Nissan Micra stands out from the rest. If you want, you can get a Micra without:

- air conditioning
- power mirrors
- remote locking
- Bluetooth
- cruise control
- USB ports

Basically, you can get this car as Spartan as a subcompact car from 15 years ago, which is great news if you're open to the idea of voluntary simplicity.

I must admit that I have no objection to depriving myself of such gadgets...except for Bluetooth, which I need to talk and drive. I'm not ready to ditch my cell phone just yet.

I guess that means I'm not perfectly green!

Specifications

SEATING CAPACITY: 5
CARGO SPACE (MIN – MAX):
408 – 819 L (14.4 – 28.9 ft³)
WEIGHT: 1,044 kg (2,301 lb)
ENGINE:
Combined power: 109 hp (80 kW)
Torque combined: 107 lb-ft (145 Nm)

Fun to drive

Despite being a simple car, the Nissan Micra is a lot of fun to drive in the city and on the highway. It's lively, handles like a charm and might lure you to speed if you aren't paying attention. It reminds me of the Renault 5 from back in the day. Caution: This car is susceptible to side winds.

The Micra five-speed manual transmission (a dying breed) is tight and makes for a perfect pairing with the car's little four-cylinder, 1.6-liter engine.

Somewhat retro fuel consumption

This little number is obviously not at the cutting-edge of high-tech. That's why you'll find that its fuel consumption is as reasonable as one might expect. It's easy to find a cheap little car on the market. However, with a price tag lower than $10,000, you'd be hard-pressed to find one as inexpensive as the Nissan Micra.

If you want to choose a ride that stands out from the rest with its voluntary simplicity, the Micra is your best bet when it comes to gas-powered cars. When you buy a car with fewer bells and whistles, you invest in something that requires fewer raw materials, less water and less energy to produce. It's an ecologically coherent choice.

In addition, the fewer the gadgets a car has, the less likely it is to have problems. Just because it doesn't have air conditioning doesn't mean it isn't reliable!

So for Spartan spenders and those who prefer simplicity, this car seems like an obvious choice!

- Simple vehicle
- Nice drive
- Inexpensive

- Disappointing fuel economy
- Sensitive to crosswinds

PORSCHE

HYBRID

Cayenne S E-Hybrid

PRICE: C: $87,700 (CAD) – $77,200 (USD)
P: $106,600 (CAD) – $93,200 (USD)

FUEL CONSUMPTION: Gas: **C:** 10.7 L/100 km
(22 mpg) **P:** 9.4 L/100 km (25 mpg). Gas/electric:
C: 5 L/100 km (47 mpg)/**P:** 4.6 L/100 km (51 mpg)

ELECTRIC RANGE: C: 22 km (14 mi)/**P:** 26 km (16 mi)

CHARGE TIME: C: 120 V: 12 h, 240 V: 2.7 h,
P: 120 V: 10 h, 240 V: 2.3 h,

GREENHOUSE EMISSIONS: C: 163 g/km (260 g)/mi/
P: 143 g/km – 229 g/mi

GHG EMISSIONS RATING: C: 8/10/ **P:** 9/10

CALIFORNIA SMOG RATING: 6/10

* C = Cayenne, P = Panamera

Awaiting something better

DANIEL BRETON

I've always been a fan of Porsche. The little company has made a big name for itself with its Germanic rigor, specialized cars and—in contrast to Italian sports cars—reliability.

Twenty years ago, I even had the chance to own a Porsche, and it brought me a great deal of pleasure—it was worth every speeding ticket. I'm a lot wiser now, I assure you.

A plug-in hybrid: really?

Having already tested the Porsche Cayenne S, I can say that the hybrid will feel quite familiar to anyone used to the gas-powered version. The plush, comfortable interior puts you at ease instantly. The first thing to do is figure out the vast array of buttons surrounding you; fortunately, it doesn't take long, since they are quite intuitive.

With that step out of the way, it's time to take a ride.

When you turn on the Porsche Cayenne S E-Hybrid, it makes noise—in fact, it makes a racket. It's very strange. If there's one feature common to plug-in and electric hybrids, it's silence, but this Porsche is more than audible. Even more off-putting is that it's not the characteristic noise of Porsche's boxer engine, but rather the irritating sound of what seems to be a huge fan.

Specifications

SEATING CAPACITY: Cayenne: 5/Panamera: 4

CARGO SPACE (MIN – MAX):
Cayenne: 566 – 1,671 L (20.5 – 59.7 ft³)
Panamera: 335 – 1,153 L (11.8 – 40.7 ft³)

WEIGHT: Cayenne: 2,350 kg (5,181 lb)
Panamera: 2,095 kg (4,618 lb)

ENGINES (GAS/ELECTRIC):
Combined power: 416 hp (306 kW)
Torque combined: 435 ft-lb (588 Nm)

BATTERY:
Material: lithium-ion
Storage capacity: Cayenne: 10.8 kWh
Panamera: 9.4 kWh
Warranty: 8 years/160,000 km (96 months/100,000 mi)

Panamera S E-Hybrid

Equipped with a three-liter, V6 engine with 333 horsepower, coupled with a 95-horsepower electric motor, th E-Hybrid has a powerful acceleration: The 2,350-kilogram (5,181-pound) behemoth does 0 to 100 km/hr (0 to 62 mph) in six seconds. When it goes from electric to gas mode, shifting speeds is less than perfectly smooth and for a Porsche, that's a bit of a disappointment. Fortunately though, the handling is top-notch as is the braking.

Range and fuel economy

Over the 543 kilometers (337 miles) I drove in the Cayenne, I was able to get an average consumption of 3.4 L/100 km (69 mpg)—a pretty good showing from such a large, powerful vehicle. That said, when I was going 100 km/hr (62 mph), after I'd surpassed the electric range, gas consumption went up to 9 L/100 km (26 mpg)— a fairty average increase.

While driving very gently, the maximum 100-percent electric range I was able to get with the 10.8 kWh battery was 32 kilometers (20 miles).

Recharging takes 2¾ hours with the 3.6 kWh onboard charger and one hour and 20 minutes if you opt for the 7.2 kWh charger.

With a minimum price tag of $87,700 for this plug-in hybrid SUV (and even more for the Panamera S E-Hybrid!), you can buy a Tesla Model S 70D (about 400 kilometers (250 miles) of 100-percent electric range) or for a few more dollars more, a Tesla Model X. And since Porsche itself announced the arrival of a 100-percent electric car with a 500-kilometer (311-mile) range...

In the end, we want more from Porsche than what we get from these two E-Hybrids.

Cayenne S E-Hybrid

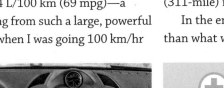

- Very powerful vehicles
- Superior handling and braking

- Disappointing range
- Noisy
- Hesitant transmission

Porsche Cayenne S E-Hybrid/Panamera S E-Hybrid

1500 EcoDiesel

ECO

PRICE: $39,895 (CAD) – $37,780 (USD)

FUEL CONSUMPTION: 10.2 L/100 km (23 mpg)
(4 x 2)

GREENHOUSE EMISSIONS: 274 g/km
(439 g/mi)

GHG EMISSIONS RATING: 4/10

CALIFORNIA SMOG RATING: 5/10

The only diesel in its class

JEAN-FRANÇOIS GUAY

The Ram 1500 sets a standard for full-size pickup trucks in terms of design and ingenuity. With its muscular look inspired by road tractors and its abundance of features, it's given the Ford F-150, the Chevrolet Silverado 1500 and the GMC Sierra 1500 (which believed themselves to be the only players in the field), reason to be very nervous.

Knowing that pickup buyers tend to be fond of diesel engines, FCA (Fiat Chrysler Automobiles) rushed to outmaneuver Ford and General Motors three years ago by introducing a 3.0-liter V6 turbo-diesel engine, which they named the EcoDiesel.

Quietness and versatility

To avoid confusion: the Ram 1500 EcoDiesel's V6 is the same engine as that found under the hood of the Jeep Grand Cherokee, which cut its ties with the Mercedez-Benz V6 turbo-diesel at the end of 2009. However, the EcoDiesel's V6 has nothing in common with the in-line six-cylinder 6.7-liter engine, which is found in the Ram 2500 and 3500 and which is built by the American company, Cummins. One thing is certain: the EcoDiesel is quieter and smoother than the Cummins.

While the Ford F-150 has relied on EcoBoost technology to get better fuel economy in its V6 engines and General Motors has upgraded its V6 and V8 gas engines in the Silverado 1500 and the Sierra 1500 by adding direct injection and cylinder deactivation, the Ram 1500 has focused

Specifications

SEATING CAPACITY: 3
CARGO SPACE: 1614 L – 57,5 ft³ (6 ft, 4 in. load)
WEIGHT: 2,308 kg (5,090 lb)
ENGINE:
  Power: 240 hp (176 kW) (V6 turbo-diesel 3.0 L)
  Torque: 420 lb-ft (569 Nm)

on improving fuel economy with its diesel engine. Developing 240 horsepower and 420 pound-feet of torque, the Ram 1500 uses one liter less per 100 kilometers (0.26 gallons per 62 miles) than the Ford V6. The Ram also has another trick up its sleeve: the V6 Pentastar, with a 3.6-liter gas engine (305 horsepower, 269 pound-feet of torque), whose fuel consumption is higher than the 2.7-liter Ford EcoBoost by only 0.6 liters per 100 kilometers (0.37 gallons per 62 miles).

Get out your calculator

To get the benefits of the EcoDiesel engine, however, there's a price to pay. Informed consumers should figure out whether it's worth spending that much money to save a liter or two every 100 kilometers (a quarter or half a gallon per 62 miles). On top of the extra cost ($5,700 [CAD]/$3,120 [USD]) over the 3.6-liter V6 Pentastar, the buyer also has to opt for a deluxe model, since the EcoDiesel isn't available in entry-level versions.

Also, greenhouse gas emissions (GHG) for diesel are 17 percent higher per liter than gas; the Ram diesel engine thus emits six percent more CO_2 than the Ford's 2.7-liter EcoBoost. That's not counting the fact that harmful emissions from a diesel engine are even higher than those of a gas engine.

Comparing the power of Ram's Pentastar V6 to its EcoDiesel V6, the EcoDiesel can tow a trailer with 12 percent more weight than a 3.55 axle ratio. Another advantage of the EcoDiesel is the option for a 3.92 axle ratio (not offered with the Pentastar), which increases towing capacity to 4,177 kilograms (9,210 pounds) according to the cabin configuration and the length of the load body.

For now, no American half-ton pickup can compete with the diesel-powered Ram 1500. The only opposition comes from the Japanese, with Nissan's new Titan XD and its turbo-diesel V8 Cummins engine. And even it consumes more than the Ram.

➕
- Low fuel consumption
- Eight-speed automatic transmission
- Active grille shutters improve the drag coefficient (C_d), so its aerodynamics are better thus improving fuel economy.

➖
- EcoDiesel engine is not offered in the basic model
- High price with the EcoDiesel option
- Heavier pickup than the competition

Ram 1500 EcoDiesel

Fortwo

smart

ECO

PRICE: $17,300 (CAD) – $14,650 (USD)
FUEL CONSUMPTION: 6.5 L/100 km (36 mpg)
GREENHOUSE EMISSIONS: 154 g/km (246 g/mi)
GHG EMISSIONS RATING: 8/10
CALIFORNIA SMOG RATING: 7/10

Lots of improvements

DANIEL BRETON

First of all, let's acknowledge that the previous generation of the gas-powered Smart Fortwo far overstayed its welcome on the market. With reliability that may not be terrible but doesn't impress, the prohibitive costs of maintenance and repair and, above all, a transmission that is absolutely antediluvian, it was doomed to please very few, which has been reflected in its plummeting sales.

Then along came the electric version of the Smart that saved this line for Mercedes, along with helping the German manufacturer reach its requirements for CAFE (Corporate Average Fuel Economy) standards, governed by NHTSA (nhtsa.gov/fuel-economy). This standard is aimed at reducing energy consumption by improving fuel economy in its cars and light trucks in the U.S.

For the last two years, Mercedes clearly hasn't been overly eager to showcase its gas-powered Smarts, since they were completely absent from the showrooms of Detroit, Los Angeles and Montréal. Only Smart Fortwo EDs were proudly displayed on the stands.

Well, that's no longer the case. The new Smart Fortwo has arrived, and it has changed—for the better.

Equipped with a new engine and, above all, a transmission worthy of the name, it's hard to believe how much the new version has improved. It has livelier acceleration, shifting that barely resembles the inferior shifting of its predecessor, and the handling is also markedly better.

Specifications

SEATING CAPACITY: 5
CARGO SPACE (MIN – MAX): 190 – 350 L (6.7 – 12.4 ft³)
WEIGHT: 965 kg (2,127 lb)
ENGINE:
 Power: 89 hp (66 kW)
 Torque: 100 lb-ft (135 Nm)

Its suspension, too, a lot better than before.

The look of its exterior, however, is not universally loved. Its more square shape may appeal more to men, whereas women might prefer the older version (my survey sample is made up of my wife and her friends; so take that for what it's worth). The interior, however, is a crowd-pleaser across the board. It's better finished, better laid out and, above all, modern.

Unlike in the previous version, the functions that are now available in all newer cars (Bluetooth, USB port, etc.) are available with this car, even with the entry-level model. The levers are wisely placed and the finish is a step up in terms of quality.

The price of this small city car is reasonable, but it's hard to ignore the fact that the electric version goes for about the same price in areas where government rebates are also available,

making this version a good deal less attractive than its electric cousin.

That said, there simply aren't many electric models available, and the new version of the Smart Fortwo ED won't be on the market for a few months yet.

Last but not least: For a car this small with a turbocharged 0.9-liter engine, its fuel economy seems a little weak. Its combined fuel-efficiency of 6.5 L/100 km (36 mpg), compared with the 0.2 L/100 km (1,170 mpg) fuel rating for the much larger Honda Civic (which has a price tag that's not much higher) gives me pause.

Still, for a small city car that can pass and park with ease, this new Smart Fortwo is a huge step forward.

As for reliability: to be determined.

➕
- Car improved in every respect
- Reasonable price
- Transmission worthy of the 21st century

➖
- Fuel economy a little low
- Unproven reliability

Smart Fortwo gas-powered

Fortwo Electric Drive

smart

ELEC

PRICE: $26,990 (CAD) – $19,990 (USD)
ELECTRIC RANGE: 109 km (68 mi)
CHARGE TIME: 120 V: 16 h, 240 V: 6 h
GREENHOUSE EMISSIONS:
  0 g/km (0 g/mi)
GHG EMISSIONS RATING: 10/10
CALIFORNIA SMOG RATING: 10/10

Cute, inexpensive and decent

DANIEL BRETON

I remember the launch of the Smart Fortwo. It was back in 1998, almost 20 years ago now. After all these years, it's about time that the third generation came out. Unfortunately, that's not the case for the EV version: The Smart Fortwo ED inherited the same chassis, recycled from the 2015 model, unlike the gas-powered version that you see at car shows. Big disappointment.

That being said, since I know this little car very well (my wife drives one), I can sing its virtues for you. The top three: sharp handling, its 100-percent electric operation and a particularly attractive price tag (with discounts/tax credits). That makes the Smart Fortwo ED the most affordable electric car on the North American market.

A city girl that can handle the open road

The electric version of the Smart Fortwo isn't new. Actually, we're currently witnessing the third generation.

This car, as opposed to its gas-powered version, has been relieved of a transmission, which makes acceleration linear and quicker. Plus, the car's center of gravity has been lowered by housing the battery in the floor, which makes for better handling and resistance to side winds. The engineering upgrades made to the electric version make it a more attractive prospect and more fun to drive.

Specifications

SEATING CAPACITY: 2
CARGO SPACE (MIN – MAX): 220 – 340 L (7.8 – 12,0 ft³)
WEIGHT: 900 kg (1,894 lb)
MOTOR:
  Power: 74 hp (55 kW)
  Torque: 96 lb-ft (130 Nm)
BATTERY:
  Material: lithium-ion
  Storage capacity: 17.6 kWh
  Warranty: 8 years/160,000 km (96 months/100,000 mi)

Its biggest drawback is its dry suspension, which you'll come to be intimately aware of on imperfect roads.

Recharging this car is a six-hour affair with a 240-volt terminal, or 16 hours with a 120-volt outlet. It's surprising—even though this car is 100-percent electric, it isn't equipped with a fast-charge port. Forget long trips with the electric Fortwo.

Good range for day-to-day travel

You can hardly use this car to travel far, but its 109-kilometer (68-mile) maximum range is more than enough to get you from point A to point B for everyday trips. Remember that the average commute is a 60-kilometer (35-mile) round trip, which means the Fortwo has got most of us covered there.

In chillier climes (-30°C/-22°F), the car's range drops to somewhere between 85 to 90 kilometers (53 to 56 miles). Having tested it during a particularly difficult winter, I can attest to that.

It's worth mentioning that this is *the only* electric car in Canada that you can get as a convertible. I recommend it wholeheartedly: It's a lot of fun, plus the retractable roof is very well designed.

For those of you who live in colder climates, you'll appreciate the heated seats that are standard, but I suggest you also opt for the cruise control and GPS.

In a nutshell, this little EV really earns its title of cute, inexpensive and decent!

- Very affordable
- Well-designed convertible top

- Dry suspension
- No fast-charge port

Smart Fortwo Electric Drive

Crosstrek Hybrid

HYB

PRICE: $30,495 (CAD) – $26,395 (USD)
FUEL CONSUMPTION: 7.9 L/100 km (30 mpg)
GREENHOUSE EMISSIONS:
176 g/km (282 g/mi)
GHG EMISSIONS RATING: 8/10
CALIFORNIA SMOG RATING: 9/10

In last place

JACQUES DUVAL

Among Asian car manufacturers, Subaru lags behind its popular and more aggressive competitors. However, the brand has acquired a good reputation, thanks to its performance in large, international rallies. It can also be credited with continuous loyalty to all-wheel drive and a flat engine ("boxer") architecture similar to that of Porsche. Its creations in the small-car-big-inspiration category are the WRX and WRX XTI.

Subaru sets itself apart by customer loyalty. Respect for the brand is high in the eastern U.S. and Canada, as their models are particularly well adapted to winter conditions. To get in step, Subaru recently added a crossover hybrid to its line: the Crosstrek hybrid.

This model won't make history and its greenish color might bring about more unkind comments than admiring winks.

Pitiful performance

The Crosstrek is disappointing due to its desire to be economical with hybrid motorization in the form of a gasoline-powered engine and an electric motor. This electrical package adds 13.4 horsepower to the 148 from a two-liter engine, for.a total of 161 horsepower. That's pretty meager fare for a vehicle weighed down by an extra 104 kilograms (229 pounds) due to hybrid motorization. The start/stop system is so jerky that my passenger asked me if I'd stalled the engine when I stopped at a red light. This trick would usually allow you to reduce consumption, but these savings turned out to

Specifications

SEATING CAPACITY: 5
CARGO SPACE(MIN – MAX): 609 – 1,422 L (21.5 – 50.2 ft³)
WEIGHT: 1,595 kg (3,516 lb)
ENGINES (GAS/ELECTRIC):
  Combined power: 160 hp (118 kW)
  Torque: 163 lb-ft (221 Nm)
BATTERY:
  Material: nickel-metal hydride (NiMH)
  Storage capacity: 0.55 kWh
  Warranty: 8 years/160,000 km (96 months/100,000 mi)

be insignificant. Our test resulted in the unenviable consumption of 9 L/100 km (26 mpg) and a 10-second acceleration time between 0 and 100 km/h (62 mph).

Don't plan on using the electric mode for very long in the Crosstrek hybrid; I had a hard time going faster than 20 km/h (12 mph) without the gasoline-powered motor switching on. As if that wasn't enough, know that the CVT-type transmission falters, certainly not helping the motor's sluggishness.

The Crosstrek was developed to allow Subaru to have a presence in the compact all-wheel drive crossover market: a category dominated by the Toyota RAV4 and Honda CR-V. Subaru's version doesn't stack up, even if its comfort and behavior (closer to a car than a truck) are praiseworthy. You also can't complain about its handling, but braking causes serious pitching when you try to stop too quickly.

A better interior

The Crosstek seems to be a greater success on the inside despite the manual settings that feel a bit mismatched in a car that's trying to be luxurious. Points also go to the steering-wheel phone, audio system and speed control commands. The only negative aspect here is the rearview camera that's too far away and too small. As for spaciousness, luggage space is hindered by the raised floor designed to make room for electrical components. Since the spare tire has disappeared, you might worry about having to use an emergency kit to repair a tire.

The Subaru Crosstek hybrid is the least attractive vehicle in this category.

- Nice interior look
- Useful steering-wheel commands
- Precise handling

- Failed hybridization
- Abhorrent start/stop
- Sluggish motor
- Should be forgotten

Subaru Crosstrek Hybrid

Impreza PZEV

ECO

PRICE: $19,995 (CAD) – $19,090 (USD)
FUEL CONSUMPTION: 7.6 L/100 km (31 mpg)
GREENHOUSE EMISSIONS: 177 g/km (284 g/mi)
GHG EMISSIONS RATING: 8/10
CALIFORNIA SMOG RATING: 9/10

All-wheel drive plus decent fuel economy

DANIEL BRETON

Some people swear by all-wheel drive. Not me. I'm not one of those who think that you need to be sitting in an all-wheel drive vehicle to drive with total safety. Particularly since this system seems to inspire a false sense of safety in some drivers who then proceed to drive too quickly, forgetting the basic fact that all-wheel drive doesn't give you the ability to brake any faster to avoid a crash.

A false sense of safety

Consider that the next time you take a look around during a snowstorm. You'll notice with astonishment that four-wheel-drive cars and pickup trucks are skidding and sliding right off the road.

Why? Because their owners are driving too fast.

What is the PZEV system?

PZEV means Partial Zero Emissions Vehicle. (Note: It's easy to confuse polluting emissions and greenhouse gas emissions).

The PZEV classification was introduced following negotiations between the California Air Resource Board (CARB) and automobile manufacturers, to allow manufacturers to slow the introduction of zero-emission vehicles (polluting and greenhouse gas emissions from the exhaust), both electric and hydrogen.

Subaru's PZEV system reduces air pollution from the exhaust, such as carbon monoxide, volatile organic compounds, fine particulates and NOx, that contribute to cancer and lung

Specifications

SEATING CAPACITY: 5
CARGO SPACE (MIN – MAX): 638 – 1,485 L (22.5 – 52.4 ft³) (hatchback); 340 L (12.0 ft³) (sedan)
WEIGHT: 1,365 kg (3,009 lb)
ENGINE:
  Power: 148 hp (109 kW)
  Torque: 145 lb-ft (196 Nm)

and heart disease. Thus, its antipollution system is one of the most effective on the market, although it isn't the only one out there: There are other manufacturers that offer systems just as effective or even superior.

However, Subaru's PZEV system does *not* reduce CO_2 emissions that contribute to global warming. You must keep in mind that antipollution systems actually can't filter CO_2; On the contrary, the more constraining a filter is, the more it tends to increase fuel consumption in a vehicle. These systems, therefore, increase CO_2 emissions, which are directly proportionate to fuel consumption.

A simple, practical car to battle the elements

The Subaru Impreza probably won't turn a lot of heads. Visually, it's fairly ordinary, and it has one of the blandest interiors in the industry. That said, the instrumentation has undergone improvement, and you can now see your instant and average fuel consumption, which is helpful for managing your eco-driving.

This small car shows impressive drivability when conditions are bad. Its admired all-wheel drive and relatively low center of gravity make driving very reassuring, if you stay within reasonable bounds.

I managed to average 6.2 L/100 km (38 mpg) on the highway, which is very decent for an all-wheel drive vehicle. Its combined fuel consumption is about 7.6 L/100 km (31 mpg).

The upshot? If you really need all-wheel drive, this car is a good bet.

- Respectable all-wheel drive
- Fairly good fuel consumption
- Reasonable price

- The PZEV system doesn't lower GHG
- Reduced cargo space

Subaru Impreza PZEV

PRICE: 70: $95,300 (CAD) – $70,000 (USD)
70D: $101,900 (CAD) – $75,000 (USD)

ELECTRIC RANGE: 70: 370 km (230 mi)
70D: 385 km (239 mi)

CHARGE TIME:
70: 120 V: 71 h, 240 V: 8 h, fast-charge:
400 V: approx 1 h 30, Supercharger: 50 min
70D: 120 V: 74 h, 240 V: 8 h 15,
400 V: approx 1 h 30, Supercharger: 54 min
GREENHOUSE EMISSIONS: 0 g/km (0 g/mi)
GHG EMISSIONS RATING: 10/10
CALIFORNIA SMOG RATING: 10/10

The revenge of the nerds

DANIEL BRETON

A few months ago, I had the chance to test-drive the all-new Tesla Model S 70D, a 100-percent electric all-wheel-drive car whose fully electric range is over 400 kilometers (249 miles). Those who have already driven a Tesla Model S already know that the acceleration in this car is very impressive (for any version), that it holds to the road and that it seems to have an unshakeable stability. All these qualities have already received plenty of attention. And its crash test safety rating, established by the National Highway Traffic Safety Administration (NHTSA) is pretty good to boot.

What really impressed me is that rare combination of power and silence. Traditionally, almost all manufacturers of high-performance cars seem to feel they absolutely must produce noise to prove their worth; It's kind of like how college football players feel compelled to bellow and holler while drinking, unsure that their burly physique will sufficiently show the world how manly they are.

The Tesla Model S, on the other hand, has an almost intellectual aura—think of it as the revenge of the nerd who has had enough of getting intimidated and pushed around by bullies at school.

And in glorious silence, the Tesla Model S demolishes cars with noisy engines. Whether

Specifications

SEATING CAPACITY: 5 or 7

CARGO SPACE (MIN – MAX): 744.7 – 1,645 L
(26 – 58 ft^3) + 150 L (1.8 ft^3) in front

WEIGHT: 2,100 – 2,400 kg (4,630 – 5,291 lb)

MOTORS:
Power: **70:** 315 hp, **70D:** 518 hp
Torque: **70:** 325 lb-ft, **70D:** 387 lb-ft

BATTERY:
Material: lithium-ion
Storage capacity: 70 kWh or 90 kWh
Warranty: 8 years unlimited engine and battery

it's a 70D, a P85D or a P90D, it's more powerful than it needs to be.

Good storage space

If you don't need all-wheel drive, you can opt for the Tesla Model S70, which offers more baggage space at a lower cost.

Both the Tesla Model S 70 and the S 70D have plenty of storage space, but is that an important factor for potential buyers of this type of car? If people looked at the numbers they would see that this kind of car has more storage than many SUVs.

Luxury you can afford

If you drive more than 50,000 kilometers (30,000 miles) per year and you're longing to buy an Audi, a BMW or a Mercedes for $40,000 (CAD)/$30,000 (USD) or more, you could easily buy a Tesla Model S 70 instead, since all the money you would save on gas and maintenance with the Tesla would balance out the cost, or even outweigh it—and you would no longer create exhaust pollution.

Hard to enter

Despite all that, the car isn't perfect. Getting in is a bit of a nuisance due to the low roof line. Sitting in the rear is even worse: my head touches the roof, and I'm not very tall. But believe it or not, I've seen the same problem in some SUVs.

Yes, the central console is as good as any other car's, and more intuitive to boot, but it's so big that it can be a real distraction. Also, the quality of the finish is very uneven; it seems that it is a work in progress.

In summary, the Tesla Model S 70 and S 70D are two cars that deserve to be at the top of your list of potential buys if you're looking for performance, cargo space—and true electric driving.

- The quintessential electric car
- Unparalleled performance
- Unequaled range
- Unmatched safety
- The least expensive Tesla

- Difficult to get in
- Uneven finish quality
- Range diminished in cold weather

Tesla Model S 70/70D

ELEC

🌿🌿🌿🌿🌿🌿🌿🌿🌿🌿

PRICE: n/a

ELECTRIC RANGE:
  85: 426 km (265 mi)

CHARGE TIME:
  85: 120 V: 81 h – 240 V: 9 h 10 –
  400 V: approx 1 h 50 – Supercharger: 1 h

GREENHOUSE EMISSIONS: 0 g/km (0 g/mi)

GHG EMISSIONS RATING: 10/10

CALIFORNIA SMOG RATING: 10/10

Miles and miles in my Tesla Model S: Wow!

SYLVAIN JUTEAU

March 13, 2013, will be forever etched in my mind, since that was the day I received my Tesla Model S. It was the 6,004th sedan built by Tesla, that exceptional Californian company.

In under three years, the Tesla—of which I'm the proud owner—has already been driven 190,000 kilometers (118,000 miles). This car's greatest feature is its ability to rejuvenate itself via occasional software updates.

Also, since it's aluminum, the body of my Tesla hasn't rusted at all, so it looks as gorgeous as it did when it left the plant. One of the many other advantages is its top-tier fuel economy: No exaggeration. I would have burned about $25,000 (CAD)/$18,800 (USD) worth of gas in an average car.

And of course there are other savings, like maintenance costs, which are very minimal, and lower insurance premiums for green cars.

Yet myths persist that say you can't go very far with an electric vehicle. For me, the opposite is true.

When driving costs next to nothing, you feel the urge to go farther and farther. At 190,000 kilometers (118,000 miles), many gas vehicles would be outdated or worn out, and some of the mechanical components defective.

Specifications

SEATING CAPACITY: 5 or 7
CARGO SPACE (MIN – MAX): 744.7 – 1,645 L
(26 – 58 ft³) + 150 L (1.8 ft³) in front
WEIGHT: 2,100 – 2,400 kg (4,630 – 5,291 lb)
MOTORS:
  Power: **85:** n/a
  Torque: **85:** n/a
BATTERY:
  Material: lithium-ion
  Storage capacity: 85 kWh
  Warranty: 8 years unlimited engine and battery

But like wine, my Tesla seems to improve with age. I've never had a major problem, and I've driven it a great deal. The few minor problems I've encountered were quickly resolved by Tesla Motors, which provides exceptional customer service.

When the sunroof started making a strange noise, Tesla fixed the problem quickly, loaning me a courtesy car in the interim—a Tesla Model S, of course. The same thing happened when the manufacturer had to completely replace the powertrain, also because of a noise it was making.

Tesla's service and its eight-year unlimited-mile warranty are effective. I've always ended up pleasantly surprised at the speed with which the company resolved any problems I had.

One day, when the odometer was at 130,000 kilometers (80,778 miles), I ran out of power. People from Tesla came to get me and towed the car to a garage. Do you know what the problem was? The 12-volt battery! Now, consider this: How many automobile manufacturers are there who would change a 12-volt battery, under warranty, and loan you a courtesy car that's equivalent to your own for the wait time?

As for concerns about lack of range, I can attest that I have never run out of electricity, even driving from Montréal to Florida or Detroit. Indeed, the tools for planning range and the network of charging stations in North America are so effective that I didn't feel the slightest bit concerned about running out of power.

Ultimately, I think Tesla has revolutionized the luxury car industry. I would never go back.

➕
- Innovative car
- Range does not decrease after 200,000 km
- Good road handling

➖
- Some small problems with noise

Tesla Model S 85

Model S P85D/P90D

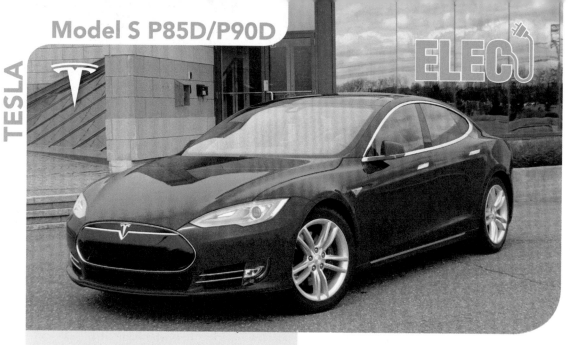

ELEC

PRICE: P90D: $146,400 (CAD) – $108,000 (USD)
ELECTRIC RANGE:
 P90D: 407 km (253 mi)
CHARGE TIME:
 90D: 120 V: 77 h 45 – 240 V: 8 h 45 –
 400 V: approx 1 h 45 – Supercharger: 58 min
GREENHOUSE EMISSIONS: 0 g/km (0 g/mi)
GHG EMISSIONS RATING: 10/10
CALIFORNIA SMOG RATING: 10/10

No such thing as perfection?

JACQUES DUVAL

Who could have guessed that five years ago a little company in southern California was getting ready to sell what experts—like Consumer Reports and the National Highway Traffic and Safety Administration—now call the best car in the world?

The revolutionary vehicle in question is the Tesla Model S, which you can get in several versions. I have owned and loved both the P85 and P85D. I must add that out of all the cars I've owned in my life, nothing has come close to the perfection that is the Model S.

We know the pros: safety, 424 kilometers (263 miles) without recharging the batteries; spaciousness (seating for up to seven); phenomenal handling; performance (the fastest sedan in the world); luxury; comfort; and construction so solid it's a stranger to rattles. As for its weaknesses, let's mention the killjoy price and incomplete equipment. The central screen does eliminate all buttons, but the fact that you can use it to access the Internet while driving is dangerous. There's also no CD player. The interior could be taken up a notch, and the center console isn't included unless you pay extra (now standard).

The new seats (an option that popped up a year ago) are certainly more comfortable, but they also make it more difficult to buckle your seatbelt when wearing layers. The car

Specifications

SEATING CAPACITY: 5 or 7
CARGO SPACE (MIN – MAX): 744.7 – 1,645 L
(26 – 58 ft³) + 150 L (1.8 ft³) in front
WEIGHT: 2,100 – 2,400 kg (4,630 – 5,291 lb)
MOTORS:
  Power: **P90D:** 463 hp
  Torque: **P90D:** 713 lb-ft
BATTERY:
  Material: lithium-ion
  Storage capacity: 70 kWh or 90 kWh
  Warranty: 8 years unlimited engine and battery

accelerates so seamlessly that you can often drive up close to the car in front of you at excessive speed, forcing a slam on the brakes at the last second.

The D in the Model S means that the car has four-wheel drive and handles so well it practically accelerates as fast on snow as on a dry road. As for the P90D, it has all the properties of the 85, while cutting off 0.3 seconds from the P85D's 3.1 second 0-100 km/h (0-62 mph) sprint.

Even with four people aboard on the ICAR circuit, it blew my passengers away.

What can be said about Auto Pilot?

Auto Pilot is a new feature that was activated on my car nine months after I bought it.

One morning—as Tesla often does—I found that they'd installed a whole series of new features on my car electronically overnight. This included a revised dashboard and software that allowed me to switch on Auto Pilot!

I became a passive driver, keeping my hands close to the steering while the car led itself, both on secondary roads and on highways. Be careful, you'll quickly notice that the magic is in its infancy. The car's equipped with many cameras and it must read the road and its markings for direction. That means the screen may ask you to take the wheel if you come across debris or heavy traffic.

In the end, guidance issues still need fixing, and Auto Pilot is (for the time being) only a gadget to impress your passengers...while giving you a few new frights.

- Minimal electricity consumption
- Great performance
- Extended range
- Optimal safety

- Prohibitive pricing
- Learning curve
- Distracting screen
- Incomplete equipment
- Auto Pilot still in development

Tesla Model S P85D/P90D

TESLA

ELEC

PRICE: n/a

ELECTRIC RANGE: 402 km (250 mi)

CHARGE TIME:

P90D: 120 V: 78 h – 240 V: 8 h 50 –
400 V: approx 1 h 40 – Supercharger: 55 min

GREENHOUSE EMISSIONS: 0 g/km (0 g/mi)

GHG EMISSIONS RATING: 10/10

CALIFORNIA SMOG RATING: 10/10

Cross your fingers

JACQUES DUVAL AND SYLVAIN JUTEAU

In Jacques Duval's opinion:

Tesla's much-talked-about Model X is finally on the road—although the phrase doesn't give you the whole picture, since in theory this SUV is capable of tackling much more difficult terrain, thanks to its all-wheel drive and its 18-inch (46 cm) adjustable ground clearance. But these characteristics are almost trivial compared to the features that make the Model X a true innovator.

The 21st-century wizard Elon Musk, founder of Tesla, broke into his mighty cache of resources to make the Model X a vehicle that veers far from the beaten path—you guessed it, both figuratively and literally. The result is definitely not as aesthetically pleasing as the Model S, but it has plenty to make it stand out from the SUVs of its competitors. It starts with a panoramic windshield that offers unprecedented visibility for any vehicle, reaching around toward the rear seats. The effect is incredible. But...where's the sun visor?

And there's the rub: To shield your eyes from the setting sun, you have to move an arm attached by magnet above the door and swing it forward to the mirror, where another magnet holds it in place. The operation is neither ergonomic nor safe when the vehicle is in operation. Also, forget about a sunroof and roof rack. It is possible, however, to attach a bracket to the rear bumper to remedy this problem. And the Model X can pull a 2,268-kilogram (5,000-pound) load, which puts it in the SUV category. Something to think about is that the misfortune of a rock bouncing

Specifications

SEATING CAPACITY: 5 or 7
CARGO SPACE (MIN – MAX): n/a
WEIGHT: n/a
MOTOR:
  Power: n/a
  Torque: n/a
BATTERY:
  Material: lithium-ion
  Storage capacity: 90 kWh
  Warranty: 8 years unlimited engine and battery

into the windshield would cost an arm and a leg in replacement cost.

Elaborate choreography of opening

The most spectacular aspect of Tesla's most recent creation is still its irresistible intelligent falcon-wing doors, intended to facilitate access to the rear seats. When they do their thing, these doors attract curious looks. But in using them, I found that their complexity created problems. I wondered if some engineers involved had to face their worst nightmare: Elon Musk having to reckon that the design for the Model X may have gone too far. Besides being slow in their elaborate choreography of opening, I wonder if they will be able to withstand the harsh conditions of winter with snow and ice.

However, I loved the front doors which opened by themselves, and of course the comfortable seating and all that the car inherited from the Model S: for instance, the presence of two electric motors, one in the front and one in the back, that combine to produce 762 horsepower, making the Model X the fastest SUV on the planet.

Buyers can opt for an interior layout that seats five, six or seven, although one wonders where a group of this number would put their bags. We met a man who had recently purchased the vehicle and settled on six seats and an all-white interior, which is less extreme than you might think.

Happy owners

Asked about his experience, the new Model X owner told us about having to visit the service center for problems with the electronic key and its various commands. "You have to expect these kinds of issues with a vehicle that's this new and

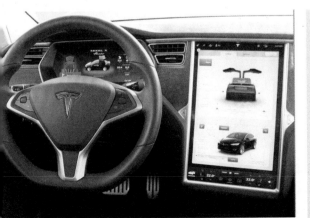

- Innovative solutions
- Mind-boggling power
- Amazing road handling
- Unobtrusive sound level

- Unproven reliability
- Braking that could be improved
- Questionable windshield
- Excessive price

Tesla Model X P90D

packed with futuristic accessories," he said. He had no intention of be getting rid of his recent acquisition, however. Another point of criticism is the lack of storage space in the cabin. Instead, the area has a Hepa filter to purify the air, like you would in an operating room.

The vehicle is a dream to drive, with phenomenal performance, superb handling, engaging steering and total silence. Only the braking seemed a little limited on occasion, I thought. I would also avoid the 22-inch tires, which are noisier and stiffer on bad roads.

There's no denying that the Model X is expensive—very expensive—but it's hard to find such a high-performing SUV that ranks as one of the safest on the market. Not to mention that it will give you almost 410 kilometers (255 miles) for free, every day. Can anyone claim to do better?

In Sylvain Juteau's opinion:
For me, this is the car of the year, regardless of the category. We've waited for this beautiful 100-percent electric goddess for a long time.

And finally it's possible to drive it—and I had more than a brief encounter.

With my friend Jacques Duval, I had the opportunity to drive this formidable SUV 1,200 kilometers (746 miles) in Florida over three days. A big thanks to my friend Mark Templeton, who generously loaned out his Model X P90D with the "Ludicrous" mode option and all the features—Founder's Edition, if you please!

The eighth wonder of the world
I can hardly find the words. But then, I've been a fan of Tesla for a long time now... To start with,

it's like you're driving a performance sedan, but with the comfort and space of an SUV.

On the drag strip, you're dealing with a veritable racing car that can beat out the vast majority of sports cars on the 0 to 100 km/h (62 mph) sprint, while seating seven adults and towing as much as 2,268 kilograms (5,000 pounds).

In short, you have all the advantages of the Tesla Model S (which won almost every award in the world for Best Car of the Year in every category), but with the convenience of a large SUV. On top of that, there's a windshield that's more expansive than that of a helicopter, autopilot, a huge 17-inch screen, articulated falcon-wing doors, and so on. Not to mention the almost nonexistent gas consumption! What more could you possibly ask for?

In my view, the falcon-wing doors are quite useful: as the father of three wonderful children, I love being able to "board" standing up in the second row while being protected from the wind and rain by the doors. I can then buckle up the oldest one and put in the baby seats, even in the pouring rain. Being able to access the third row of seats without performing spine-wrenching gymnastics is also greatly appreciated.

To my mind, if you live less than 100 kilometers (62 miles) from a Tesla service center and you are already someone who buys in the luxury SUV category, it isn't even a question. Forget the Porsche Cayenne, BMW X5, Range Rover and Audi Q7. They don't hold a candle to the Tesla Model X.

That said, it isn't perfect, and as with any jewel of technology, there will be bugs. But Tesla's after-sale service is in a class of its own. They correct the bugs with automatic upgrades and other adjustments. They are also reasonable in terms of prices for parts.

Replacing the supersized windshield (if you have an accident) won't cost you $10,000 as some detractors have suggested, but just $2,500, installation included. Changing ordinary windshields at many rival luxury car companies is more expensive than that.

I'll venture a prediction: The Model X will be the vehicle of 2016, and this will be unanimous. The only strike against it, for me, is its price in Canada. On his Twitter account, Elon Musk promised that the price difference for the Model S would be $5,000 (USD), but it's actually $20,000 to $30,000 (CAD), depending on the configuration chosen.

Tesla Model X P90D

TOYOTA

HYB

Avalon Hybrid

🍃🍃🍃🍃🍃🍃💧💧💧

PRICE: Camry: $28,710 (CAD) – $26,790 (USD)
Avalon: n/a (CAD) – $36,650 (USD)
FUEL CONSUMPTION: Camry: 5.7 L/100 km
(41 mpg)/Avalon: 5.9 L/100 km (40 mpg)
GREENHOUSE EMISSIONS: Camry: 134 g/km
(215 g/mi)/Avalon: 139 g/km (223 g/mi)
GHG EMISSIONS RATING: 9/10
CALIFORNIA SMOG RATING: 9/10

Cars that won't break...but may bore

DANIEL BRETON

If you take a look at the type of vehicles used by taxi drivers in major North American cities (and even in Paris), you'll find that many are hybrids—specifically, Prius, Prius V and Camry, almost exclusively Toyota-made cars.

There's a simple reason for that. These vehicles pay for themselves, since they save these drivers several thousand dollars per year, and, no less important, are considered some of the most reliable on the market.

That said, not everyone is a taxi driver. We don't want to buy cars because just they're economical or reliable. If we did, a number of auto manufacturers that have been producing unreliable vehicles for years, even decades (often resulting in prohibitive repair costs) would have gone bust long ago.

This proves that when it comes to purchasing decisions, other factors come into play: look, color, social status, performance, novelty. That's where cars like the Camry hybrid and the Avalon hybrid are clearly losing ground.

Struggling to make a mark

Despite some efforts, these two cars are having a harder and harder time competing in the hybrid game, even though they are more powerful than their single four-cylinder engine

Specifications

SEATING CAPACITY: 5

CARGO SPACE: Camry: 370 L – 13.1 ft³
Avalon: 396 L – 14.0 ft³

WEIGHT: 1,550 kg (3,417 lb)

ENGINES (GAS/ELECTRIC):
Combined power: 200 hp (147 kW)
Torque: gas: 156 lb-ft (211 Nm),
electric: 199 lb-ft (270 Nm)

BATTERY:
Material: nickel-metal hydride (NiMH)
Storage capacity: 1.6 kWh
Warranty: 8 years/160,000 km – 96 months/100,000 mi

Camry Hybrid

counterparts. The Ford Fusion hybrid and Hyundai Sonata hybrid have fuel economy ratings as good as those of Toyotas (5.5 - 5.9 L/100 km (40 - 43 mpg)) but these two rivals provide superior driving enjoyment.

In addition, the look of the Fusion and Sonata is distinctly more modern than that of the Camry and Avalon, in terms of both the interior and the exterior. If only the Camry's interior was as refined as that of the Lexus... But that wouldn't be possible, since Lexus is the luxury division of Toyota.

If we consider that Ford offers a plug-in hybrid version of its Fusion (Fusion Energi), with a 100-percent electric range that is about 35 kilometers (22 miles), the Camry is literally left in the dust. That said, the Fusion Energi has the major drawback of taking up a lot

of (maybe too much) space in the trunk. Hopefully, Ford will solve this design flaw that is sure to detract from interest in this car. I don't know many people who would be satisfied with a sports car-size trunk in a midsize car.

The Camry and Avalon hybrids do, however, have the advantage of being very comfortable and extremely reliable. If what you want is to avoid problems, you can feel safe in buying one of these models, but you may experience the somewhat paradoxical problem of being a little bored behind the wheel.

In summary: If you want to keep your vehicle for a long time or you drive a taxi, either of these cars is a good choice. On the other hand, if you want a more energy-efficient vehicle or a more engaging driving experience, think about getting another model.

Camry Hybrid

➕
- Good fuel economy
- Extraordinary reliability
- Improved design

➖
- A bit of a bore to drive

Toyota Camry Hybrid/Avalon Hybrid

HYB

TOYOTA

PRICE: $45,755 (CAD) – $47,890 (USD)
FUEL CONSUMPTION: 8.4 L/100 km (28 mpg)
GREENHOUSE EMISSIONS: 200 g/km (320 g/mi)
GHG EMISSIONS RATING: 7/10
CALIFORNIA SMOG RATING: 8/10

The definition of a true crossover

JEAN-FRANÇOIS GUAY

The Highlander has never had an easy time at Toyota. Along with having to go up against models from competing brands, it has to stand out from its own family members, the 4Runner, the RAV4, the Sequoia, the Sienna and the Venza. To hold its own among its siblings, the Highlander spares no effort, combining the cargo space and comfort of a van and the off-road capability and towing capacity of an SUV. As for the hybrid version of the Highlander, it has the virtue of having the same fuel-efficiency of a compact SUV.

Before the arrival of the new Volvo XC90 T8 and the BMW X5 xDrive 40e, the Highlander was one of the few hybrid-powered full-size SUVs in the market, along with the Lexus RX 450h.

All versions of the Highlander have perfectly fit the definition of a crossover: a cabin that can seat up to eight, front-wheel or all-wheel drive, high towing capacity, different trim levels and multiple equipment groups.

Three electric motors

The Highlander Hybrid is only offered with all-wheel drive and CVT transmission. It is driven by a 3.5-liter Atkinson-cycle V6 mated to two electric motors, one in the front and one in the rear, for a combined power of 280 horsepower—10 more than the conventional 3.5-liter V6 Highlander. Due to a lack of buyers, the bulky 2.7-liter four-cylinder (185 horsepower) is no longer available in Canada, but can still be found in the U.S.

Specifications

SEATING CAPACITY: 7 or 8

CARGO SPACE (MIN – MAX): 390 – 1,198 – 2,370 L
(13.7 – 42.3 – 83.7 ft³)

WEIGHT: 2,170 kg (4,784 lb)

ENGINES (GAS/ELECTRIC):
Combined power: 280 hp (209 kW)
Torque: gas: 215 lb-ft (292 Nm)
electric: 247 lb-ft (335 Nm)

BATTERY:
Material: nickel-metal hydride (NiMH)
Storage capacity: 1.9 kWh
Warranty: 8 years/160,000 km (96 months/100,000 mi)

With its last redesign in 2014, a new optional all-wheel drive was installed in the conventional Highlander, with an automatic six-speed transmission, for better fuel economy. The Highlander previously had five-speed transmission and full-time all-wheel drive. The system now delivers 100 percent of the power to the front wheels, under normal conditions, and can send up to 50 percent of the capacity to the rear wheels when you want to compensate for loss of traction.

For driving on soft ground, you have the option of locking front and rear torque distribution at 50:50 at speeds up to 40 km/h (25 mph). As for the Highlander Hybrid, it has kept its "FWD-i" drive, which uses a rear electric engine for extra traction when the front wheels are slipping.

Towing capacity

The Highlander does well in snow and on icy slopes. The platform and the mechanics of the Highlander Hybrid are strong enough to tow 1,587 kilograms (3,500 pounds) while the conventional gas V6 pushes towing capacity to 2,268 kilograms (5,000 pounds).

As for cargo space, the presence of batteries doesn't equal loss of cargo space; all Highlanders have the same interior size.

With average combined fuel consumption rated at 8.4-L/100 km (28 mpg), the Highlander Hybrid is the most energy-efficient non-plug-in vehicle that can fit up to eight people.

If you're really in need of a vehicle this big, the Highlander Hybrid is worth considering.

- Very large cabin
- A smooth, quiet ride
- All-wheel drive and towing capacity
- Strong fuel economy

- Sluggish CVT transmission
- No skid plates (off-road)

ECO

PRICE: $21,165 (CAD) – $19,995 (USD)
FUEL CONSUMPTION: 7.4 L/100 km (32 mpg)
GREENHOUSE EMISSIONS: 174 g/km (278 g/mi)
GHG EMISSIONS RATING: 8/10
CALIFORNIA SMOG RATING: 7/10

More of the same under a great brand

DANIEL RUFIANGE

Everybody knows it: There's a positive correlation between the Toyota empire's diverse vehicle offering and hybridization. Nonetheless, the Japanese manufacturer is well aware that not all consumers have deep enough pockets for some of the more attractive hybrid models out there. That is why the arrival of this model into the Toyota brand is welcome.

Compact newcomer

Luckily there are options. One such alternative is a newcomer to Toyota—the iM. In Europe, they call it Toyota Auris, and its latest re-engineering hit the continent back in 2012. You might say that we're being served a bit of leftovers.

This compact car is propelled by a tireless four-cylinder, 1.8-liter, 137-horsepower engine with 126 pound-feet of torque. Not bad, but you'd think that a brand-new product would merit more modern equipment. The only technology boasted by the Toyota iM is its Valvematic system, borrowed from the Corolla's Eco Mode, which maximizes power and fuel-efficiency by constantly varying the opening of valves.

Safety onboard

Inside the iM, you're in for a technological treat. Two screens come standard and provide you with myriad specs, there's a plug for any device imaginable, dual-zone climate control and a reverse camera to boot. Security was not

Specifications

SEATING CAPACITY: 5
CARGO SPACE: 588 L (20.8 ft³)
WEIGHT: 1,335 kg (2,943 lb)
ENGINE:
  Power: 137 hp (101 kW)
  Torque: 126 ft-lb (171 Nm)

left by the wayside for this Toyota and it's been outfitted with plenty of driving aids. Let's just say that there are eight airbags.

At the wheel

When you get behind the wheel, you'll notice that it's not exactly powerful, but still fun to drive. It's important to credit the engineers behind the iM for the aggressive calibrations they've made to the chassis. The CVT option is recommended for maximal fuel economy. For more fun behind the steering wheel, you can opt for the six-speed manual transmission. Funnily enough, the iM with CVT makes for a more interesting performance on the road.

Test-drives demonstrated average fuel consumption of 7 L/100 km (33.5 mpg), which is an acceptable figure at best.

Luckily, the price point is respectable: $21,165 for manual transition and $21,990 for CVT.

On the other hand, when you take a closer look at Toyota Group's selection, you'll find the Prius C, which is an intriguing subcompact with a starting price similar to that of the iM. The difference? Its average fuel economy falls slightly below 5 L/100 km (47 mpg).

It all comes down to what you need. The iM is a bit more spacious. Toyota has got a truly interesting product to offer consumers—but will they buy? Besides, bringing this model formerly known as Scion (Scion Brand) to the Toyota brand is full of promise.

- Practical vehicle
- Generally good road handling

- Expensive base price

Toyota iM

HYB

PRICE: $26,305 (CAD) – $24,200 (USD)
FUEL CONSUMPTION: 4.5 L/100 km (52 mpg)
GREENHOUSE EMISSIONS: 106 g/km (170 g/mi)
GHG EMISSIONS RATING: 10/10
CALIFORNIA SMOG RATING: 9/10

The standard for hybrids: a pioneer reinvented

JACQUES DUVAL AND DANIEL BRETON

In Jacques Duval's opinion:
You have to credit the Toyota Prius for being the first hybrid car on the market and the first to bring the energy-efficient automobile into the public eye. That's no small accomplishment. My first encounter with the 2016 Prius took place in Japan, but it was so brief and in such a confined environment that I didn't get a lot out of it. My next opportunity, on North American soil, was a much better eye opener.

Panoramic view

The first thing that strikes you is the size of the windshield, which offers an expansive view of the landscape as well as a valuable addition in terms of safety. But while front visibility is excellent, the two-paneled rear window only provides a vague suggestion of whatever's happening behind you. For this reason, the 360-degree back-up camera is essential.

As per previous models, the 2016 Prius is a liftback with front-wheel drive. Its hatch opens up a roomy cargo space that has been increased by 56 liters (2 cubic feet). Making the world's best-selling hybrid six centimeters (2.4 inches) longer has been widely praised as a definite improvement.

Inside, some will be intimidated by the array of instrumentation, which is center-mounted to accommodate both left- and right-hand driving—a placement chosen to save on costs. It presents a barrage of information on operating

Specifications

SEATING CAPACITY: 5
CARGO SPACE: 697 L (24.6 ft³)
WEIGHT: 1,395 kg (3,075 lb)
ENGINES (GAS/ELECTRIC):
   Combined power: 121 hp (74 kW)
   Torque combined: 105 lb-ft (142 Nm)
BATTERY:
   Material: nickel-metal hydride (NiMH) or lithium ion
   Storage capacity: 1.3 kWh
   Warranty: 8 years/160,000 km (96 months/100,000 mi)

the vehicle, offering a dangerous temptation that draws your eye to the many details appearing on the screen while you drive. The whitish plastic on the console and part of the steering wheel contrasts strikingly with the black interior. You'll love it or hate it, depending on your taste.

Modest performance

Mechanically, it's noteworthy that this Prius rests on an entirely new platform called Toyota New Global Architecture (TNGA). Needless to say it does well for those famous parameters. Noise, vibration and harshness, and rigidity has been improved have 60 percent, which translates into better road handling.

Under the Prius's hood, the 1.8-liter four-cylinder Atkinson-cycle engine has gone from 131 to 124 horsepower, managed by a CVT transmission. This slight reduction has no impact on acceleration, since all electrical components were made lighter. Acceleration is still in the 10.6 seconds range, which is a disappointment. At midrange, the torque amps things up a bit, and there's no shortage of power for passing: I got 7.3 seconds going from 80 to 120 km/h (50 to 75 mph).

In any event, no one is buying this car for its performance, but rather to save at the pump. With its electric motor powered by a lithium-ion battery located under the backseat, you can reach surprising speeds in strictly electric mode. We contacted an engineer who cited speeds of 105 km/h (65 mph), which, in our view, is no mean feat. At the end of our trip, our average fuel consumption was 4.5 L/100 km (52 mpg).

- A nice improvement over previous versions
- More enjoyable to drive
- Excellent safety rating
- Spacious

- No plug-in version
- Terrible rear visibility
- Modest power
- Confusing dashboard

Toyota Prius

In Daniel Breton's opinion:

How, in 2016, can a car claim to be "green" (as if any car can be truly green) when it's merely a hybrid, while so many new electric car models are hitting the market? Well, it turns out hybrids still have their place.

Exceptional fuel economy

Toyota has succeeded in improving the engine's thermal efficiency to 40 percent, a new high for the automobile industry, and reduced its weight by 100 kilograms (220 pounds). Thus this midrange automobile can get respectable acceleration and, above all, a fuel consumption that is peerless among non-plug-in vehicles.

According to official U.S. government data (see fueleconomy.gov), the fuel consumption for the all-new Toyota Prius is 4.4 L/100 km (53 mpg), city; 4.7 L/100 km (50 mpg), highway; and 4.5 L/100 km (52 mpg), combined.

As for the Prius Eco (only available in the U.S.), its fuel consumption is 4.4 L/100 km (53 mpg), city; 4.4 L/100 km (53 mpg), highway; and 4.2 L/100 km (56 mpg), combined. That's slightly better than the previous version.

But where the Prius stands out is the ease with which those ratings can be achieved and even surpassed. With the third-generation Prius, I could get about 3.8 L/100 km (62 mpg) practicing eco-driving, but with this hybrid vehicle I was able to get exceptional fuel consumption: in the mountains, 4 L/100 km (59 mpg), and combining city and highway driving, 2.9 L/100 km (81 mpg)!

An affordable price tag

Starting at about $26,000 in Canada, this car goes for about the same price as traditional midsize cars (in their standard version), but the fuel economy and GHG emissions of these midsize cars (Honda Accord, Ford Fusion and Hyundai Sonata) are 75 percent worse than those of the Prius.

A tale of two batteries: NiMH and Li-ion

If you purchase a basic Prius, you'll end up with the traditional (and indestructible) NiMH battery. If you opt for one of the better-equipped versions, you get the Li-ion battery.

And saying "better-equipped" is a bit of an understatement. With a pedestrian-detection system, a pre-collision system and a lane departure alert via cameras and the dashboard screen, the car is now fitted out for this day and age, packed with equipment that's now seen as indispensable for a high-tech car.

Impressive handling

While the previous three versions were thoroughly dull to drive, the Prius 4 is extremely enjoyable on winding roads. It is much better at taking curves, thanks to a new suspension, a lower center of gravity and a wider stance.

Its body has been made more rigid, which has a decisive impact, especially when driving in power mode. While the Toyota Prius hasn't exactly become a highway car, driving pleasure has been added to the mix—better late than never. Let's not forget that this car has been on the market for 19 years.

At the head of the pack

The Toyota Prius and its technology have not yet been surpassed. For those who can't plug in their car or who must drive long distances and need a vehicle that's practical and affordable (even without subsidies) and is superb for fuel economy, this is the benchmark.

Meanwhile, the Prius Prime was recently unveiled...with a disapointing electric range of only 35 kilometers (22 miles).

Prius C

HYB

PRICE: $21,055 (CAD) – $19,950 (USD)
FUEL CONSUMPTION: 4.7 L/100 km (50 mpg)
GREENHOUSE EMISSIONS: 111 g/km (178 g/mi)
GHG EMISSIONS RATING: 10/10
CALIFORNIA SMOG RATING: 8/10

A winner!

DANIEL BRETON

The Prius C is one of those small cars that didn't make a huge splash right off the bat, but appreciation for its character has been growing steadily. This hybrid subcompact has been gaining attention through its ever-increasing use in carpool and car-sharing services.

An original look

Having a look meant to stand out from the crowd, the Prius C seems to have a wider appeal than that of its big sister, the Toyota Prius. The interior is intended to feel modern, but it's not an especially good look: With its lines and gaudy colors, it's not a success. The central flaw is the material, which has too much plastic to suggest quality.

The dashboard, on the other hand, is practical and well designed, packed with very useful information to help with effective eco-driving. It allows you to clearly see and regulate your fuel consumption and your driving habits, which is an important aspect of driving a hybrid.

The Bluetooth system is quite easy to activate, and the functions are intuitive. The graphics, however, seem rather cheap—almost reminiscent of an old video game you might see at a flea market.

The hybrid system

It's pretty well-known—almost taken for granted: I'm referring, of course, to Toyota's hybrid system, which has definitely earned its stripes. It is the high-water mark for hybrid systems.

Reliable—verging on indestructible—this system will serve you well year after year; so

Specifications

SEATING CAPACITY: 5
CARGO SPACE (MIN – MAX):
  260 – 484 L (9.2 – 17.1 ft³)
WEIGHT: 1,132 kg (2,496 lb)
ENGINES (GAS/ELECTRIC):
  Combined power: 99 hp (74 kW)
  Torque: gas: 82 lb-ft (111 Nm)
        electric: 125 lb-ft (169 Nm)
BATTERY:
  Material: nickel-metal hydride (NiMH)
  Storage capacity: 0.9 kWh
  Warranty: 8 years/160,000 km (96 months/100,000 mi)

much so that a several expert bodies have named the Prius the most reliable vehicle over 300,000 kilometers (185,000 miles).

The pint-sized Prius C is no exception to the rule. It is very reliable, and what's more, its price is competitive, so not having enough cash to buy a hybrid is no longer a fear.

Its closest gas-powered competitors use at least 40 percent more gas, and the Prius C costs a little more than (or may be the same price as) these cars. And 40 percent more gas equals 40 percent more CO_2 emissions.

When I took it out on the highway, going 100 km/h (62 mph), I easily reached an average of 4.3 L/100 km (55 mpg), and the temperature hovered around 0°C (32°F). I had about the same fuel consumption in the city.

It's logical therefore to expect that you can obtain an average consumption of less than 4.5 L/100 km (52 mpg) over time. In this respect, the Prius C has only been out-performed by the now-defunct first-generation Honda Insight.

The Prius C is no racing car, but it's the most fun ride of the whole Prius family, thanks to its smaller size, which boosts its agility greatly. Its road handling is also amazingly stable, making it as comfortable on the highway as in the city.

In short, this little car is a winner and deserves to be more popular. For those who are looking for a less-polluting car, but are unable to buy an electric car (no way to plug it in, overly long distances to travel, etc.), it is the best choice for subcompacts that still use gas.

➕
- Very reliable car
- Unmatched fuel economy
- Competitive price

➖
- Overly plastic interior finish
- Sensitive to crosswinds
- Modest power

Toyota Prius C

TOYOTA

PRICE: $29,090 (CAD) – $26,675 (USD)
FUEL CONSUMPTION: 5.6 L/100 km (42 mpg)
GREENHOUSE EMISSIONS:
  132 g/km (211 g/mi)
GHG EMISSIONS RATING: 9/10
CALIFORNIA SMOG RATING: 8/10

V is for versatile

DANIEL BRETON

Nobody does a double take when the rather nondescript Prius V drives by. Nobody gets excited when driving a Prius V. And nobody gets worked up talking about the Prius V. It just doesn't awaken any deep-seated passion in car lovers. The Prius V's acceleration is totally unremarkable, the handling somewhat soft, although it is still safe.

But, if there's one energy-efficient, space-saving and reliable car out there, it's definitely this one. If you need proof, take a look at the taxis in your city. As time goes by, more and more cab drivers choose the Prius V, which is completely logical. It's almost a minivan, but not quite, almost a car, but not quite. This crossover is spacious enough to seat five passengers and their luggage comfortably.

Unrivaled fuel economy

Not everyone can buy a 100-percent electric car. Some simply can't connect their vehicle at home, while others need greater freedom.

That's why, unless you switch to a plug-in car, no crossover (even a subcompact car) is as fuel-efficient as the Toyota Prius V. Only the Ford C-MAX hybrid comes close, but even it's smaller and less roomy than the V.

With a combined fuel consumption of 5.6 L/100 km (42 mpg), it pleases users who need more space, while still ensuring their car's frugality and low CO_2 emissions.

That said, it is far from perfect. Its engine is not very powerful and therefore you can expect thundering acceleration. It is quite noisy and its interior also seems to have more plastic

Specifications

SEATING CAPACITY: 5
CARGO SPACE (MIN – MAX): 971 – 1,906 L (34.3 – 67.4 ft³)
WEIGHT: 1,505 kg (3,340 lb)
ENGINES (GAS/ELECTRIC):
  Combined power: 136 hp (100 kW)
  Combined torque: gas: 105 lb-ft (142 Nm)
                            electric: 153 lb-ft (207 Nm)
BATTERY:
  Material: nickel-metal hydride (NiMH)
  Storage capacity: 1.3 kWh
  Warranty: 8 years/160,000 km (96 months/100,000 mi)

than the entire living room of my late aunt. Its dashboard is not intuitive and the display indicating the current consumption is *less* effective than before.

Unparalleled reliability

This vehicle's other strong suit, actually very strong suit, is the flawless reliability of Toyota's hybrid system. Several tests, studies and surveys revealed that *the* most reliable vehicle on the market after 300,000 kilometers (186,411 miles) bears the name Prius. Clearly, the Prius V has good genes.

This car is obviously not without its flaws. If you enjoy driving on winding roads, if you appreciate luxury and little extras, if you delight in the comfort of form-hugging seats, ride right past this one because you'll be disappointed.

However, if you're more the rational, pragmatic, practical type, and its format suits your needs, I'm convinced that you'll be thoroughly satisfied with this versatile, reliable and fuel-efficient vehicle's "performances." Also, nobody will be able to say that you're not doing your part to reduce your carbon footprint!

If you're considering a plug-in alternative, take a look at the Ford C-MAX Energi, a crossover that drives about 30 kilometers on 100-percent electricity.

That said, don't ask yourself if the Prius V's battery lasts a long time. It lasts a *very* long time.

V is for versatile...for a real *green* car.

- Practical vehicle
- Impressive fuel economy
- Very reliable

- Very plastic interior
- Weak engine power
- High noise level

Toyota Prius V

RAV4

PRICE: $34,465 (CAD) $29,270 (USD)
FUEL CONSUMPTION: 7.1 L/100 km (33 mpg)
GREENHOUSE EMISSIONS:
 169 g/km (270 g/mi)
GHG EMISSIONS RATING: 8/10
CALIFORNIA SMOG RATING: n/a

Twenty years already

JACQUES DUVAL

Among the 13 hybrid vehicles (a record) offered by the Toyota/Lexus tandem, the RAV4 is the best-seller in its category. In 1996, it introduced a new type of vehicle to the market: the compact SUV. People loved it from the get-go because it had almost all the same qualities as its heftier, older siblings, while spacing out stops at the pump. Toyota wanted to sell it in a hybrid version. A comparative test of the two versions (hybrid and non-hybrid) highlighted the superiority of the one equipped with an electric motor.

With its 2.5-liter (0.66-gallon) four-cylinder Atkinson-cycle gas engine and electric counterpart, the car boasts a combined power of 194 horsepower, as opposed to only 176 with the strictly gas-powered version. And let's not forget that a second electric motor is located on the rear axle, where it only activates the back two when necessary, like during fast acceleration or on low-adherence surfaces. There's no mechanical link between the main engine or transmission and the back wheels, meaning no driveshaft.

The transmission itself is continuously variable and, during the test, was easily forgotten while doing its job.

The RAV4 is modeled on the vehicles in its family, except for the prominent front end that seems to be Toyota's new signature, giving their cars a pretty terrible profile. But let's focus on the driving. While it might not be stimulating, the hybrid version seemed more lively to me, as

Specifications

SEATING CAPACITY: 5
CARGO SPACE (MIN – MAX): 99 – 1,982 L (35.6 – 70.6 ft³)
WEIGHT: 1,780 kg (3,925 lb)
ENGINES (GAS/ELECTRIC):
  Combined power: 194 hp (143 kW)
  Torque: gas: 206 lb-ft (279 Nm)
  electric: 199 lb-ft (270 Nm)
BATTERY:
  Material: nickel-metal hydride (NiMH)
  Storage capacity: 1.6 kWh
  Warranty: 8 years/160,000 km (96 months/100,000 mi)

if the RAV4 was designed in two steps with greater thought going into the fuel-efficient model. For example, the engine sound itself is more discreet, although noise level increases considerably in the rain. Its performance is slightly better than that of the gas-powered version, with an 8.7-second 0 to 100 km/h (0 to 62 mph) and a fuel consumption of 6.2-to-7.8L/100 km (30 to 38 mpg). Impressive results for an all-wheel-drive vehicle that's roomier than a car of the same size. We're talking about an approximately 20-percent savings, which is far from negligible.

The interior has undergone considerable changes and now has a very nice dashboard. However, after an hour at the wheel, I would have liked the seats to be more comfortable. I also had to search to find the rearview mirror adjuster, which is very low on the driver's left side.

The high-end model has the trappings of a luxury car: 18-inch wheels (compared to 17 inches on the basic model), a wide rearview camera, power lift-gate, three driving modes, pedestrian detectors, heated steering wheel and parking assist sensors. I'd like to add that both the front and back cameras could benefit from a spray to clean them off in bad weather, as the lenses quickly get dirty, making them unusable. In spite of its small size, the RAV4 has about a 990-liter (35-cubic-foot) trunk and a larger passenger compartment than the Ford Escape. And it can haul 795 kilograms (1,750 pounds); that is, 113 kilograms (250 pounds) more than the gas model.

Even if you wish that Toyota had taken the RAV4's electrical system further by offering a rechargeable version, don't forget about all its assets. The car's handling isn't particularly entertaining, but it has the best security rating in its class.

- Guaranteed reliability
- Notable efficiency
- Advanced safety
- Substantial equipment
- Towing capacity

- Uncomfortable seats
- No rechargeable version
- Unchallenging handling

Toyota RAV4

e-Golf

HYBR

PRICE: n/a (CAD) – $28,995 (USD)
ELECTRIC RANGE: 134 km (83 mi)
CHARGE TIME: 120 V: + 20 h, 240 V: 4 h
  fast recharge: ½ h to 80%
GREENHOUSE EMISSIONS: 0 g/km (0 g/mi)
GHG EMISSIONS RATING: 10/10
CALIFORNIA SMOG RATING: n/a

Volkswagen makes amends

JACQUES DUVAL

If there's a vehicle that can make up for Volkswagen's infamous trafficked diesel-engine scandal, it's certainly the e-Golf, one of the best electric cars on the market. However, the German manufacturer still has the wrong attitude when it comes to marketing, as it isn't sold in the Canadian provinces or American states where "zero emissions" legislation has yet to be enacted. That means there are only a dozen states where you can get the e-Golf.

This is even more objectionable in the province of Québec, which has always been fertile ground for the sale of VW products. Québec makes up one-third of the brand's total Canadian sales. And let's not forget that this part of North America is most enthusiastic about electric cars. Once again, it's up to consumers, mainly future electric car buyers, to pressure the company to rectify the situation.

At the wheel

The e-Golf, which I have had the opportunity to drive twice, is actually a real gem with a range varying between 110 and 145 kilometers (68 and 90 miles), and a charge time of less than four hours. So I was pleasantly surprised by this car's fuel economy. The range meter read 119 kilometers (74 miles) at the beginning of one of my many drives. After a quick 7.4 kilometers (4.6 miles), the e-Golf's range only dropped by 3.2 kilometers (2 miles) below the

Specifications

SEATING CAPACITY: 5
CARGO SPACE (MIN – MAX): 272 – 1,162 L (9.6 – 41 ft³)
WEIGHT: 1,550 kg (3,400 lb)
ENGINES (GAS/ELECTRIC):
　Combined power: 115 hp
　Combined torque: 199 lb-ft
BATTERY:
　Material: lithium-ion
　Storage capacity: 24.2 kWh
　Warranty: 8 years/160,000 km (96 months/100,000 mi)

original reading. That was also after driving without much regard for efficiency. Now that's a 24.2 kWh battery that can stock up!

You can do even better by opting for Eco or Eco+ mode. It's best if you're not in a rush, as the 150 km/h (93 mph) top speed drops to around 95 km/h (59 mph), which can be restrictive on the road.

Reminder of the BMW i3

Without reaching this maximum, the 115-horsepower engine is sufficient to push the e-Golf to 100 km/h (62 mph) in 10 seconds, which is comparable to the competition. In this respect, this Golf reminded me of the BMW i3.

The transmission is also not automatic or manual, since it's direct drive or, if you prefer, single-ratio.

The main thing I learned about this electric Volks is that it preserves initial driving enjoyment, thanks to solid handling and fun maneuverability. Finally, an exclusive spoiler, 16-inch rims and LED headlights that ensure safe driving after dark add to the e-Golf's esthetic value.

We have to give it to Volkswagen for this winning car and its enjoyable combo of comfort, luxury, economy and sportiness. Now they just need to make it available everywhere with a certain level of concern for the environment.

- Reliable
- Good handling
- Golf's assets intact
- Quiet ride

- Considerably high price
- Lacking power
- Limited availability

VOLKSWAGEN

HYB

PRICE: $36,895 (CAD) – $31,120 (USD)
FUEL CONSUMPTION: 5.3 L/100 km (44 mpg)
GREENHOUSE EMISSIONS: 125 g/km (200 g/mi)
GHG EMISSIONS RATING: 9/10
CALIFORNIA SMOG RATING: 9/10

Thumbs up or down?

DANIEL BRETON

While the storm of the diesel Volkswagen scandal continues to cause damage, it's easy to forget that the manufacturer also makes electric and hybrid cars. The company itself doesn't seem to put a lot of focus on them—a surprising fact, given that it can no longer sell diesel cars.

A true German highway car

When it comes to hybrid technology, the word "boring" tends to come up pretty often.

Hybrids are outdated, yawn-inducing when driving, unexciting. Despite this common view, it isn't the case with the Volkswagen Jetta Turbo Hybrid, which has very impressive acceleration for a midsize car, on par with any other model with a six-cylinder engine. This is a result of its turbocharger and electric engine, which assists the 1.4-liter four-cylinder engine.

There's also the matter of the very persuasive road handling of Volkswagens. It's a treat to tear up the roads, taking curves without easing up much on the speed and enjoying the precision of the steering, in a car that is a tried and true German vehicle—a champion of the Autobahn. No hybrid car on the market gives you better driving pleasure.

Acceptable fuel economy

In terms of gas consumption, this Jetta compares favourably to the hybrid versions of all its rivals (the Camry, the Sonata and the Fusion) except the Prius, which does much better, particularly the new version. Note that the hybrid version of the Jetta has better fuel economy than its diesel-

Specifications

SEATING CAPACITY: 5
CARGO SPACE: 320 L (11.3 ft³)
WEIGHT: 1,547kg (3,411 lb)
ENGINES (GAS/ELECTRIC):
  Combined power: 170 hp (125 kW)
  Combined torque: 184 lb-ft (249 Nm)
BATTERY:
  Material: lithium-ion
  Storage capacity: 1.1 kWh
  Warranty: 8 years/160,000 km (96 months/100,000 mi)

engine sister—and emits much less air pollution and GHG.

Why did Volkswagen update the hybrid version of the Jetta, which uses less fuel and creates less pollution than the diesel version, while putting so much emphasis on selling its diesel engines? I think the answer lies in the fact that despite its good qualities, the Jetta suffers from two handicaps:

1- Its price. Offered at a starting price that's much higher than that of the competition—for example, $7,000 (CDN)/$5,250 (USD) more than a Hyundai Sonata Hybrid or a Ford Fusion Hybrid, and a whopping $10,000 (CDN)/$7,500 (USD) more than the Toyota Prius—the Jetta Hybrid really comes up short. At a cheaper price, you could buy, for example, a Chevrolet Volt, which performs just as well but has much better fuel economy and is more practical in terms of cargo space.

2- Its trunk. With the battery located in the trunk, the Jetta Hybrid has the same problems as the Ford Fusion Hybrid: a trunk that has sacrificed a large chunk of its space and an inability to lower the rear seats. This gives the Jetta Hybrid a major disadvantage over the regular version and creates a real handicap when compared with the Toyota Prius and the Chevrolet Volt, both of which are hatchbacks.

As for style, all Volkswagen products feel a little conservative for my taste, and this Jetta is no exception. But given the brand's sales figures, it's pretty clear that many people feel differently.

So if, like some of my friends, you're a fan of Volkswagen, this Jetta may be the car for you. If not, you can do just as well, if not better, looking elsewhere.

- Reasonable fuel consumption
- Pleasant to drive

- High price
- Unknown reliability

NEWCOMERS AND RARE GEMS

This section is devoted to models that have recently arrived on the market, are coming soon or are simply so rare that few of us will ever see a single one. New models of electric vehicles are now being developed at such a pace that this list is sure to grow by the day.

And that's a very good sign.

Enjoy discovering these vehicles!

ELEC

Tesla Model 3

Not even the legendary Ford Mustang incited the kind of fervor that accompanied the unveiling of the Tesla Model 3. According to some sources, more than 300,000 people paid $1,000 each to reserve a Model 3, the diminutive successor to the Tesla Model S. And this despite the fact that it will only be available to buyers starting with the 2018 model year.

So what explains the excitement surrounding a car about which we know nothing, except that it will be 100-percent electric? The answer is simple and reflects the reputation earned by the Californian manufacturer whose Model S has been named Best Car in the World by the venerable Consumer Reports organization.

Tesla Motors has always been known as a manufacturer of expensive—very expensive—cars, to be admired without any reasonable hope of actually owning one. The Model 3's mission is to reach a wider audience, drivers who want to go electric without emptying their wallets. The Model 3 is the company's response to the multiple consumer surveys that indicate a widespread readiness to make the jump to electric cars so long as the price is reasonable

and the range is at least 300 kilometers (186 miles). For $35,000 USD, the Model 3 meets these requirements and more, with 335 kilometers (208 miles) between charges and a 0-100 km (62-mile) acceleration of under six seconds. And that's not to mention the more streamlined versions that will give the Model 3 an official place in the sports sedan category. To get around the lack of rear passenger room (a common problem for cars of this format), the designers have made use of the space made available by the absence of a front-mounted motor to create an innovative cabin area. Some, however, may miss the more practical hatchback architecture.

What else can we say? Only that this mass-produced car makes Tesla the fourth largest automobile manufacturer in North America, a spot coveted by many companies that just don't have the material resources for it. Can Tesla change the game? Many think so, for the same reasons that the public believes in Elon Musk, who—shades of Steve Jobs—is in the process of changing the world.

JACQUES DUVAL

Newcomers and rare gems

BMW X5 xDrive 40e

Few manufacturers offer plug-in hybrid versions in the luxury SUV category. Aside from Porsche, with its Cayenne E-Hybrid, and Volvo, with its XC90 Plug-In Hybrid, Mitsubishi will be giving us a plug-in hybrid version of the Outlander, but it will undoubtedly be less luxurious than a BMW or a Porsche.

This BMW SUV, the X5 xDrive40e, has two engines that combine for 308 horsepower: a four-cylinder twin-turbo engine and a 111-horsepower electric motor.

The electric range is very modest: less than 25 kilometers (16 miles), according to the EPA. Even though the battery eats up cargo space, the SUV is roomy. With 0-100 km (62-mile) acceleration in seven seconds, BMW fans will feel at home in terms of performance, handling and comfort.

DANIEL BRETON

Chrysler Pacifica PHEV 2017

Although there are more and more hybrid, plug-in hybrid and electric cars on the market, SUVs with partial- or full-electric technology are still rare. What's more, you won't find any minivans that use this technology.

However, SUVs and minivans are both very popular. The two sides just don't add up—and the inconsistency persists today.

This year, however, Chrysler will bring out its all-new 2017 Pacifica in a plug-in hybrid version. With a totally new platform, this descendant of the respected Dodge Caravan little resembles the "bread box" of 20 years ago. Distinctly modern, the Pacifica PHEV could be very popular with families who need a legitimately practical vehicle (much more practical than the vast majority of SUVs, in fact) that can handle the everyday travel needs in 100-percent electric mode.

Thanks to a 16 kWh battery, Chrysler has announced a 50-kilometer (31-mile) electric range, which seems altogether feasible. The Pentastar V6 engine, coupled to an electric motor, has been re-designed to improve efficiency. That's a good thing, since it's not setting any records for fuel economy in its current incarnation.

DANIEL BRETON

HYB 🔋

Ferrari LaFerrari

What an amusing name for the ultimate Ferrari and flagship of the most prestigious car brand in the world. This model is being included here because it uses hybrid technology that adds 163 horsepower for a total of 963, making it fly—witness the 15-second acceleration time to top 300 kilometers (186 miles) per hour.

Much better looking than its predecessor, the Enzo, the Ferrari LaFerrari is built with the secrets of Formula 1 machinery and is manufactured on the same assembly line.

This Ferrari pushes the limits of technology with achievements like a lighter, more rigid chassis. To minimize weight, the seats are incorporated right into the chassis tub. Only 499 were made, making them highly sought-after in the collector car market.

True to the company's history, the gas engine is a V12 that develops 800 horsepower with 9,250 RPM, controlled by a seven-speed dual-clutch automatic transmission.

The only drawbacks are its scarcity and price. And let's not forget fuel economy, particularly the effect of its hybrid power on its average fuel consumption: 14.2 L/100 km (16.5 mpg). That's a disappointment. Personally, I'd opt for the Yaris instead!

JACQUES DUVAL

H

Honda FCV

The Honda FCV, a second-generation hydrogen car and descendant of the FCX Clarity, will hit the California market this year, featuring a more classic look than its predecessor.

Equipped with a hatchback, the FCV has a more spacious (and more practical) interior than the Honda Accord. With 134 horsepower, the FCV is no racecar, but it accelerates decently—and silently.

Honda has managed to cut the cost of its hydrogen tank by 90 percent compared with that of the FCX Clarity, allowing it to drop the price of the car a great deal. Also, while the FCX tank had a maximum pressure of 350 bar (5,000 psi), the new tank has a maximum of 700 bar (10,000 psi). With this new tank, the car will have a range of more than 500 kilometers (300 miles). California will be the first state to sell the model, to be followed later by a few other states. Will Ontario make the list of places where you can buy the FCV? It's too early to say.

DANIEL BRETON

Newcomers and rare gems

ACURA NSX

The Honda/Acura group made an audacious move in 1990 when it launched what would become a serious rival to Ferrari: the NSX. The car's panache should have given it a fighting chance against the famous Italian car; but Ferrari simply remains untouchable.

This year, Acura brings us an updated NSX tailored to meet today's concerns—most especially about the environment, a subject of major importance to those of us writing this book and far outweighing any interest in, say, the differences in acceleration between Ferrari and NSX.

Nonetheless, with its Japanese approach, the NSX strikes the right balance between a pure sports car and a car for daily use, in the same vein as the Audi R8. The American-built NSX is probably a little too heavy, but it has all-new characteristics in line with its being a hybrid with a 3.5-liter V6 turbo gasoline engine with 573 horsepower, assisted by three electric motors (two on the front axle and one between the engine and the nine-speed dual-clutch gearbox that controls the all-wheel drive). This appreciable power system propels the NSX to 100 km/h (62 mph) in less than four seconds, or up to 70 km/h (40 mph) in complete silence if you drive "economically" in electric mode. The dry-sump engine is modeled on those Honda uses in racing, as is the carbon-fiber floor of the body, and the steel and aluminum frame. It all should be enough to please those environmentalists who still need a little touch of oil from time to time.

JACQUES DUVAL

Hyundai Ioniq

Sometime this year, Hyundai will release the Ioniq, an all-new car with three powertrain options, a rival to the Prius. Thus, much like Ford with its Fusion and C-MAX, the new Korean car will be available in two types of electrification (plug-in hybrid and hybrid), but will go a step further by offering a 100-percent electric version that can be fully charged in less than 4½ hours on a 220-volt outlet or to 80 percent in 24 minutes at a fast-charging station. The other two models are fitted with a 1.6-liter four-cylinder 104-horsepower engine; in the plug-in hybrid version—which has been promised for 2017—this engine, paired with a 60-horsepower electric engine will develop 164 horsepower.

The Ioniq is a sedan with a relatively conventional look—plain, in fact. In its basic hybrid version, it will have a combined output of 139 horsepower. This is the first version that will be released; it's scheduled to hit the market next fall. This version will be followed by the 100-percent electric version with a 170-kilometer (106-mile) range, which is slightly better than the Leaf.

The Ioniq will have enough space for four, although the rear seats may be a little tight. However, the tailgate makes it more practical to load baggage, since the space will exceed 0.57 cubic meters (20 cubic feet).

JACQUES DUVAL

H

Tucson Fuel Cell

The Korean manufacturer's compact SUV is now offered in a hydrogen fuel cell electric version. Like the gas-powered model, this version is powered by a 134-horsepower engine with 221 pound-feet of torque. Its range is around 400 kilometers (249 miles).

The maximum speed is 160 km/h (99 mph) and its acceleration is a little weak: Hyundai's figures tells us it goes 0 to 100 km/h (62 mph) in 12.5 seconds.

This is another car that was being sold only in California (and more recently in Ontario), but it is offered only as a lease—purchasing is not an option.

P.S. I was taken aback to see that Hyundai—on the website for this model—compares the filling time for this vehicle to that of an electric car—taking care to omit the charging time for an electric vehicle at a level 3 station. Only charging time for levels 1 and 2 are mentioned (see hyundaiusa.com/tucsonfuelcell).

Perhaps, ladies and gentlemen of Hyundai, a little more rigor is in order.

DANIEL BRETON

Newcomers and rare gems

Kia Niro

After giving us the Soul EV and the Optima Hybrid, in a few months Kia will introduce the Niro 2017. It will be available in three electric versions: hybrid, plug-in hybrid and electric. The hybrid version will be fitted with an

Atkinson cycle 1.6-liter four-cylinder engine, coupled to an electric motor fed by a 1.56 kWh battery, generating a total power of 146 horsepower.

You'll find no CVT transmission here; what you will find is a six-speed dual-clutch automatic transmission. According to Kia, the Niro's fuel economy will be equal to that of the best Toyota hybrids. And while its cousin, the Hyundai Ioniq, will be a compact hatchback, the Niro will be a compact SUV.

If this partially or fully electric little SUV is offered at a price that's as reasonable as we expect, it could be a hit.

DANIEL BRETON

Kia Optima Hybrid and PHEV 2017

I was quite impressed with the previous generation of the Kia Optima. The hybrid version, however, wasn't particularly effective compared with the competition represented by Camry, Fusion, Jetta and other midsize cars available in a hybrid version.

That's why, in 2017, Kia will introduce two partly electric versions of the Optima: a retooled hybrid and a plug-in hybrid.

The good-looking cousin of the Hyundai Sonata Hybrid, this Kia Optima Hybrid will have its 2.4-liter engine replaced by a two-liter direct-injection engine that, combined with its electric motor, will produce a total of 193 horsepower. According to Kia, it will have 20 percent higher efficiency.

Like the Sonata Plug-in Hybrid, the Kia Optima PHEV will come with a 9.8 kWh lithium-ion polymer battery, giving it a fully electric range of about 40 kilometers (25 miles). After testing the Sonata PHEV, that seems entirely possible.

DANIEL BRETON

HYBRID

BMW i8

With high-level embedded technology and a nifty carbon-fiber body, BMW has created a veritable laboratory on wheels with its i8 hybrid. The vehicle made its debut two years ago, and the German company wanted to make it an exclusive model—a status ensured by its limited-production run. Some believe that the i8 will become a collector's car. In fact, a certain West Palm Beach dealership decided to sell it for tens of thousands of dollars over the manufacturer's suggested price for that reason.

The main attraction of this rare specimen is a small three-cylinder 1.5-liter (91-cubic-inch) TwinPower turbocharged engine with no less than 231 horsepower. Coupled to an electric motor with an additional 131 horsepower and an automatic six-speed transmission, the i8 doesn't skimp on performance, but doesn't match the sheer awesomeness of the Tesla Model S's "Ludicrous" mode. The i8 manages the 0-100 km/h (62 mph) sprint in a mere four seconds. Using electric mode only adds six

seconds to that time. Access is fairly easy, despite swan-wing doors that seem a touch awkward. You have to be careful not to get too close to another car when in a parking lot. The seating inside is comfortable, but I found that the dashboard could be improved by distinguishing it more from non-environmentally-oriented BMW models.

Va-Va-Vroom!

An amusing detail: BMW came up with a synthetic engine sound to push noise levels to those of a race car—the shape of which the i8 is meant to evoke. It's an...interesting idea.

In a brief test, I found that the steering feels a little disengaged from road conditions at the front end and that braking takes time to kick in when you press the pedal.

There's a lot to say about the operation of this very special hybrid, but there's no need to go on—and it would also be essentially a billboard for the BMW i3, that is more thoroughly described among the road tests earlier in the book.

JACQUES DUVAL

Chevrolet Malibu Hybrid

General Motors has produced very poor hybrids over the years such as the 2008/2009 Chevrolet Malibu Hybrid. So, in light of this, I was not especially eager to acquaint myself with the new Malibu Hybrid. All I can say is, I'm amazed.

The 2016 Malibu is a totally new vehicle: new chassis, new, smaller engines (1.5- and 2-liter, turbocharged) in the regular versions, and a new 1.8-liter engine in the hybrid version. More spacious than its predecessor, it's also 136 kilograms (300 pounds) lighter, making it the lightest midsize sedan in its category.

With 182 horsepower and 277 pound-feet of torque, the Malibu Hybrid won't break any records for acceleration, but it is particularly good on fuel economy. Its fuel-efficiency ratings of 5 L/100 km (47 mpg) in the city and 5.1 L/100 km (46 mpg) on the highway make it one of the most energy-efficient midsize hybrid sedans, beating out the Camry, the Sonata, the Optima, the Fusion and the Jetta.

To give you some idea of the improvement that's been made: the 2008 Malibu Hybrid used 70 percent more fuel than the 2016 Malibu Hybrid. Furthermore, it has no transmission. Its power distribution was inspired by the Volt, with the electric motor driving the car. Its battery is the same type of lithium-ion battery found in the Volt, but in a smaller, 1.5 kWh version; small enough to allow the trunk to be practical since the rear seats fold down.

By practicing eco-driving in mountainous areas (Victoria, B.C.), I reached an average of 4.2 L/100 km (56 mpg). That's a great result. The regenerative braking is smooth, but it can be made more aggressive by shifting the lever to the "L" position. Featuring a 4G LTE connection (enabling voice-to-text messaging), packed with all the latest security features, matching the superior road handling of most of its competitors, sold at a competitive price in all its variations ($28,850 CAD, plus a destination freight charge of $1,650 for Canada), and, most important, now truly energy-efficient, the 2016 Chevrolet Malibu Hybrid should satisfy those who can't plug in their car, yet want a vehicle with terrific fuel economy.

P.S. A plug-in version is not available—and that's where the Volt comes in.

DANIEL BRETON

HYB

Lexus LC 500h 2018

Once again, Lexus has "hybridized" one of its models. This time, however, they've taken a whole new approach: essentially, this car is a sports-hybrid.

Indeed, with its two engines combining for a whopping 354 horsepower, no one can accuse the LC 500h hybrid of being boring.

For a greater feeling of control while driving, Lexus has also complemented the CVT system with a four-speed transmission. Different drive modes will be available, ranging from Eco to Sport. The car can be driven in 100-percent electric mode up to speeds of 140 km/h (87 mph).

With the system it inherited from the RX 450h, fuel economy is promising to be good—possibly better than 7.5 L/100 km (31 mpg).

A strong look, sporty driving—and good fuel economy.

Will this Lexus charm fans of sporty driving?

We'll find out soon enough.

DANIEL BRETON

HYB

2017 Lincoln MKZ Hybrid

Once again, Lincoln attempts a fresh start with its MKZ. Though well-made, this car seems unable to captivate the public, if the number of makeovers the manufacturer has given it recently is anything to go by. Gone is the "winged" front grille, replaced with a more feline design. With this grille, reminiscent of the Jaguar XF, the MKZ has shed its very refined look for something more muscular (if only in appearance).

As for the hybrid power, it seems that the same system as that of the previous generation is being offered: a 2.5-liter four-cylinder engine combined with an electric motor and CVT transmission, for a total of 188 horsepower and combined fuel consumption of 5.69 L/100 km (50 mpg), which is excellent for a midsize luxury hybrid.

The only thing missing now for the MKZ is a plug-in hybrid version.

DANIEL BRETON

Mercedes B 250 e

With a 28 kWh battery and a 132 kW electric motor, this crossover is in direct competition with the slightly smaller BMW i3. Like the i3, this 100-percent electric Mercedes has vigorous acceleration and clings to the road like few other crossovers.

Luxurious, with a high-quality finish, the B 250 e is a practical vehicle, with interior space and cargo space that are very well designed. That said, its charging system is poorly executed with a too-short cord for the charging kit. Since Mercedes recommends you don't use an extension cord, it's a real problem if you want to plug into a 120-volt outlet.

Based on the EPA's stats, the range of the B 250 e is a little higher (140 kilometers/87 miles) than that of the BMW i3 (130 kilometers/80 miles). That said, the BMW has the undeniable advantage of being offered in a version with a range extender.

DANIEL BRETON

Mitsubishi Outlander PHEV

This four-wheel-drive SUV will be mainly for electric driving and will be as spacious as the gas-powered version. We're told it will have a 12 kWh battery, giving it an electric range of 35 to 45 kilometers (22 to 28 miles), depending on conditions. This will be the only plug-in hybrid that will offer fast charging—an undeniable advantage. The car has already become a success in Europe.

This plug-in SUV hybrid, however, seems to be stuck in the "coming-soon" stage. Introduced in 2014 and advertised for distribution in North America last year, it remains unclear when exactly in 2016 it will be available. We are being told it will be this summer—time will tell.

But at the rate things are going, this Outlander risks being technologically out-of-date by the time it appears, with the Bolt and other competing models on the horizon.

DANIEL BRETON

Toyota Mirai (hydrogen)

I took this so-called masterpiece for a spin; not a long one, but long enough to tell you that it's a luxury car (with the exception of the gray-cloth lining the roof) with all its attending softness and quietness. Its hydrogen fuel cell produces a sound closer to a hum than to Tesla's turbine-like humming. The first acceleration has some bite, but still not on par with the Model S. Also, like many gasoline-powered cars, there's an unsatisfying dead time when you press the accelerator.

My brief introduction allowed me to appreciate its comfortable seats and its neutral cornering. At the same time, steering is so smooth you almost think you're running on empty. Fuel consumption ratings were not provided to us, but the average seems to be 3.5 L/100 km (67 mpg).

A number of experts, including my colleague Pierre Langlois, were greatly surprised that Toyota chose hydrogen as fuel, given the lack of infrastructure and the fact that its production is not particularly harmless.

In any event, the Mirai may go largely unnoticed, since only a small quantity will be made available, and only in the Californian market. Rumors have it that the price will be in the range of $60,000 (USD)

JACQUES DUVAL

HYBR

Volvo XC90 PHEV

The Volvo XC90 PHEV, a luxury SUV, has everything that a large, affluent family, with some awareness of the impact of their lifestyle on the environment, could want:

• a vehicle that can seat seven safely and comfortably
• a vehicle whose active and passive security is among the best in the industry
• a vehicle that can get you around in 100-percent electric mode
• a vehicle whose fuel consumption in combustion mode is still reasonable, given the size of the vehicle

That said, a 100-percent electric range of less than 25 kilometers/9 miles (according to the EPA, 23 kilometers/14 miles) is not groundbreaking. It will take more to impress those who really want to make the change to electric driving. Volvo has also announced that this type of plug-in hybrid setup will be available on all their future models. Stay tuned.

DANIEL BRETON

Newcomers and rare gems

THE *GUIDE'S* MEDALISTS
by type of technology

ELEC

100-percent electric

The *Guide's* definition: any vehicle with one or more electric motors, powered by a battery (or a fuel cell).

WINNING ALL CATEGORIES

Gold: *Chevrolet Bolt*
• 320 km (200-mi) electric range

The electric vehicle of the year. Even with its practical approach and great range it is really fun to drive. The Bolt EV, along with Tesla Model 3, is writing a new chapter in the history of the automobile. It deserves its title.

Silver: *Tesla S 70*
• 377 km (234-mi) electric range

The Tesla S 70 is an excellent vehicle for anyone who wants to drive an S model with fewer bells and whistles.

Bronze: *Nissan Leaf 30 kWh*
• 172 km (107-mi) electric range

The update to the Leaf is a success. Its range and practicality have been substantially improved, which presumably will only add to its popular appeal.

List of vehicles in this book covered by category: BMW i3 • Chevrolet Spark • Fiat 500e • Ford Focus EV • Hyundai Ioniq EV • Kia Soul EV • Kia Niro EV • Mercedes B250 e • Mitsubishi i-MiEV • Porsche Mission-e • Smart Fortwo Electric Drive • Tesla Model S 70D • Tesla Model S 85 • Tesla Model S P85D • Tesla Model S P90D • Tesla Model X P90 • Toyota Mirai • Volkswagen e-Golf

HYBRID

Plug-in hybrid or electric vehicle with range extender

The *Guide's* definition: any vehicle powered by electricity and gas that can be plugged into a power outlet.

Gold: Chevrolet Volt

- 85 km (53-mi) electric range
- 2.2 L/100 km (107 mpg combined (gas-electric)
- 5.6 L/100 km (42 mpg) combined city/highway (gas)

A success in almost every way: range, fuel economy, driving enjoyment and price. This car has a growing fan base. It was remarkably well conceived and designed from the get-go, and the second generation is even better. The only thing left is to make it a true five-seater.

List of vehicles in this book covered by category: Acura NSX • Audi A3 e-tron • BMW i8 • BMW X5 xDrive40e • Cadillac ELR • Ferrari LaFerrari • Ford C-MAX Energi • Ford Fusion Energi • Hyundai Ioniq • Kia Niro • Kia Optima PHEV • Mitsubishi Outlander PHEV • Porsche Panamera S E-Hybrid and Cayenne S • Volvo XC90 PHEV

Silver: BMW i3 with range extender

- 115 km (71-mi) electric range
- 2 L/100 km (118 mpg) combined (gas-electricity)
- 6 L/100 km (39 mpg) (gas)

The use of carbon fiber in the mass production of the i3 is reason enough to see the kernel of a future revolution in the manufacturing of electric vehicles. Also, its modest range extender is helping to dispel fears of a lack of "brute force" and to win people over to electric vehicles.

Bronze: Hyundai Plug-in Sonata

- 43 km (27-mi) electric range
- 2.4 L/100 km (98 mpg) combined (gas-electric)
- 5.9 L/100 km (40 mpg) combined city/highway (gas)

The surprise of the year: A car of good breeding that combines interior space, reasonable range, fuel economy and a classic look. The only real sticking point is the rather high price.

The Guide's medalists by type of technology

HYB

Hybrid

The *Guide's* definition: any vehicle primarily powered by an internal-combustion engine (gas), which is also equipped with an electric motor to provide support, but which can't be plugged into power outlet.

Gold : Toyota Prius
• 4.5 L/100 km (52 mpg) combined

The venerable Prius has undergone a facelift, making it fully relevant again as energy-efficient vehicles are becoming more popular with drivers who cannot charge their cars close to home.

List of vehicles in this book covered by category: Acura RLX hybrid • Ford C-MAX hybrid • Ford Fusion hybrid • Honda CR-Z • Hyundai Ioniq hybrid • Kia Niro hybrid • Kia Optima hybrid • Lexus CT 200h • Lexus ES 300h • Lexus GS 450h • Lexus LS 600h • Lexus NX 300h • Lexus RX 450h • Lincoln MKZ hybrid • Subaru Crosstrek hybrid • Toyota Avalon hybrid • Toyota Camry hybrid • Toyota Highlander hybrid • Toyota Prius C • Toyota Prius V • Toyota RAV4 hybrid • Volkswagen Jetta Turbo hybrid

Silver: Chevrolet Malibu Hybrid
• 5.1 L/100 km (46 mpg) combined

From the bottom of the charts, the new version of the Malibu has climbed to the top. Beating out all rivals except the Prius in efficiency. Being well-equipped and with a new lower price, it deserves praise.

Bronze : Hyundai Sonata Hybrid
• 5.7 L/100 km (41 mpg) combined

Another much-improved hybrid car is the Hyundai Sonata. Much more user-friendly than before, comfortable and spacious, it deserves a place on the podium.

ECO

Fuel efficient

The *Guide's* definition: any vehicle powered solely by an internal-combustion engine whose fuel consumption is among the lowest for solely gas-powered vehicles.

Gold: Honda Civic
- 6.7 L/100 km (35 mpg) combined city/highway fuel efficiency in gasoline mode

Among the range of cars that use traditional technology, the Civic was updated to make it more practical, economical and enjoyable to drive, earning it first place in the *Guide* for energy-efficient vehicles—not to mention the real improvement to its finish.

List of vehicles in this book covered by category: Chevrolet Silverado • Chevrolet Trax • Fiat 500X • Ford F-150 EcoBoost • Ford Fiesta and Focus • Ford Mustang EcoBoost • Honda Fit • Honda HR-V • Mazda 3 • Mazda CX-3 • Mazda MX-5 • Nissan Juke • Nissan Micra • Toyota iM • Smart Fortwo

Silver: Subaru Impreza PZEV
- 7.6 L/100 km (31 mpg) combined city/highway fuel efficiency in gasoline mode

For those who need an all-wheel-drive car, the small Impreza PZEV proves to be both practical (particularly the hatchback version) and solid on the road—and, even better, economical at the pump, all for a very reasonable purchase price.

Bronze: Ram 1500 EcoDiesel
- 10.2 L/100 km (23 mpg) combined city/highway fuel efficiency in 2WD gasoline mode
- 10.7 L/100 km (22 mpg) combined city/highway fuel efficiency in 4WD gasoline mode

For those who use a pickup for work, a Hemi would be a step beyond their needs. That's where the Ram 1500 EcoDiesel comes in, offering the necessary power and torque while using much less fuel than its competitors. Its Ford rival, the F-150 EcoBoost, doesn't have comparable fuel economy.

The Guide's medalists by type of technology

ELECTRIC CARS *VS.* FOSSIL FUELS: REBATES, TAX BREAKS, GOVERNMENT BENEFITS AND SHORTCOMINGS

DANIEL BRETON

The following text was written for people who are against rebates, tax breaks and other incentive measures that encourage private and public electric transit on the basis they unduly favor industry to the detriment of taxpayers.

100 years of subsidies... for oil companies

In March 2012, the Obama administration issued a press release entitled:

"It's Time to End the Taxpayer Subsidies for Big Oil"

In it, the White House stated, *"The United States has been subsidizing the oil industry for a century. In fact, some of the oldest tax breaks for the oil companies date back to 1913–a time when there were only 48 states in the Union and Ford was still producing the Model T."*

Nonetheless, on March 29, 2012, the vote to put an end to subsidies for oil companies was shot down. President Obama had been trying for years to phase them out through budgetary measures but failed *each and every time*.

The oil industry is still heavily subsidized the world over. The International Energy Agency evaluated fossil fuel energy subsidies (oil, gas and coal) at **$543 billion** in 2013, amounting to nearly four times the amount spent on subsidizing renewable energy.

In November 2015, the Overseas Development Institute released a study that placed the figure that G20 countries spend on fossil fuel production subsidies at **$450 billion**.

"Special" taxes for EVs

Some American states have adopted legislation that requires hybrid and electric car consumers to pay extra. These states cite the potential impact of the increasing number of EVs on infrastructure (which is largely financed through fuel taxes), and legislated to pay for it thusly.

American states that tax hybrid and electric vehicles (2015)

- Georgia
- Idaho
- Michigan
- Wyoming
- Colorado
- Nebraska
- North Carolina
- Washington state

Support for electric transport

At the other end of the spectrum, an increasing number of nations around the world are legislating in favor of research and development as well as purchasing and leasing cars that are partially or totally electric. Obviously lobbies differ from one country to the next, so incentive measures vary widely. Some jurisdictions only allow an exemption for emissions inspections, while others offer aggressive bonuses upon purchase.

Coercive measures for EV expansion

While some jurisdictions offer rebates or tax incentives for partially or 100-percent electric cars, others resort to coercive measures to foster the expansion of greener vehicles on their roadways.

Zero Emission Vehicle Program: Implemented in California back in 1990, the program aims to enforce sales quotas on automobile manufacturers to produce zero emission vehicles.

California zero-emission quota objectives for major automobile manufacturers:
- 4.5% of sales in 2018
- 7% of sales in 2019
- 9.5% of sales in 2020
- 12% of sales in 2021
- 14.5% of sales in 2022
- 17% of sales in 2023
- 19% of sales in 2024
- 22% of sales for 2025 onward

The California Air Resource Board (CARB), a state governmental organization, has been the global reference in the fight against atmospheric pollution for 40 years. It raises the possibility of imposing a 100-percent plug-in car quota for 2030. It's safe to say that the battle between the state and manufacturers will be fierce.

American states that have adopted zero-emission legislation based on California's:
- Connecticut
- Maine
- Maryland
- Massachusetts
- New Jersey
- New York
- Oregon
- Rhode Island
- New Mexico
- Vermont

As of this book being written, not a single Canadian jurisdiction had enacted similar legislation.

Bonus-malus: A measure mostly implemented in Europe, bonus-malus legislation is designed to discourage gas-guzzling and heavily polluting vehicles in favor of fuel-efficient and greener ones. That means someone buying an SUV might have to pay a surtax of up to 200 percent of the purchase price (as in Norway), and someone buying an electric car could get an "eco-bonus" of up to 6,300 euros (as in France), or a tax exemption.

Canada vs. the world

While the federal government in the U.S. offers its citizens a tax credit of up to $7,500 when they buy an electric vehicle, the government of Canada offers its people **absolutely nothing**.

While countries like Austria, China, the Czech Republic, Denmark, Estonia, Finland, France, Germany, Iceland, India, Ireland, Italy, Japan, Luxembourg, Monaco, the Netherlands, Norway, Portugal, Romania, Spain, Sweden, Switzerland and the UK have various incentive measures on offer to expand EV sales, Canada is off doing its own thing, supporting the expansion of gas and oil infrastructure.

Electric cars vs. fossil fuels: rebates, tax breaks, government benefits and shortcomings

Thus, in Canada, the provinces had to take the lead when it comes to encouraging the presence of EVs.

Quebecers: get rebates of up to $8,000 for the purchase or lease of a partially or entirely electric vehicle. Rebates are also offered to individuals, corporations and merchants for the purchase and installation of charging stations.
http://vehiculeselectriques.gouv.qc.ca/particuliers/vehicules-electriques.asp

Ontarians: get rebates of up to $13,500 for the purchase or lease of a partially or entirely electric vehicle. Plus, rebates are offered to individuals for the purchase and installation of charging stations.
http://www.mto.gov.on.ca/english/vehicles/electric/index.shtml

British Columbians: get rebates of up to $5,000 for the purchase or lease of a partially or entirely electric vehicle. There's also a rebate of up to $6,000 for the purchase of a fuel cell vehicle. Add that to the province's *Scrap-it7* program and British Columbians can get up to $8,250 back. Plus, rebates are offered to individuals for the purchase and installation of charging stations.
http://www.livesmartbc.ca/incentives/transportation/

USA: huge variations from state to state

Besides the federal government's tax break, there are a variety of measures related to EVs and hydrogen vehicles in the U.S. from one state to another, and they tend to vary in scope.

The following is an exhaustive inventory of such measures as detailed on the National Conference of State Legislatures' website:
http://www.ncsl.org/research/energy/state-electric-vehicle-incentives-state-chart.aspx#wa

Arizona

High Occupancy Vehicle (HOV) Lane Exemption: Qualified alternative fuel vehicles may use designated HOV lanes regardless of the number of occupants in the vehicle.

Electric Vehicle Equipment Tax Credit: Maximum of $75 available to individuals for installation of EV charging outlets.

Reduced Alternative Fuel Vehicle (AFV) License Tax: Reduction in the annual vehicle license tax for an electric vehicle to a minimum of $5 per year.

Alternative Fuel Vehicle Tax Exemption: SB 1413, enacted in 2014, exempts certain alternative fuels such as natural gas, electricity and hydrogen from the state use tax.

Vehicle Emissions Inspection Exemption: HB 2226 and HB 2580 (2014) exempt qualified plug-in electric vehicles from an annual emissions inspection for the first five registration years.

Plug-In Electric Vehicle (PEV) Charging Rates: The Arizona Public Service Company offers a residential time-of-use plan to customers who own a qualified PEV. The pilot program was available through Dec. 31, 2015. Additionally, the Salt River Project offers an experimental reduced rate time-of-use plan for certain plug-in hybrid and electric vehicle owners.

California

HOV Lane Exemption: Qualified alternative fuel vehicles—including hydrogen, hybrid and electric vehicles—may use designated HOV lanes regardless of the number of occupants in the vehicle. Qualified vehicles are also exempt from toll fees in High Occupancy Toll (HOT) lanes.

Alternative Fuel Vehicle Rebate Program: The Clean Vehicle Rebate Project (CVRP) offers rebates for the purchase or lease of qualified vehicles. The rebates offer up to $2,500 for light-duty zero emissions and plug-in hybrid vehicles that the California ARB has approved or certified.

Sales Tax Exclusion for Manufacturers: California's Alternative Energy and Advanced Transportation Financing Authority (CAEATFA) provides a sales tax exclusion for advanced manufacturers and manufacturers of alternative source and advanced transportation products, components or systems. These incentives expire on June 30, 2016.

Alternative Fuel Vehicle Rebate Program: The San Joaquin Valley Air Pollution Control District administers the Drive Clean! Rebate Program, which provides rebates of up to $3,000 for the purchase or lease of eligible new vehicles, including qualified natural gas and plug-in electric vehicles.

Alternative Fuel & Vehicle Incentives: Through the Alternative and Renewable Fuel Vehicle Technology Program (ARFVTP), the California Energy Commission provides financial incentives for businesses, vehicle and technology manufacturers, workforce training partners, fleet owners, consumers and academic institutions with the goal of developing and deploying alternative and renewable fuels and advanced transportation technologies.

Insurance Discount: Farmer's Insurance offers a discount of up to 10 percent on certain insurance coverage for HEV and AFV owners.

PEV Charging Rate Reductions: The Sacramento Municipal Utility District (SMUD), Southern California Edison (SCE), Pacific Gas & Electric (PG&E), Los Angeles Department of Water and Power (LADWP), and San Diego Gas & Electric (SDG&E) provides discounted rate plans to residential customers for electricity used to charge qualified electric vehicles.

Electric Vehicle Supply Equipment Rebate: The Los Angeles Department of Water and Power (LADWP) Charge Up L.A.! Program provides rebates to residential and commercial customers who install level 2 (240 Volt) chargers. Rebates are offered to the first 2,000 customers who apply. Glendale Water and Power (GWP) also offers a $200 rebate to residential customers owning an electric vehicle and installing a level 2 charging station. Certain restrictions apply.

Free Parking: Sacramento offers free parking to individuals or small businesses certified by the city's Office of Small Business Development that own or lease EVs with an EV parking pass in designated downtown parking garages and surface lots. Vehicles must be 100-percent electric to qualify.

Free Parking: Free metered parking in San Jose, Hermosa Beach and Santa Monica for electric vehicles displaying a Clean Air decal.

Alternative Fuel Vehicle Parking: The California Department of General Services (DGS) and California Department of Transportation (DOT) must provide 50 or more parking spaces and park-and-ride lots owned and operated by DOT to incentivize the use of alternative fuel vehicles.

Connecticut

Hydrogen and Electric Vehicle Rebate: The Hydrogen and Electric Automobile Purchase Rebate (CHEAPR) Program provides up to $3,000 for the purchase or lease of a hydrogen fuel cell electric vehicle (FCEV), all-electric vehicle, or plug-in hybrid electric vehicle. Rebates are offered on a first-come, first-served basis.

Alternative Fuel Vehicle Funding: The Connecticut Clean Fuel Program provides funding to municipalities and public agencies that purchase, operate and maintain alternative fuel and advanced technology vehicles, including those that operate on compressed natural gas, propane, hydrogen and electricity. The Connecticut Department of Energy and Environmental Protection also provides funding to municipalities and state agencies for the project cost and installation of electric vehicle supply equipment.

Electric Vehicle Emissions Inspection Exemption: Vehicles powered exclusively by electricity are exempt from state motor vehicle emissions inspection.

Reduced Registration Fee: Electric vehicles are eligible for a reduced vehicle registration fee of $38.

Alternative Fuel and Hybrid Electric Vehicle Parking: Free parking on all city streets for qualified AFVs and HEVs registered in New Haven.

Delaware

Vehicle-to-Grid Energy Credit: Retail electricity customers with at least one grid-integrated electric vehicle may qualify to receive kilowatt-hour credits for energy discharged to the grid from the EV's battery at the same rate that the customer pays to charge the battery.

District of Columbia

Alternative Fuel and Fuel-Efficient Vehicle Title Tax Exemption: Qualified alternative fuel vehicles are exempt from the excise tax imposed on an original certificate of title.

Reduced Registration Fee: A new motor vehicle with a U.S. Environmental Protection Agency estimated average city fuel economy of at least 40 miles per gallon is eligible for a reduced vehicle registration fee of $36. This reduced rate applies to the first-time registration only.

Alternative Fuel Vehicle Tax Credit: An income tax credit of 50 percent—up to $19,000 per vehicle—is available for the incremental or conversion cost for qualified vehicles. A tax credit is also available for 50 percent of the equipment costs for the purchase and installation of alternative fuel infrastructure. The maximum credit is $1,000 per residential electric vehicle charging station and $10,000 for each public fueling station.

Florida

HOV Lane Exemption: Qualified alternative fuel vehicles may use designated HOV lanes regardless of the number of occupants in the vehicle. The vehicle must display a Florida Division of Motor Vehicles issued decal, which is renewed annually. Vehicles with decals may also use any HOV lane designated as a HOV toll lane without paying the toll.

Electric Vehicle Supply Equipment (EVSE) Financing: Property owners may apply to their local government for funding to help finance EVSE installations on their property or enter into a financing agreement with the local government for the same purpose.

Electric Vehicle Supply Rebate: Orlando Utilities Commission (OUC) offers a rebate of up to $1,000 for the purchase and installation of a commercial electric vehicle supply equipment. The rebate amount varies by program year and expires on Sept. 30, 2016.

Electric Vehicle Rebate: Jacksonville Electric Authority (JEA) offers rebates of up to $1,000 for new PEVs purchased or leased on or after September 18, 2014.

Georgia

HOV Lane Exemption: Qualified EVs and plug-in hybrid EVs (PHEVs) may use designated HOV lanes regardless of the number of occupants in the vehicle.

Alternative Fuel Vehicle Tax Credit: An income tax credit is available to individuals who purchase or lease a new dedicated AFV or convert a vehicle to operate solely on an alternative fuel. The amount of the tax credit is 10 percent of the vehicle cost, up to $2,500.

Zero Emission Vehicle Tax Credit: An income tax credit is available for 20 percent or up to $5,000 for individuals who purchase or lease a new zero-emissions vehicle. The credit only applies to vehicles purchased before July 1, 2015.

Electric Vehicle Supply Equipment Tax Credit: An income tax credit of 10 percent of the cost of the electric vehicle charging equipment, up to $2,500.

PEV Charging Rate Incentive: Georgia Power offers a time-of-use electricity rate for residential customers who own a hybrid or electric vehicle.

Electric Vehicle Registration Fee: HB 170 (2015) imposes a $200 annual fee on all non-commercial electric vehicles and $300 on all commercial electric vehicles.

Hawaii

HOV Lane Exemption: Qualified EVs and PHEVs may use designated HOV lanes regardless of the number of occupants in the vehicle.

Parking Fee Exemption: Qualified vehicles with electric vehicle license plates are exempt from certain parking fees charged by any non-federal government authority.

Parking Requirement: Public parking systems with 100 parking spaces or more must include at least one designated parking space for EVs and provide an EV charging system.

PEV Charging Rate Incentive: Hawaiian Electric Company offers time-of-use rates for residential and commercial customers who own an electric vehicle. This pilot program is offered to customers on Oahu and the island of Hawaii and in Maui County.

Idaho

Vehicle Inspection Exemptions: Hybrid and electric vehicles are exempt from state motor vehicle inspection and maintenance programs.

Alternative Fuel Annual Fee: HB 312 (2015) creates a $140 annual fee on all-electric vehicles and $75 on certain hybrid vehicles.

Illinois

Alternative Fuel Vehicle and Alternative Fuel Rebates: The Illinois Alternate Fuels Rebate Program provides a rebate of 80 percent, or up to $4,000, of the cost of purchasing an alternative fuel vehicle or converting a conventional vehicle. *This rebate program is currently suspended.*

Electric Vehicle Supply Equipment Rebates: The Illinois Department of Commerce and Economic Opportunity provides rebates to offset the cost of level 2 EVSE. The maximum possible total rebate award is $49,000 or 50 percent of the total project cost for up to 15 EVSE, whichever is less. *This rebate program is currently suspended.*

Electric Vehicle Registration Fee Reduction: The owner of an EV may register for a discounted registration fee not to exceed $35 for a two-year registration period or $18 for a one-year registration period.

Electric Vehicle Emissions Inspection Exemption: Vehicles powered exclusively by electricity are exempt from state motor vehicle emissions inspections.

Indiana

Plug-In Electric Vehicle Charging Rate Incentive: Indianapolis Power & Light Company (IPL) offers special plug-in EV charging rates for residential and fleet customers who own a licensed electric or plug-in electric vehicle.

Electric Vehicle Supply Equipment Credit and Charging Incentive: Northern Indiana Public Service Company (NIPSCO) IN-Charge Electric Vehicle

Program offers a credit of up to $1,650 to purchase and install residential EVSE, as well as free plug-in electric vehicle charging during off-peak hours. This program is in effect until Jan. 31, 2017.

Louisiana

Alternative Fuel Vehicle and Fueling Infrastructure Tax Credit: An income tax credit is available for 50 percent of the cost of converting or purchasing an alternative fuel vehicle or constructing an alternative fueling station. Alternatively, a tax credit of 10 percent of the cost of the motor vehicle, up to $3,000 is available for alternative fuel vehicles registered in the state.

Authorization for Alternative Fuel Vehicle Loans: The Louisiana Department of Natural Resources will administer the AFV Revolving Loan Fund to provide loan assistance to local government entities, including cities, parishes, school boards and local municipal subdivisions for the cost of converting conventional vehicles to operate on alternative fuels, or the incremental cost of purchasing new AFVs.

Maryland

HOV Lane Exemption: SB 33 (2014) allows qualified alternative fuel vehicles to use designated HOV lanes regardless of the number of occupants in the vehicle.

Plug-in Electric Vehicle Tax Credit: Effective July 1, 2013, through June 30, 2014, a tax credit of up to $1,000 was available against the excise tax imposed for the purchase of a qualified plug-in electric vehicles. Effective July 1, 2014, through July 1, 2017, HB 1345 and SB 908 (2014) replace the existing tax credit by providing a tax credit equal to $125 times the number of kilowatt-hours of battery capacity of the vehicle, or up to $,3000.

Electric Vehicle Supply Equipment Tax Credit and Rebate: The Maryland Energy Administration (MEA) offers an income tax credit equal to 20 percent of the cost of qualified EVSE. The credit may not exceed the lesser of $400 or the state income tax imposed for that tax year. MEA also offers an EVSE rebate program for the costs of acquiring and installing qualified EVSE. Rebate amounts vary, but may not exceed 50 percent of the costs of acquiring and installing qualified EVSE. Offer was valid between July 1, 2014, and June 30, 2016.

Massachusetts

Plug-In Electric Vehicle Rebates: The Massachusetts Department of Energy Resources has a program called Massachusetts Offers Rebates for Electric Vehicles (MOR-EV), which offers rebates of up to $2,500 to customers purchasing PEVs.

Alternative Fuel Vehicle and Infrastructure Grants: The Massachusetts Department of Energy Resources' Clean Vehicle Project provides grant funding for public and private fleets to purchase alternative fuel vehicles and infrastructure, as well as idle reduction technology.

Electric Vehicle Emissions Inspection Exemption: Vehicles powered exclusively by electricity are exempt from state motor vehicle emissions inspections.

Michigan

Vehicle Inspection Exemption: Alternative fuel vehicles are exempt from emissions inspection requirements.

Electric Vehicle Supply Equipment Rebate: Indiana Michigan Power provides rebates of up to $2,500 to residential customers who purchase or lease a new plug-in electric vehicle and install a level 2 EVSE with a separate meter. Customers must also sign up for the Indiana Michigan Power PEV time-of-use rate. The rebate is available to the first 250 qualified customers who submit a completed application. Consumers Energy Company provides qualified customers with a reimbursement of up to $2,500 to cover the purchase, installation and wiring for qualified level 2. Additionally, DTE Electric Energy Company will provide up to $2,500 for the purchase and installation of separately metered EVSE to the first 2,500 qualified customers who purchase PEVs and enroll in the DTE PEV rate.

Plug-In Electric Vehicle Charging Rate Reduction: Indiana Michigan Power, Consumers Energy and DTE Energy offer a special time-of-use rate option to residential customers who own a qualified PEV.

Minnesota

Electric Vehicle Charging Tariff: HB 2834 (2014) requires each public utility selling electricity to file a tariff that allows a customer to purchase electricity solely for the purpose of recharging an electric vehicle. The tariff must include either a time-of-day or off-peak rate.

Plug-In Electric Vehicle Charging Rate Reduction: Dakota Electric offers a discounted rate for electricity used to charge electric vehicles during off-peak times. Connexus Energy also offers a reduced rate and a $270 rebate to install a time-of-day meter.

Mississippi

Revolving Loan Fund: The Mississippi Development Authority established a revolving loan program to provide zero-interest loans for public school districts and municipalities to purchase alternative-fuel school buses and other motor vehicles, convert school buses and other motor vehicles to use alternative fuels,

purchase alternative fuel equipment, and install fueling stations. Loans provide up to $300,000 for the purchase of vehicles and up to $500,000 for the purchase and installation of fueling infrastructure.

Missouri

Alternative Fueling Infrastructure Tax Credit: Between Jan. 1, 2015, and Jan. 1, 2018, SB 729 (2014) provides an income tax credit for the cost of installing a qualified alternative fueling station. The credit provides 20 percent or up to $15,000 for residential and $20,000 for commercial installation of qualified refueling property.

Vehicle Inspection Exemption: Alternative fuel vehicles are exempt from state emissions inspection requirements.

Alternative Fuel Vehicle Decal: The state motor fuel tax does not apply to vehicles that are powered by an alternative fuel, if they obtain an AFV decal. For a passenger vehicle weighing less than 18,000 pounds, the decal fee is $75.

Montana

Alternative Fuel Vehicle Conversion Tax Credit: Businesses or individuals are eligible for an income tax credit of up to 50 percent of the equipment and labor costs for converting vehicles to operate using alternative fuels.

Nebraska

Alternative Fuel Vehicle and Fueling Infrastructure Loans: The Nebraska Energy Office administers the Dollar and Energy Saving Loan Program, which provides low-cost loans for a variety of alternative fuel projects, including the replacement of conventional vehicles with AFVs, the purchase of new AFVs, the conversion of conventional vehicles to operate on alternative fuels, and the construction or purchase of a fueling station or equipment.

Alternative Fuel Vehicle Registration Fee: Nebraska requires a $75 fee for the registration of an alternative fuel vehicle that operates on electricity or any other source of energy not otherwise taxed under the state motor fuel tax laws.

Nevada

HOV Lane Exemption: The Nevada Department of Transportation may establish a program allowing federally certified low emission, energy-efficient, and alternative fuel vehicles to operate in HOV lanes regardless of the number of passengers.

Plug-In Electric Vehicle Charging Rate Incentive: NV Energy offers discounted electricity rates to residential customers who charge electric or plug-in hybrid electric vehicles during off-peak hours.

Vehicle Inspection Exemption: Alternative fuel vehicles are exempt from emissions testing requirements. A new HEV is exempt from emissions inspection testing for the first five years, after which the vehicle must comply with emissions inspection testing requirements on an annual basis.

Parking Fee Exemption: All local authorities with public metered parking areas within their jurisdiction must establish a program for AFVs to park in these areas without paying a fee.

New Jersey

Vehicle Toll Incentive: The New Jersey Turnpike Authority offers a 10 percent discount from off-peak toll rates on the New Jersey Turnpike and Garden State Parkway through NJ EZ-Pass for drivers of vehicles that have a fuel economy of 45 miles per gallon or

higher and meet the California Super Ultra Low Emission Vehicle standard. The discount will expire Nov. 30, 2018.

Zero Emission Vehicle Tax Exemption: ZEVs sold, rented or leased in New Jersey are exempt from state sales and use tax.

New York
Rebate up to $2,000 for the purchase of an electric or hydrogen vehicle.

HOV Lane Exemption: Through the Clean Pass Program, qualified vehicles may use the Long Island Expressway HOV lanes regardless of the number of passengers in the vehicle.

Alternative Fuel Vehicle Recharging Tax Credit: SB 2609 and AB 3009, passed in 2013, provide a tax credit for 50 percent of the cost, up to $5,000, for the purchase and installation of alternative fuel vehicle refueling and electric vehicle recharging property. The credit is available through Dec. 31, 2017.

Alternative Fuel Vehicle Toll Incentive: Through the Clean Pass Program, qualified vehicles have a $6.25 toll rate during off-peak hours at Port Authority crossings.

Electric Vehicle Emissions Inspection Exemption: Vehicles powered exclusively by electricity are exempt from state motor vehicle emissions inspections.

Plug-In Electric Vehicle Rate Reduction: Residential Con Edison customers pay a reduced price for electricity used during the designated off-peak period.

North Carolina

HOV Lane Exemption: Qualified alternative fuel vehicles may use designated HOV lanes regardless of the number of occupants in the vehicle.

Vehicle Inspection Exemption: Qualified PEVs are exempt from state emissions inspection requirements.

Alternative Fuel Tax Exemption: The retail sale, use, storage and consumption of alternative fuels is exempt from the state retail sales and use tax.

Plug-In Electric Vehicle Fee: SB 402 (2013) requires electric vehicle owners to pay an annual registration fee of $100.

Ohio

Alternative Fuel and Fueling Infrastructure Incentives: The Alternative Fuel Transportation Grant Program may provide grants and loans for up to 80 percent of the cost of purchasing and installing fueling facilities offering alternative fuels.

Emissions Inspection Exemption: Vehicles powered exclusively by electricity, propane or natural gas are exempt from state vehicle emissions inspections after receiving a one-time verification inspection.

Oklahoma

Alternative Fueling Infrastructure Tax Credit: A tax credit is available for up to 75 percent of the cost of installing alternative fueling infrastructure, including electric vehicle charging stations.

Oregon

Alternative Fueling Infrastructure Tax Credit for Residents: Through the Residential Energy Tax Credits program, qualified residents may receive a tax credit for 25 percent of alternative fuel infrastructure project costs, up to $750.

Alternative Fueling Infrastructure Tax Credit for Businesses: Business owners and others may be eligible for a tax credit of 35 percent of eligible costs for qualified alternative fuel infrastructure projects.

Pollution Control Equipment Exemption: Dedicated original equipment manufacturers of natural gas and electric vehicles are not required to be equipped with a certified pollution control system.

Pennsylvania

Alternative Fuel Vehicle Funding: The Alternative Fuels Incentive Grant (AFIG) Program provides financial assistance for qualified projects and information on alternative fuels, including PHEVs. The AFIG Program also offers Alternative Fuel Vehicle Rebates to assist with the incremental cost of the purchase of new AFVs. Rebates of $3,000 are available for qualified EVs and PHEVs.

Plug-In Electric Vehicle Rebate: PECO Energy Company provides rebates of $50 to residential customers who purchase a new, qualified PEV.

Rhode Island

Alternative Fuel Vehicle Tax Exemption: The town of Warren may allow excise tax exemptions of up to $100 for qualified AFVs registered in Warren.

Electric Vehicle Emissions Inspection Exemption: Vehicles powered exclusively by electricity are exempt from state emissions control inspections.

South Carolina

Fuel Cell Vehicle Tax Credit: Residents who claim the federal fuel cell vehicle tax credit are eligible for a state income tax credit equal to 20 percent of the federal credit.

Tennessee

HOV Lane Exemption: Qualified alternative fuel vehicles may use designated HOV lanes regardless of the number of occupants in the vehicle.

Electric cars vs. fossil fuels: rebates, tax breaks, government benefits and shortcomings

Texas

Alternative Fuel Vehicle Rebate: Qualified vehicles purchased or leased may be eligible for a rebate of up to $2,500. The Light-Duty Motor Vehicle Purchase or Lease Incentive (LDPLI) Program was available until June 26, 2015, or until total funding of $7.75 million was awarded. Only purchases made on or after May 13, 2014, are eligible to apply for the rebate.

Alternative Fueling Infrastructure Grants: The Texas Commission on Environmental Quality administers the Alternative Fueling Facilities Program, which provides grants for 50 percent of eligible costs, up to $600,000, to construct, reconstruct or acquire a facility to store, compress or dispense alternative fuels, including electricity, in Texas air quality nonattainment areas.

Vehicle Replacement Vouchers: The Texas Commission on Environmental Quality administers the AirCheckTexas, Drive a Clean Machine program, which provides vouchers of $3,500 to qualified individuals for the purchase of hybrid, electric or natural gas vehicles.

Electric Vehicle Supply Equipment Incentive: Austin Energy customers who own a plug-in electric vehicle are eligible for a rebate of 50 percent or up to $1,500 of the cost to purchase and install a qualified level 2 EVSE.

Utah

HOV Lane Exemption: Qualified vehicles may use designated HOV lanes regardless of the number of occupants in the vehicle. Vehicles must display a special clean fuel decal issued by the Utah Department of Transportation.

Alternative Fuel Tax Exemption: Propane, compressed natural gas, liquefied natural gas, electricity and hydrogen used to operate motor vehicles are exempt from state fuel taxes, but subject to a special fuel tax at the rate of three-nineteenths of the conventional motor fuel tax.

Alternative Fuel and Fuel Efficient Vehicle Tax Credit: HB 15 (2015) provides that new clean fuel vehicles purchased between Jan. 1, 2015, and Dec. 31, 2016, that meet air quality and fuel economy standards may be eligible for a credit of 35 percent of the purchase price, up to $1,500, including certain electric and hybrid electric vehicles. New plug-in hybrid vehicles are eligible for a tax credit of $1,000. An income tax credit is also available for 50 percent or up to $2,500 of the cost to convert a vehicle to run on propane, natural gas or electricity that meets air quality and fuel economy standards.

Free Electric Vehicle Parking: Free metered parking in Salt Lake City for electric vehicles displaying a Clean Air license plate.

Vermont

Alternative Fuel and Vehicle Research and Development Tax Credit: Vermont businesses that qualify as a high-tech business involved exclusively in the design, development and manufacture of alternative fuel vehicles, hybrid electric vehicles, all-electric vehicles, or energy technology involving fuel sources other than fossil fuels are eligible for up to three of the following tax credits: 1) payroll income tax credit; 2) qualified research and development income tax credit; 3) export tax credit; 4) small business investment tax credit and 5) high-tech growth tax credit.

Virginia

HOV Lane Exemption: On HOV lanes serving the I-95/I-395 corridor, registered vehicles displaying Clean Special Fuel license plates issued before July 1, 2006, are exempt from HOV lane requirements. On HOV lanes serving the I-66 corridor, registered vehicles displaying Clean Special Fuel license plates issued before July 1, 2011, are exempt from HOV lane requirements.

Plug-In Electric Vehicle Charging Rate Reduction: Dominion Virginia Power offers discounted electricity rates to residential customers who charge electric vehicles during off-peak hours.

Vehicle Inspection Exemption: Alternative fuel and hybrid electric vehicles are exempt from emissions testing.

Alternative Fuel Vehicle Fee: SB 127 (2014) requires that alternative fuel vehicles and all-electric vehicles—hybrid vehicles are excluded—registered in the state pay an annual vehicle license tax of $64. Electric vehicles must also pay a $50 annual license tax.

Washington

Alternative Fuel Vehicle Tax Exemption: New passenger cars, light-duty trucks and medium-duty passenger vehicles that are dedicated alternative fuel vehicles are exempt from the state motor vehicle sales and use taxes.

Electric Vehicle Infrastructure Exemptions: Public lands used for installing, maintaining and operating EV infrastructure are exempt from leasehold excise taxes until Jan. 1, 2020. Additionally, the state sales and use taxes do not apply to EV batteries; to labor and services for installing, repairing, altering or improving EV batteries and EV infrastructure; or to the sale of property used for EV infrastructure.

Electric Vehicle Supply Equipment Return on Investment Incentive: HB 1853 (2015) allows utilities to petition the Washington Utilities and Transportation Commission (UTC) for a rate of return of an additional two percent above the standard return on equity on EVSE installed for the benefit of ratepayers. The expenditures may not increase ratepayer costs more than 0.25 percent.

Vehicle Inspection Exemption: Alternative fuel and hybrid electric vehicles are exempt from emissions testing.

Electric Vehicle Supply Equipment Rebate: Puget Sound Energy (PSE) provides a rebate of $500 to qualified customers for the purchase and installation of level 2 EVSE. PSE expects the rebate program to remain open until Nov. 1, 2016, depending on available funds.

Plug-In Electric Vehicle Fee: Electric vehicle owners must pay an annual vehicle registration fee of $100. The fee will expire if the legislature imposes a vehicle-miles-traveled fee or tax in the state.

Wyoming

Plug-In Electric Vehicle Fee: HB 9 (2015) requires owners of plug-in electric vehicles to pay an annual decal fee of $50, effective July 1, 2015.

I hope that this article sets the record straight regarding the large monetary amounts dedicated to fossil fuel subsidies, and also the measures and subsidies in place for buyers of electric vehicles. Armed with this information, you can evaluate your purchasing decision from both a personal and planetary perspective.

Electric cars vs. fossil fuels: rebates, tax breaks, government benefits and shortcomings

REFERENCES

Bonus-malus in France, developpement-durable. gouv.fr/Bonus-Malus-definitions-et-baremes.html

Bonus-malus in Norway, evnorway.no

Bossel, U., "Does a Hydrogen Economy Make Sense?," Proceedings of the IEEE, Vol. 94, n° 10, October 2006, pages 1826 to 1837 (see Figure 9 of this article)

CAFE (standards), nhtsa.gov/fuel-economy

Cost comparison between a gas-powered and an electric car, energy.gov/articles/egallon-how-much-cheaper-it-drive-electricity

International Council on Clean Transportation, theicct.org/laboratory-road-2015-update

International Energy Agency, worldenergyoutlook. org/resources/energysubsidies

Kelley Blue Book, kbb.com

Le Devoir, "Technologies vertes: Volkswagen investira plus de 85 milliards d'ici 2016," ledevoir. com/economie/automobile/331608/en-bref-technologies-vertes-volkswagen-investira-plus-de-85-milliards-d-ici-2016

Libération, "Le diesel est cancérogène, c'est officiel. Et il se passe quoi maintenant?" liberation.fr/societe/2012/06/14/le-diesel-est-cancerogene-c-est-officiel-et-il-se-passe-quoi-maintenant_826081

Melaina, M. and Penev, M., "Hydrogen Station Cost Estimate," technical report, NREL/TP-5400-56412, National Renewable Energy Laboratory, September 2013 (see Table 3, page 5)

National Conference of State Legislatures (NCSL), ncsl.org/research/energy/state-electric-vehicle-incentives-state-chart.aspx#wa

National Highway Traffic Safety Administration, nhtsa.gov

Nealer, R., Reichmuth, D. and Anair, D., "Cleaner Cars from Cradle to Grave. How Electric Cars Beat Gasoline Cars on Lifetime Global Warming Emissions," Union of Concerned Scientists, November 2015. ucsusa.org/sites/default/files/attach/2015/11/Cleaner-Cars-from-Cradle-to-Grave-full-report.pdf

Nykvist, B. and Nilsson, M., "Rapidly falling costs of battery packs for electric vehicles," Nature Climate Change, Vol. 5, April 2015, pages 329 to 332

Overseas Development Institute, "Empty promises: G20 subsidies to oil, gas and coal exploration," odi. org/sites/odi.org.uk/files/odi-assets/publications-opinion-files/9957.pdf

Ramsden, T. et al., "Hydrogen Pathways," technical report, NREL/TP-6A10-60528, National Renewable Energy Laboratory, March 2013 (see Figure ES1, page ix)

Scrap-it (British Columbia program), scrapit.ca

The White House (Washington), "It's time to end the taxpayer subsidies for Big Oil," whitehouse.gov/blog/2012/03/28/it-s-time-end-taxpayer-subsidies-big-oil

ZEV standards (new California standards), arb.ca. gov/msprog/zevprog/zevregs/1962.2_clean.pdf

PHOTO CREDITS

Every effort has been made to indicate the source and owner of the rights to each photo. Juniper Publishing apologizes for any errors or omissions in this regard.

Legend : (t) top, (b) bottom, (l) left, (r) right, (m) middle

Acura: p. 86, 87, 214
AddÉnergie, Québec, 2015: p. 38
Antoine Antoniol/Bloomberg via Getty Images: p. 55
Archives de la STM: p. 16, 25
Audi: p. 88, 89
BMW: p. 12-13, 77 (tr), 93, 212 (t)
Cadillac: p. 95 (b)
Chevrolet: p. 20, 26, 52, 84-85, 97 (b), 99, 100, 101, 102, 103, 104, 105, 107 (t), 109 (b), 223 (m)
Chrysler: p. 212 (b)
Communauto: p. 80
Daniel Breton: p. 218, 224 (t)
Dodge: p. 79 (b)
Fiat: p. 110, 111 (t), 112, 113
Ford: p. 28, 114, 115, 116, 117, 118, 119, 120, 121, 122, 123, 124, 125
Honda: p. 78 (tr), 126, 127, 128, 129, 130, 131, 213 (b)
Hyundai: back cover (r); p. 48, 132, 133, 134, 135, 215, 223 (b), 224 (b)
Jacques Duval: cover (b); back cover (l); p. 7, 10, 19, 27, 31, 46, 51, 70, 74, 77 (br), 79 (t), 90, 91, 92, 94, 95 (t), 96, 97 (t), 98, 106, 108, 109 (t), 111 (b), 136, 137, 138, 139 (b), 140, 147 (b), 151 (t), 156, 157, 159, 162, 163, 165, 174, 175, 176, 177, 184, 185, 186, 187, 188 (t), 189 (l), 196, 197, 198, 206, 213 (t), 217, 222 (m, b), 223 (t), 224 (m)
Justin Sullivan/Getty Images: p. 30

Kia: p. 139 (t), 216
Leonard G.: p. 78 (tl)
Lexus: p. 78 (bl), 141, 142, 143, 144, 145, 147 (t), 148, 149, 150, 151 (b), 219 (t)
Lincoln: p. 219 (b)
Louise Bilodeau: p. 239 (b)
Mazda: p. 152, 153, 154, 155
Mercedes-Benz: p. 77 (bl), 220 (t)
Mitsubishi: p. 158, 220 (b)
Natal Witness Archives/Gallo Images/Getty Images: p. 15
Nissan: p. 160, 161, 164, 166, 167
Nova Bus: p. 17
Patrick T. Fallon/Bloomberg via Getty Images: p. 33 (t)
Photo Hydro-Québec: p. 47, 50
Porsche: p. 72, 168, 169
Ram: p. 170, 171, 225 (b)
Roberto Machado Noa/LightRocket via Getty Images: p. 69
Roulezelectrique.com: p. 41
Shutterstock: p. 6, 9, 11, 18, 24, 29, 34, 35, 37, 40, 42, 44, 53, 54, 58, 59, 60, 61, 63, 64, 67, 68, 76, 181, 222 (t)
Smart: p. 172, 173
Subaru: p. 178, 179, 225 (t)
Sylvain Juteau: p. 183 (t), 239 (tl)
Tesla Motors: cover (t); back cover (m); p. 23, 45, 180, 182, 183 (b), 188 (b), 189 (r), 211
Toyota: p. 56, 57, 78 (br), 190, 191, 192, 193, 194, 195, 199, 200, 201, 202, 203, 204, 205, 221 (t), 225 (m)
Universal History Archive/UIG via Getty Images: p. 14
Volkswagen: p. 77 (tl), 207, 208, 209
Volvo: p. 221 (b)
Yalcin/Anadolu Agency/Getty Images: p. 33 (b)

Printed by Marquis Imprimeur inc.

ACKNOWLEDGEMENTS

We would like to extend our thanks to the following people, who helped bring this book to fruition, and who have helped promote the electrification of transportation for the world of today and tomorrow.

Our "electrifying" associate: Sylvain Juteau, the third person behind the book project, and a key collaborator.

Sylvain is the founder of the specialized blogs focusing on the electrification of transportation, roulezelectrique.com and evandmore. com. Collaborating with other experts, he has been sharing his expertise in electric vehicles since 2011. He is also the president of Roulez Électrique (roulezelectrique. com), which promotes the electrification of transportation, in Trois-Rivières, Québec—where he installed Canada's very first charging service station.

Contributors

Jean-François Guay: Educated as a lawyer and criminologist, Jean-François began his career as an automobile reviewer in 1983. Widely recognized for his expertise, he conducts road tests, reports on auto news and provides consultation to a variety of media sources. In his legal work, he specializes in the application of the Highway Safety Code and consumer protection.

Pierre Langlois: With a PhD in physics, Pierre wrote the book *Rouler sans pétrole* in 2008 (Éditions Multimondes) and has authored numerous reports and analyses. In 2013, he acted as consultant to the government of Québec for the development of a policy for the electrification of transportation. He makes regular appearances in media, particularly roulezelectrique.com, on electric vehicles.

Daniel Rufiange: Professor of history by training and a passionate automobile reporter, Daniel is a fan of anything with wheels. With his love of history, he has a special interest in vintage cars, but he also follows new models and the latest technologies, including those involving the electrification of transportation and hybrid power.

Pioneers on the electric path

Jennifer St-Yves-Lambert, Elvire Toffa Juteau and Ève-Mary Thaï Thi Lac, each of whom, in their own way, supports the development of the electrification of transportation—and drives electric!

Trailblazers

Pierre Couture, Raymond Deshaies and Karim Zaghib have worked all their lives on the electrification of transportation and the advancement of clean and effective technological solutions to polluting vehicles.

Almost 25 years ago, Pierre Couture invented a wheel-motor plug-in hybrid car at Hydro-Québec's research institute IREQ and developed a high-speed monorail, and is responsible for an array of other electric inventions and advancements.

Karim Zaghib has been developing batteries for electric cars for more than 20 years and is a leader in the field.

Raymond Deshaies introduced the first diesel-electric hybrid bus in 1966. He has devoted much of his life to producing cleaner public transport by continuously improving generations of electric buses.

We would also like to thank:

AddÉnergie, Communauto, Le Circuit Électrique, Gad Elmoznino, Émilie Folie-Boivin, Romaric Lartilleux, Charles Rivard, George Saratlic, Steve Spence, Mark Templeton and Melanie Testani.